Essays on Renaissance Philosophies of Music

Books by David Whitwell

The Sousa Oral History Project
The Art of Musical Conducting
The Longy Club: 1900–1917
La Téléphonie and the Universal Musical Language
Extraordinary Women
A Concise History of the Wind Band
Essays on the Modern Wind Band
Essays on Performance Practice
A New History of Wind Music
The College and University Band
The Early Symphonies of Mozart
Music of the French Revolution
Stories from the Podium

On Composers
Wagner on Bands
Berlioz on Bands
Chopin: A Self-Portrait
Liszt: A Self-Portrait
Schumann: A Self-Portrait in His Own Words
Mendelssohn: A Self-Portrait in His Own Words

On Education
Philosophic Foundations of Education
Foundations of Music Education
Music Education of the Future

Aesthetics of Music

Aesthetics of Music in Ancient Civilizations
Aesthetics of Music in the Middle Ages
Aesthetics of Music in the Early Renaissance
Aesthetics of Music in Sixteenth-Century Italy, France and Spain
Aesthetics of Music in Sixteenth-Century Germany, the Low Countries and England
Aesthetics of Baroque Music in Italy, Spain, the German-Speaking Countries and the Low Countries
Aesthetics of Baroque Music in France
Aesthetics of Baroque Music in England

The History and Literature of the Wind Band and Wind Ensemble Series

Volume 1 The Wind Band and Wind Ensemble Before 1500
Volume 2 The Renaissance Wind Band and Wind Ensemble
Volume 3 The Baroque Wind Band and Wind Ensemble
Volume 4 The Wind Band and Wind Ensemble of the Classical Period (1750–1800)
Volume 5 The Nineteenth-Century Wind Band and Wind Ensemble
Volume 6 A Catalog of Multi-Part Repertoire for Wind Instruments or for Undesignated Instrumentation before 1600
Volume 7 Baroque Wind Band and Wind Ensemble Repertoire
Volume 8 Classical Period Wind Band and Wind Ensemble Repertoire
Volume 9 Nineteenth-Century Wind Band and Wind Ensemble Repertoire
Volume 10 A Supplementary Catalog of Wind Band and Wind Ensemble Repertoire
Volume 11 A Catalog of Wind Repertoire before the Twentieth Century for One to Five Players
Volume 12 A Second Supplementary Catalog of Early Wind Band and Wind Ensemble Repertoire
Volume 13 Name Index, Volumes 1–12, The History and Literature of the Wind Band and Wind Ensemble

Ancient Voices

Ancient Views on Music and Religion
Ancient Views on the Natural World
Ancient Views on What Is Music
Contemporary Descriptions of Early Musicians
Early Views of Music and Ethics
Early Thoughts on Performance Practice
Music Performance in Ancient Societies

Renaissance Voices

Essays on Renaissance Philosophies of Music
Renaissance Men on Music

www.whitwellbooks.com

David Whitwell

Renaissance Voices
Views on Music by
Renaissance Writers

Essays on Renaissance Philosophies of Music

Edited by Craig Dabelstein

WHITWELL PUBLISHING • AUSTIN, TEXAS, USA

Renaissance Voices: Views on Music by Renaissance Writers
Essays on Renaissance Philosophies of Music
Dr. David Whitwell

WHITWELL PUBLISHING
AUSTIN, TX 78701
WWW.WHITWELLPUBLISHING.COM

© 2014 by David Whitwell
All rights reserved. First edition 2014

Composed in Bembo Book.
Published in the United States of America.
All images used in this book are in the public domain except where otherwise noted.

ISBN-13: 9781936512799

Cover design by Daniel Ferla.

Contents

	Acknowledgement	ix
Part 1:	**The Dawning of a New Era**	
1	On Music and Society in the Fourteenth Century	3
2	On the 'Well-Rounded Man'	13
3	In Praise of Women	23
Part 2:	**Commentary on the New Renaissance Values**	
4	On Music and Society in the Fifteenth Century	33
5	Johannes Tinctoris on Music	45
6	On Music and Society in the Sixteenth Century: The Opposition by the Church	57
7	Polyphony, the Child of Mathematics, Is Left on the Steps of the Church	73
8	On Music and Society in the Sixteenth Century: The Spread of Italian Humanism	83
9	Erasmus on Humanism	95
10	On Music and Society in the Sixteenth Century: The Growing Irrelevance of the Universities	105
11	On Sixteenth-Century German Music Treatises	115
Part 3:	**Commentary on Performance**	
12	Contemporary Reflections on the Aesthetic Values of Music	137
13	Contemporary Comments on Performance Practice	149
14	Comments on Renaissance Improvisation	163
	Bibliography	171
	About the Author	183
	About the Editor	185

Acknowledgments

I am indebted to my friend and colleague, Craig Dabelstein, for his help in preparing this book for publication.

David Whitwell
Austin, Texas

PART I
THE DAWNING OF A NEW ERA

On Music and Society in the Fourteenth Century

Today everyone in the field of music associates the beginning of the fourteenth century as being synonymous with the beginning of the Renaissance. In university classes we put a chalk line on the blackboard, under a heading, '1300,' followed by the name Machaut (who conveniently enough was born in the year 1300) and here, we say, begins the Renaissance.

But the term itself, 'Renaissance,' was only first coined in 1840,[1] so in absence of this term (and the chalk line moving across the sky) one has to wonder what the persons actually living in the fourteenth century were aware of. To appreciate their perspective one has to first recall that the first one thousand years of the Christian Era was a period in which the Church, in assuming the role of speaking for mankind, attempted to control the thought, education and very lives of men. No one, we think, has characterized so well and succinctly this atmosphere than the nineteenth-century scholar, Francesco de Sanctis, writing in defense of Boccaccio's *The Decameron* (Boccaccio having been accused of having ruined the moral life of the Italians).

> The essential quality of the Middle Ages was transcendence: a sort of ultrahuman and ultranatural 'beyond' outside of nature and man, the genus and the species outside the individual, matter and form outside their unity, the intellect outside the soul, perfection and virtue outside life, the law outside consciousness, the spirit outside the body, and the purpose of life outside the world …
>
> The natural product of this exaggerated, theocratic world was asceticism. Life here on earth was losing its seriousness and value, so that while man continued to dwell here, his spirit was in the next life …
>
> Feeling, as the product of human or natural propensity, was always considered a sin. Passions were banned and poetry was considered the mother of lies. The theater was the food of the Devil and stories and romances were regarded as profane types of literature. All these things were called by one name: 'the senses' …
>
> But a state of tension and imbalance like this cannot last. Art and culture, the knowledge and experience of life, work to modify it and transform it. Thus art, by seizing this world, had begun to humanize it, bring it closer to man and nature …[2]

This long and dark period was followed by a kind of 'Pre-Renaissance,' which is our term for the twelfth and thirteenth centuries. This is when the curtain of the 'Dark Ages' really parted and it was a period that included the crusades with their impact of opening trade with the East, the building of the great cathedrals, the birth of the modern universities, the translation and dissemination of the 'lost' books of the ancient Greek philosophers, in literature the French Romances and the Minnesinger poetry and in music the troubadours. In sum, it was a period of great enthusiasm, hope and the discovery of a new ability of man to think of

---

[1] By Jules Michelet.

[2] Francesco de Sanctis, 'Boccaccio and the Human Comedy,' quoted in *The Decameron*, trans. Mark Musa and Peter Bondanella (New York: Norton, 1977), 216ff.

himself apart from the Church and to speak for himself. The result was a great sense of self-confidence, which was a necessary prerequisite to many of the advances in science and the arts. These new attitudes, which were all essential parts of Humanism, rapidly repaid society with accomplishments which the Church had been unable to achieve in one thousand years. In a relatively short period of time come the achievements of da Vinci, Michelangelo, Newton, Galileo, Copernicus and Gutenberg.

All of these wonderful changes, so Renaissance in spirit, are before we arrive at the 'Renaissance' of music history texts, the fourteenth century. And all of this is generally given short notice, if mentioned at all, in texts on Renaissance music. Also absent, generally, in these texts is any discussion of the extraordinary developments in civic and court music of the twelfth, thirteenth *and* fourteenth centuries. Neither is there acknowledgement of the breadth of composition; not all composers wore ecclesiastical garments. Gustave Reese, for example, points to an early madrigal of Jacopo da Bologna (fl. 1340–1360) in which the text mentions that 'everyone is writing ballades, madrigals, and motets.'[3] And he was not alone. Franco Sacchetti (1330–1400) complains,

> The world is full of people who want to make rhymes...so it is with songs too: without any skill.[4]

And, similarly, a madrigal by Landini observes,

> Everyone wants to arrange musical notes,
> To compose madrigals, *cacce*, *ballate*,
> Believing that his own are fine.[5]

Another fundamental change which is rarely discussed in traditional texts is that the old Church separation of 'speculative music' and 'practical music' was taking a new direction, even though these terms are still frequently found during the fourteenth century. Marchetto of Padua (1305–1326), for example, uses a new expression, 'the art and science' of music:

> Music is an art [*ars*] both admirable and delightful; it resounds in heaven and on earth.
> Moreover, music is that science [*scientia*] which consists in numbers, proportions, consonances, intervals, measures, and quantities.[6]

The original by-laws of the first minstrel guild in Paris, founded in 1321, uses a similar expression, 'the science and music of minstrelsy.'

To say it another way, the old medieval 'practical music,' meaning the actual performance of music, as opposed to theory, was now gaining recognition as an art form. The importance of this is evident in the language of civic documents, as for example in a document of 1395 of

---

3   Gustave Reese, *Music in the Middle Ages* (New York: Norton, 1940), 371.
4   Quoted in John Larner, *Culture and Society in Italy, 1290–1420* (New York: Scribner's, 1971), 172.
5   Ibid.
6   Marchetto of Padua, *Lucidarium*, trans. Jan W. Herlinger (Chicago: University of Chicago Press, 1985).

the relatively small town of Treviso, in which we read that money will be given to the civic musician Pietro di Bartolomeo Boldrani to buy a trumpet, 'for the presence of artists increases the honor of the whole community.'[7] This surely is the spirit, also, of a document found in Florence dated July 1333, which mentions,

> Since in almost every noble city, whether in Lombardy or Tuscany, fine singers are retained for the delight and joy of the citizens.[8]

In the general absence of all of this, where then in fourteenth-century life do modern music history texts find the Renaissance? We suspect that the first musicologist who drew the now traditional chalk line on the blackboard must surely have been strongly influenced by the very titles of two fourteenth-century music books, the *Ars Nova* by Philippe de Vitry (1291–1361) and the *Ars nove musice* by Jean de Muris (ca. 1290–1350). Indeed music history calls the 'new' Renaissance composers 'ars nova,' in distinction to their teachers and previous generation whom they style, 'ars antiqua.' But anyone who reads these books with the expectation of discovering a brave call for a new kind of music will be disappointed. These books are nothing but new theory books, discussing only the grammar of music, by two very traditional writers of the old scholastic mold. These books are only a continuation of the old medieval mathematical discussion on music and it was the association of mathematics and music which allowed Muris to write, 'no [other] science is hidden from him who knows music well.'[9]

Muris seems particularly old-fashioned in his condemnation of the new musical practice in abandoning the foundation of 'perfection,' music based on the number three.[10]

> All music, especially mensurable music, is founded in perfection, combining in itself number and sound. The number, moreover, which musicians consider perfect in music is … the ternary number. Music, then, takes its origin from the ternary number.[11]

As his rational support of this, he offers an extensive list of 'proofs,' including not only the Trinity, but the three aspects of time of celestial bodies, the three attributes of the stars and sun, the three attributes of the elements, the three intellectual operations, the three terms in the syllogism and many more.[12]

---

7   Quoted in Don L. Smithers, *The Music and History of the Baroque Trumpet* (London: Dent), 75ff.

8   Quoted in Ibid., 171.

9   Quoted in Oliver Strunk, *Source Readings in Music History* (New York: Norton, 1950), 179.

10   Ibid., 173.

11   Ibid., 174.

12   Ibid., 173.

In discussing what shapes the notes should be, de Muris again looks to the past, observing, 'the wiser ancients long ago agreed and conceded that geometrical figures should be the symbols of musical sounds.'[13] This he follows with an extraordinary omission, which, had he filled it, would be worth more to us than the entire rest of his treatise.

> For reasons which we shall pass over, their symbols did not adequately represent what they sang.

Well, you won't find the Renaissance in these books. But the people living early in the fourteenth century were hearing something sufficiently new in church music to coin the label, 'ars nova.' And they did recognize some distinction, as we see in a work by Machaut. Here, in a discussion of after dinner music, he not only makes a distinction between playing from notes versus improvisation, but specifically recognizes the old and new style of music.

> After they had performed an estampie, the ladies and their company went off by twos and threes, holding hands, to a very beautiful room; and there all the men and women alike who wanted to relax, dance, sing, or play at backgammon, chess or parsons found all they needed at hand and ready for games, singing, and music [*par notes, ou par sons*]. And there were musicians more skilled and knowledgeable in both the new and old styles.[14]

What were they hearing that caused them to distinguish between the old and the new? Ironically, our most helpful clues are found among the complaints of those being disenfranchised, those old-fashioned, conservative men we call *ars antiqua*. It is in their objections to the 'new music' that we must seek to identify what they heard as being new.

Perhaps a clear place to begin is the papal bull, 'Docta Sanctorum,' issued in 1324–1325 by Pope John XXII, which included a specific attack on the *ars nova* church music. First, the pope attacks the faster note values he was hearing, a reference to the practice advocated by Philippe de Vitry, and a reflection of a new livelier style of church music reflecting the new livelier mood of society. And he seems to imply that he was hearing improvisation, which he no doubt was, for there is other documentation of improvisation over chant. He didn't like this either, of course, and he calls it 'lubricating the melodies with counterpoints.'

It is clear that the strongest objection the pope had to the new style was the addition of secular melodies in the upper voices. This was a serious issue with church music, for everyone must have recognized that the old chant could not compete with the popular styles found in secular music, music clearly already tonal and with strong modern metric organization. Even the Church officials must have recognized this problem, as indeed one prelate so famously said, 'Why does the devil have all the good melodies?'

We wish we could hear today whatever it was the pope was hearing in the way of more interesting melodies, for on this point he becomes very exercised:

---

[13] Ibid., 175.

[14] 'Remedies for Fortune Fair and Foul,' trans. Conrad Rawski (Bloomington: Indiana University Press, 1991), 392.

> Their voices are incessantly running to and fro, intoxicating the ear, not soothing it, while the men themselves endeavor to convey by their gestures the sentiment of the music which they utter. As a consequence of all this, devotion, the true end of worship, is little thought of, and wantonness, which ought to be eschewed, increases. Thus, it was not without good reason that Boethius said: 'A person who is intrinsically sensuous will delight in hearing these indecent melodies, and one who listens to them frequently will be weakened thereby and lose his virility of soul.'[15]

Wanton!? It seems an awfully strong word to describe *ars nova* church music. Curiously, this same word was also used by another member of the *ars antiqua*, a Church scholastic theorist named Jacques de Liege, in his 'Speculum Musicae' written in about 1313. In complaining about the music of the *ars nova* he asks,

> What profit can there be in adding to a sound old doctrine a wanton and curious new one.[16]

If we had to guess what the pope and de Liege meant by 'wanton,' we would guess that they were hearing more feeling, more emotion—something the Church had been paranoid about for one thousand years. They didn't see the chalk line, but they *were* hearing the Renaissance.

Perhaps 'paranoid' is also an appropriate term to call some members of the *ars antiqua*, or perhaps we should be generous and just call them uncomfortable. Certainly this is clear in the case of Jacques de Liege, for in his treatise we have a man crying out for the respect which he feels is due the older practice.

> Now in our day have come new and more recent authors, writing on mensurable music, little revering their ancestors, the ancient doctors; nay, rather changing their sound doctrine in many respects, corrupting, reproving, annulling it, they protest against it in word and deed.
>
> ......
>
> Should the men who composed and used these [older] sorts of music, or those who know and use them, be called rude, idiotic, and ignorant of the art of singing?
>
> ......
>
> I do not deny that the moderns have composed much good and beautiful music, but this is no reason why the ancients should be maligned and banished from the fellowship of singers.[17]
>
> ......
>
> Should the ancients be called rude for using perfections, the moderns subtle for using imperfections?[18]

---

[15] The full text of this passage can be found in H. E. Wooldridge, *The Oxford History of Music*, second edition (London, 1929), 294ff.

[16] Strunk, Source Readings in Music History, 181, 183.

[17] Quoted in Strunk, Ibid., 181, 185, 189.

[18] Ibid., 184ff.

One also has to remember that de Liege was carrying a lot of heavy scholastic baggage. For him music could not be just an aesthetic experience, music was an expression of Reason, a cornerstone in a Church structure carefully constructed on order, mathematics and other imagined earthly manifestations of God. He was being asked to give all this up for the pleasure of the senses.

> There must be a place for what accords with Reason and with Art, since this lives by Art and Reason in every man. Reason follows the law of nature which God has implanted in rational creatures.[19]

Therefore, he says, let us return to Reason, 'let the well reasoned art [*refloreat rationabilis ars*] of the ancients flower forth again.'[20]

During his discussion of the new music, de Liege admitted that he has delighted in their 'song, singers, music, and musicians,'[21] but he complains of the new music that it accomplished 'by many means what can be conveniently accomplished by few.'[22] However, it is as an old-fashioned, scholastic churchman that de Liege is most uncomfortable. Art, he says, must be judged on moral grounds.

> For though art is said to be concerned with what is difficult, it is nevertheless concerned with what is good and useful, since it is a virtue perfecting the soul through the medium of the intellect.[23]

From this it follows that the value of art is in its influence on the character of man.

> For, if I may say so, the old art seems more perfect, more rational, more seemly, freer, simpler, and plainer. Music was originally discreet, seemly, simple, masculine, and of good morals; have not the moderns rendered it lascivious beyond measure? For this reason they have offended and are offending many judicious persons skilled also in music.[24]

And, of course, reaching back to a basic tenet of Church music maintained by most of the early Church fathers, de Liege reaffirms the principle that in Church music it is the *words* which are most important.

> Wherein does this studied lasciviousness in singing so greatly please, by which, as some think, the words are lost, the harmony of consonances is diminished, the value of the notes is changed, perfection is brought low, imperfection is exalted, and measure is confounded?

---

[19] Ibid., 182.
[20] Ibid., 189.
[21] Ibid., 182.
[22] Ibid., 181.
[23] Ibid., 184.
[24] Ibid., 189.

> In a great company of judicious men, when motets in the modern manner were being sung, I observed that the question was asked, what language such singers were using, whether Hebrew, Greek, Latin, or some other, because it could not be made out what they were saying.[25]

Another representative of the *ars antiqua* who was apparently uncomfortable to some degree was the famous Petrarch (1304–1374). In a letter to Boccaccio he despairs,

> O inglorious age! that scorns antiquity, its mother, to whom it owes every noble art,—that dares to declare itself not only equal but superior to the glorious past.[26]

Even as a representative of Church thought with her ancient structure based on Reason, and with her tying music to mathematics, and as a musician himself, how could Petrarch make this nonsensical statement?

> A deaf person can know the tones and numbers characterizing the intervals of fifth and octave, as well as the other proportions of the musical scale with which musicians work. Although one does not hear the sounds of the human voice, of strings or the organ, he nevertheless may understand in his mind their fundamental canon and, doubtless, will prefer the intellectual pleasure to a mere titillation of the ear.[27]

In another place Petrarch mentions, almost with a sense of surprise, the esteem for music held by the ancients. Here, he concedes that appreciating music represents a measure of refinement, but, as in the case of painting and sculpture, he cautions against the listener being *too* involved.

> JOY: It is pleasant to sing.
> REASON: What gives you pleasure now once gave pleasure to the Greeks. Among them anyone who could not sing or play instruments was considered ignorant. This, Cicero writes, happened to Themistocles of Athens, the most illustrious of the Greeks, when he refused to play the lyre at banquets … It is amazing that a Socrates should in his old age devote his efforts to the harp. But it should not surprise us that Alcibiades was made to study the [aulos] by his uncle Pericles, because this was regarded as most worthy by the ancients and, in fact, was even taught among the liberal arts …
>
> In the present age such an ardent zeal for music has as yet not come to possess the mind of every prince, but it has taken possession of the hearts of a few, particularly the worst ones. For Caligula was extremely fond of singing and dancing. As for Nero, it is unbelievable how much he was devoted to the study of the kithara and what pains he took with his voice. But it is stupid and utterly ridiculous when in the very night that was the last one of his life … he should grievously bewail again and again the downfall, not of such a great prince, but of such a great musician. I omit others. Even today, in your own age, we find here and there that pleasure of the ear which to enjoy honestly and soberly constitutes a measure of humane refinement. Yet to be overwhelmed and voluptuously possessed by it is nothing but sheer foolishness.[28]

---

[25] Ibid., 189ff.

[26] Letter to Boccaccio, quoted in James Robinson, *Petrarch, The First Modern Scholar and Man of Letters* (New York: Putnam, 1914), 208.

[27] Ibid., II, xcvii, 241.

[28] Ibid., I, xxiii, 71ff.

This *ars antiqua* perspective seems so strange to us, for Petrarch was an avid singer, singing his own love poetry. We wonder, did he feel he could not risk in a published format his real thoughts? Or, did he think his love songs were sufficiently removed from 'real music,' as to not be associated with his above comments? Perhaps while voicing these views of the past he was never aware that in his personal life he was a key harbinger of Humanism, the road to the future.

In any case, in the field of music it is the arrival of Humanism which announces the Renaissance. It is a return to the understanding, and acknowledgement, that communicating feeling is what music is all about that brings down the curtain on the Church's nonsense about mathematics and music.

What the people living in the fourteenth century heard which necessitated the new term, 'ars nova,' was emotions in music. And emotions in music meant an entirely different listening experience. Nowhere in medieval literature do we find a composer so fervently interested in the reaction of the listener as we do in Machaut's 'Remede de Fortune.'

> How do you like it? What do you say? ... What do you think of my song? ... What do you say? ... Won't you tell me if I sing well or poorly?[29]

Machaut returns to this theme time and time again in his writing. In one place he emphasizes the fact that music can express what nothing else can.

> So I decided that I would compose, according to my feelings towards you and in praise of you, a lai, a *complainte*, or original song; for I did not dare or know how to tell you otherwise how I felt, and it seemed to be better to tell in my new song what was oppressing and wringing my heart than to try by some other method.[30]

He returns to this in his 'Remede de Fortune.'

> And since I was not always in one mood, I learned to compose chansons and lais, ballades, rondeaux, virelais, and songs, according to my feelings, about love and nothing else; because he who does not compose according to his feelings falsifies his work and his song.[31]

At the end of the song, Machaut once again returns to feeling.

> But I composed it to her praise in accord with the skill I possessed, and as near to my feelings as I well could.[32]

---

[29] Guillaume de Machaut, 'Remede de Fortune,' trans. James Wimsatt and William Kibler (Athens: The University of Georgia Press, 1988), 280.

[30] Ibid., 368.

[31] Ibid., 188.

[32] Ibid., 206.

We gain some insight into what 'feeling' meant to Machaut in the following passage. While the thirteenth-century troubadour also mentioned the pain of love, one does not find in that literature the emphasis on the feelings themselves that we read here—it is a hallmark of the Renaissance.

> Then, like one accustomed to sighing, I uttered a lament and sigh from the depths of my heart, accompanied by weeping and washed in tears; and with great effort I turned toward her my flushed, pale, sad, sorrowful, and weeping face, full of suffering. But I said nothing to her because I was unable to speak; instead, I gazed fixedly at her.[33]

This new emphasis on feeling in music one also finds in Boccaccio. We know today that what the common listener responds to in music is not the music itself, which would require everyone to be educated in the grammar of music to appreciate it, but the communication of feelings. Boccaccio mentions this with regard to a love song.

> Love, heed not what my voice sings, but rather how much my heart, your subject, is filled with desire.[34]

These same themes are also found throughout the works of the other great master of the fourteenth century, Chaucer. Indeed, from a scholastic perspective, he makes a subtle wave good-bye to the medieval philosophy of music in his 'Nun's Priest's Tale,' when a fox who has come to hear a rooster sing, declares that the rooster sings with more feeling in his music than Boethius or any singer.

> Therwith ye han in musyk moore feelynge
> Than hadde Boece, or any that kan synge.[35]

Later in this same passage, Chaucer observes that the best singer is one who sings from the heart.[36]

Similarly, in his 'The Book of the Duchess,' Chaucer distances himself from earlier literature which had played a fundamental role in medieval thought. When a character is speaking of whether Jubal invented music, as related in the Old Testament, or Pythagoras, another character responds that none of that matters and as for himself, 'I put my feeling into songs, to gladden my heart.'[37]

And *that* was what the Renaissance was all about.

---

33 Ibid., 254.

34 *L'Ameto*, trans. Judith Serafini-Sauli (New York: Garland, 1985), 40.

35 'Nun's Priest's Tale,' line 4483.

36 Ibid., 4491.

37 'The Book of the Duchess,' 1172.

On the 'Well-Rounded Man'

> And just see how the world has gone to seed: we put our souls in trust to the theologians, who for the most part are heretics; our bodies to the doctors, who all loathe medications and never take medicine; and our property to the lawyers, who never go to law with one another.'
> 'Spoken like a courtier,' said Pantagruel.[1]
>
> Rabelais, Pantagruel

As mentioned in the first essay, the fundamental social change in the Renaissance is found in man beginning to think of himself as an individual man and not a creature defined by the Church. This led to men beginning to think about characteristics which are to be admired in a man and they became so many that today we refer to the 'Renaissance Man' as being someone who is very well-rounded. The 'courtier,' which Pantagruel refers to above, is most usually associated with the sixteenth century and is described at length in one of the most famous books of the Renaissance, *Il Cortigiano* (*The Courtier*), by Baldassare Castiglione (1478–1529). In the most noble personification he, or she, attempts to become the perfect gentleman or lady not only through deportment but by the acquisition of education and a wide variety of skills.

We see the 'well-rounded' young man first in the fourteenth century in Giovanni Boccaccio's (1313–1375) *The Decameron*, where we are given a list of the accomplishments necessary to turn a young man into a gentleman. Here we find he must learn to both sing and play an instrument ('song and sound').

> Then, consorting with young men of condition and learning the fashions and carriage that befitted gentlemen and especially lovers, he first, to the utmost wonderment of everyone, in a very brief space of time, not only learned the first elements of letters, but became very eminent among the students of philosophy, and after ... he not only reduced his rude and rustical manner of speech to seemliness and civility, but became a past master of song and sound and exceedingly expert and doughty in riding and martial exercises, both by land and by sea.[2]

Boccaccio's view of the ideal woman, however, is still a medieval view, notwithstanding more than two centuries of the praise of women in the troubadour literature. In his *Concerning Famous Women* he perhaps is trying to mask his prejudice when he observes that talent, in a woman, 'is usually very scarce.'[3] From his perspective, then, he gives a rather clear description of his view of women's place, which includes *avoiding* singing!

---

[1] François Rabelais, *Pantagruel*, trans. Donald Frame (Berkeley: University of California Press, 1991), III, xxix.

[2] *The Decameron*, trans. Mark Musa and Peter Bondanella (New York: Norton, 1977), I, 371.

[3] 'Irene,' in *Concerning Famous Women*, trans. Guido Guarino (New Brunswick: Rutgers University Press, 1963), 131.

> If a woman is to be considered completely chaste, it is necessary above all for her to curb her lustful and wandering eyes and confine them to the fringe of her dress. Her words must be not only respectable but brief, and she must speak only at the proper time. She must avoid idleness as a sure and deadly enemy of chastity, and she must abstain from feasting, for Venus is weak without food and wine. She must avoid singing and dancing as arrows of lasciviousness, and attend to temperance and sobriety. She must take care of her house, close her ears to shameful conversation, and avoid roaming from place to place. She must reject paint, superfluous perfumes, and ornaments. She must trample with all her strength on harmful thoughts and appetites, persist in sacred thoughts, and be vigilant. And, not to discuss the entire subject of real chastity, she must love only her husband with great affection and scorn others, unless it is to love them with brotherly love. She must not go without shame in her face and breast to her husband's embrace, even when it is for the sake of procreation.[4]

In sixteenth-century Italy we find a comment by Giraldi which emphasizes one of the important themes in Castiglione's book on the courtier, that everything done through effort must appear as it had required no effort.

> Though one cannot write well without the most intense diligence and great labor (nature has not arranged for excellence to issue from us without labor), nonetheless the writer ought to strive with the utmost effort, not so that the hard work on the composition will be visible, but so that the work will appear to be done naturally.[5]

Giulio Del Bene offers a typical prescription for becoming a well-rounded man, in particular if one wants to 'alter' their minds for the better they should,

> read lectures, compose sonnets, recite orations, write tragedies, canzoni, madrigals, and every other sort of composition, discuss philosophy, and speak extemporaneously on politics, ethics, and poetics.[6]

Torquato Tasso also wrote of the breadth of knowledge needed by the courtier. Conspicuously missing in his list is music, which he may have regarded as requiring too much effort, as indeed was the view of Castiglione.

> He ought to learn mathematics and moral philosophy as well as natural science and theology, and he ought to be well acquainted with the historians,[7] the poets, the orators, and with the noble arts, such as sculpture, painting and architecture. He ought to know enough about all of these subjects so that no one can accuse him of ignorance. Such knowledge will win high honor from his prince, and goodwill will follow honor.[8]

---

4   'Sulpicia,' in Ibid., 147.

5   Giraldi Cinthio, *Discorso intorno al comporre dei romanzi*, trans. in Henry Snuggs, *Giraldi Cinthio On Romances* (Lexington: University of Kentucky Press, 1968), 120.

6   Quoted in Claude V. Palisca, *Humanism in Italian Renaissance Musical Thought* (New Haven: Yale University Press, 1985), 338.

7   Pietro Aretino, in a letter to Charles V, made the memorable remark, 'falsehood is the mother of history' [Letter of June, 1536, quoted in Samuel Putnam, *The Works of Aretino* (New York: Covici, 1926), II, 85]. Aretino (1492–1556) was one of the first authors whose books were placed on the Index of Prohibited Books, a development of the Council of Trent.

8   Torquato Tasso, 'Malpiglio, or On the Court,' in *Tasso's Dialogues*, trans. Carnes Lord (Berkeley: University of California Press, 1982), 161.

In another place, which also recognizes the great growth in the prestige of civic institutions during the Renaissance, Tasso finds the musician was one of several professions which was welcome in court.

> Poets, orators, musicians, and the professors of mathematics and natural philosophy can be courtiers just as they can be citizens …
>
> Properly speaking, however, the courtier is the active and prudent man who rules the arts and sciences in a court just as the prudent citizen does in a city.[9]

Most writers of the sixteenth century make appreciation of music an important part of the definition of the courtier, as one also finds in *The Courtier* by Castiglione. Galilei has a character say to him 'you know well how much praise the development of his musical talents brings to a gentleman, and particularly to a courtier like you.'[10] Pietro Aretino, in one of his letters, mentions overhearing a young man state that he has the necessary qualities to be a courtier: 'I am a good musician, have some learning, and I love the chase.'[11] Francesco Guicciardini (1483–1540) saw a clear value in obtaining some musical skills for use as a courtier, but one senses he failed to understand the true value of music.

> When I was young, I used to scoff at knowing how to play [an instrument], dance, and sing, and other such frivolities. I even made light of good penmanship, knowing how to ride, to dress well, and all those things that seem more decorative than substantial in a man. But later, I wished I had not done so. For although it is not wise to spend too much time cultivating the young toward the perfection of these arts, I have nevertheless seen from experience that these ornaments and accomplishments lend dignity and reputation even to men of good rank. It may even be said that whoever lacks them lacks something important. Moreover skill in this sort of entertainment opens the way to the favor of princes, and sometimes becomes the beginning or the reason for great profit and high honors. For the world and princes are no longer made as they should be, but as they are.[12]

This same writer also discusses 'grace' as the most distinguishing quality of a gentleman, much in the spirit of Castiglione's emphasis on nonchalance. Although supposing it to be a gift of God, he finds grace the chief virtue in the beauty of women, in the behavior of the gentleman, in speech and among artists. In the performance of music, he defines grace as follows.

> For in the voice as well as for instruments, one will be able to offer the same reasons for grace and melody saying, by way of definition, that singing with grace is nothing other than a close observance of the style and rules of singing and of those rules for using the voice or playing a good instrument so that it shall not be unpleasant or awkward. It is this grace that customarily brings pleasure and delight to the ears of persons of judgment. And so one can say that a person does not have a good voice but

---

9 Ibid., 187.
10 Vincenzo Galilei, *Fronimo* [1584], trans. Carol MacClintock (Neuhasen-Stuttgart: Hanssler-Verlag, 1985), Op. cit., 36.
11 Letter to Ambrogio degli Eusebii, in Thomas Chubb, *The Letters of Pietro Aretino* (New Haven: Shoe String Press [Archon Books], 1967), 103.
12 Francesco Guicciardini, *Maxims and Reflections*, trans. Mario Domandi (New York: Harper Torchbooks, 1965), C, 179.

> sings with grace as, for example, I will mention Cardinal Montalto, who played and sang with much grace and feeling even though his appearance was more martial than Apollonian, and who had a scratchy voice …
>
> And that it is true that grace in singing is a quality provided by nature and not by art … may be seen from the fact that sometimes a singer appears pleasing to one person and tiresome to another; and on the contrary a stupid singer pleases when he ought not to. And the same effect is seen also in other things, especially in the bordellos of Spain and Africa in which there is not a woman that does not find a market, however ugly she may be.[13]

Galilei makes rare references to 'grace' as applied to music. First, he observes that the lutanist might omit repeated notes 'for more grace,' and 'to furnish some novelty of the ear—which, like all the other senses, is fed by it.'[14] Similarly, that the use of rests, depending on their use, can result in 'grace' or 'dullness.'[15]

In Spanish literature Lope de Vega, in his *The Duchess of Amalfi's Steward*, presents the ideal courtier. Here a discussion ensues which lists the qualities needed by a courtier.

They include the ability to recite Latin poetry, be a skillful swordsman, fine manners, impeccable dress, and 'how well he sings!'[16]

One finds a number of references to the courtier in English literature.

Robert Greene (1560–1592) provides an interesting list, in his *The Royal Exchange* (1590), of four things necessary to be a courtier.

1. Abundance of riches.
2. Ambition and desire of honor.
3. Integrity and quickness of wit.
4. The hope of reward by service.[17]

Shakespeare gives us a portrait of a rather sophisticated courtier in his *Twelfth Night*.

> He plays the viol-de-gamba and speaks three or four languages word for word without the book.[18]

In another play, his *As You Like It*, there is a brief dialog which centers on the obsession of manners by the courtiers. As the character, Touchstone, tells a rural character that he will be damned for never having been to court, Shakespeare makes an interesting reflection of the kind of cause and effect speech often used by the Puritans.

---

[13] Vicenzo Giustiniani, *Discorso sopra la Musica* [ca. 1628], trans. Carol MacClintock (American Institute of Musicology, 1962), 73ff.

[14] Vincenzo Galilei, *Fronimo*, 171.

[15] Ibid., 54.

[16] Lope de Vega, *El mayordomo de la duquesa de Amalfi*, trans. Cynthia Rodriguez-Badendyck (Ottawa: Dovehouse, 1985), I, 249.

[17] Robert Greene, *The Royal Exchange* [1590], VII, 253.

[18] *Twelfth Night or What You Will*, I, iii, 23ff.

> Why, if thou never wast at court, thou never saw'st good manners. If thou never saw'st good manners, then thy manners must be wicked; and wickedness is sin, and sin is damnation. Thou are in a perilous state, shepherd.[19]

Several sixteenth-century writers also mention, in view of the organization of society around an absolute monarch, that the occupation of being a courtier had some dangerous aspects. Sir Thomas More, for example, has left a poem, 'To a Courtier,' which reminds us of the inherent danger of striving to be near the king.

> You often boast to me that you have the king's ear and often
> Have fun with him, freely and according to your own whims.
> This is like having fun with tamed lions—often it is harmless,
> But just as often there is the fear of harm.
> Often he roars in rage for no known reason,
> And suddenly the fun becomes fatal.
> The pleasure you get is not safe enough
> To relieve you of anxiety.
> For you it is a great pleasure.
> As for me, let my pleasure be less great—
> And safe.[20]

Tasso warns that in the presence of rulers who had gained their position by birth or battle, the courtier must be cautious in not overshadowing them in exhibiting his intellect.

> But since the intellect is meant by nature to rule, it seems that the man who possesses superior prudence ought not to be considered inferior for any reason. And this is why princes usually hate any greatness of mind. When a courtier has great intelligence, which sometimes happens, he ought to cover it up modestly, not show it off with pride. Concealment becomes the courtier more than showing off.[21]

It was in this line of thought that Giraldi warns not to just write for oneself but to remember the level of the readers.

> It is even more indecorous for the one writing to show himself a philosopher, to neglect poetic grace and beauty, and, concentrating on words and recondite—often ill-fitting mysteries—to write so as to produce something hardly understood by himself and not at all by others, not remembering that clarity, ease, and directness of thought are the glory of good poets' writings. Whereas the good poets are delightful and profitable to those who devote themselves to reading them, the others remain so odious that it could be said they do not write for others, but for themselves. Great prudence, therefore, should be exercised by those who would blend the philosophic with the poetic.[22]

---

[19] *As You Like It*, III, ii, 37ff.

[20] *The Complete Works of St. Thomas More* (New Haven: Yale University Press, 1984), III, Pt. 2, 205.

[21] Tasso, *Tasso's Dialogues*, 175.

[22] Giraldi Cinthio, *Discorso intorno al comporre dei romanzi*, 125.

Another danger, here to the character of the courtier himself, is pointed out by the greatest French writer of the sixteenth century, Michel Montaigne (1533–1592). One of Montaigne's chief objections to the function of the courtier was that his very position of personal attachment to the court prevented him from free speech.

> A courtier can have neither the right to speak nor the desire to think other than favorably of a Master who from among so many thousands of his subjects has chosen to favor him with his own hand and to elevate him. Not unreasonably such favor and preferment will corrupt his freedom and dazzle him.[23]

In another place he observed, 'When serving princes it is not enough to keep a secret: you need to be a liar as well.'[24] In general, Montaigne associates with the courtiers: ambition, covetousness, irresolution, fear and desires.[25]

Montaigne's rather dim characterization of the courtier in this past definition is shared by other writers toward the end of the sixteenth century. Some, like the English writer, John Lyly (1553–1606), merely characterize the courtiers as inept and useless persons. Lyly begins his *Euphues, or The Anatomy of Wit* (1578) by introducing a young noble of Athens, whom he says 'had more wit than wealth, and yet more wealth than wisdom.' Since he considered himself above any honest work, he spent his time engaging in what 'wits' do,

> fine phrases, smooth quoting, merry taunting, using jest without mean and abusing mirth without measure.[26]

Later he bemoans the fact that such young men, so gifted by Nature and Fortune, are only interested in 'the passions of his mind and praises of his Lady.'

> From this comes such vain poetry, such idle sonnets, such enticing songs, which are set forth to the gaze of the world and the grief of the godly.[27]

In Spanish literature we find Lope de Vega is critical of the courtier, beginning perhaps as a matter of simple honesty. He presents a courtier in *Justice Without Revenge*, for example, who observes,

> For though I show an outward pleasure, as courtesy demands, my soul is full of deep displeasure.[28]

---

[23] Michel de Montaigne, *Essays*, trans. M. A. Screech (London: Penguin, 1993), I, xxvi, 174.

[24] Ibid., III, v, 954.

[25] Ibid., I, xxxix, 268.

[26] *Euphues, or The Anatomy of Wit*, in *The Complete Works of John Lyly*, ed. Warwick Bond (Oxford: Clarendon Press, 1967), I, 184.

[27] Ibid., I, 287.

[28] Lope de Vega, *Peribanez*, trans. Jill Booty, in *Lope de Vega, Five Plays* (New York: Hill and Wang, 1961), 235.

In the *La Dorotea*, Lope de Vega makes another complaint regarding the courtier—that he appears to be more educated than he really is.

> CELIA. There's always more to know than one man can know.
> LAURENCIO. Right you are, and take my word for it: as there's an infinite amount to learn, and life is short, the most learned man knows next to nothing.
> CELIA. Has this master of yours ever studied anything?
> LAURENCIO. Enough to show off what he knows, like the bachelor of arts—the worst breed of courtier to deal with.[29]

We find another example of this rather useless courtier in Edmund Spenser, although he reports they still had some musical skills:

> Diverse delights they found themselves to please;
> Some sung in sweet consort; some laughed for joy;
> Some played with straws; some idly sat at ease.[30]

Shakespeare, in several plays, paints a much more unflattering picture of the courtier. In *The Tragedy of Troilus and Cressida*, the true character of the courtier is brought into question when Troilus says,

> I cannot sing,
> Nor heel the high la volt, nor sweeten talk,
> Nor play at subtle games—fair virtues all,
> To which the Grecians are most prompt and pregnant.
> But I can tell that in each grace of these
> There lurks a still and dumb-discursive devil
> That tempts most cunningly.[31]

In the comedy, *The Winter's Tale*, the wandering musician, Autolycus, has disguised himself as a courtier and when asked if he is indeed a courtier, he responds,

> Whether it like me or no, I am a courtier. Seest thou not the air of the court in these enfoldings? hath not my gait in it the measure of the court? receives not thy nose court-odor from me? reflect I not on thy baseness court-contempt? Think'st thou, for that I insinuate, or toaze from thee thy business, I am therefore no courtier?[32]

In *Timon of Athens* Shakespeare creates a shallow, cynical courtier, the 'opposite to humanity,' to whom he gives the name *Apemantus*.

---

[29] Lope de Vega, *La Dorotea*, trans. Alan Trueblood and Edwin Honig (Cambridge: Harvard University Press, 1985), II, v.
[30] Edmund Spenser, *The Faerie Queene*, Book II, Canto IX, xxxv.
[31] *The Tragedy of Troilus and Cressida*, IV, iv, 93ff.
[32] *The Winter's Tale*, IV, iv, 797ff.

There are two passages which refer to the contemporary custom of young men going abroad, especially to Italy, to finish their education. This was particularly attacked by the religious right in England. In one play, Shakespeare seems sympathetic to this custom. At the very beginning of *The Two Gentlemen of Verona*, Valentine desires to travel, observing 'Homekeeping youth have ever homely wits.' On the other hand, in *Richard II*, Shakespeare seems to take the other side of the question, as he has the duke of York observe,

> The open ear of youth doth always listen—
> Report of fashions in proud Italy,
> Whose manners still our tardy apish nation
> Limps after in base imitation.[33]

In this regard, perhaps we should also mention that Hamlet's parents beg him not to pursue his desire to go to school in Wittenberg, but to stay and remain as their chief courtier.[34]

Hamlet uses the playing of a recorder as metaphor for the courtier's manipulation of others. He says, 'O, the recorders! Let me see one,' and proceeds to give the courtier, Guildenstern, a lesson.

> HAMLET. It is as easy as lying. Govern these ventages with your fingers and thumb, give it breath with your mouth, and it will discourse most eloquent music. Look you, these are the stops.
> GUILDENSTERN. But these cannot I command to any utterance of harmony. I have not the skill.
> HAMLET. Why, look you now, how unworthy a thing you make of me. You would play upon me; you would seem to know my stops; you would pluck out the heart of my mystery; you would sound me from my lowest note to the top of my compass. And there is much music, excellent voice, in this little organ, yet cannot you make it speak. 'Sblood, do you think I am easier to be played on than a pipe? Call me what instrument you will, though you can fret me, yet you cannot play upon me.[35]

Another example of manipulation, in this case of women, is found when Lyly also has a character advise another on how to uncover the 'deceits of thy Lady.'

> Search every vain and sinew of their disposition, if she can not sing at sight, ask her to sing, if she has no cunning to dance request her to trip it, if no skill in Music, offer her the Lute.[36]

In *A Quip for an Upstart Courtier* (1592), Robert Greene wrote an entire book on Pride as reflected in the English scene, saying his purpose was to reflect,

---

33 *Richard II*, II, i, 20ff.

34 *Hamlet*, I, ii, 117ff.

35 *Hamlet*, III, ii, 345ff.

36 Ibid., I, 254.

the abuses that Pride had bred in England, how it had infected the Court with aspiring Ennui, the City with griping covetousness, and the country with contempt and disdain. How since men placed their delights in proud looks and brave attire, Hospitality was left off, Neighborhood was exiled, Conscience was laughed at, and Charity lay frozen in the streets.[37]

In *Mourning Garment*, Greene offers yet another criticism of English character:

> In Crete you must learn to lie, in Paphos to be a lover, in Greece a dissembler, you must bring home pride from Spain, lasciviousness from Italy, gluttony from England and carousing from the Danes.[38]

Greene, in referring to the tradition of young men in England going to Italy to study the fine arts, again points out some of the failures of Englishmen.

> I am English born, and I have English thoughts, not a devil incarnate because I am Italianate,[39] but hating the pride of Italy, because I know their peevishness: yet in all the countries where I have traveled, I have not seen more excess of vanity than we English men practice through vain glory: for as our wits be as ripe as any, so our wills are more ready than they all, to put in effect any of their licentious abuses.[40]

It is in the Renaissance that women begin that slow progress away from the prejudice under which they lived in the Church culture of the Middle Ages. We find references to this changing status in the literature, as for example in the case of Marguerite de Navarre, who describes first refusing the pleasures of Love and then abruptly changing her attitude to adopt the prerequisite court habits, including performance ability in music.

> While love endured I lived in chastity,
> Refusing all base pleasures, for I wished
> To look and act as one who, angel-like,
> Kept himself free from every mortal taint.

---

[37] Robert Greene, *A Quip for an Upstart Courtier* [1592], in *The Life and Complete Works of Robert Greene*, ed. Alexander Grosart (New York: Russell & Russell, 1964), XI, 209.

[38] Robert Greene, *Mourning Garment* [ca. 1590], in Ibid., IX, 136. Additional criticism of England by Englishmen include John Lyly, in *Euphues and his England*, ed. Morris Croll (New York: Russell & Russell, 1964), 226.

> It is the nature of that country to sift strangers. Everyone that shaketh thee by the hand is not joined to thee in heart.

And Phillip Stubbs, in *The Anatomy of the Abuses in England* [1583], ed. Frederick Furnivall (London: The New Shakespeare Society, n.d.), 23.

> There is not a people more corrupt, wicked, or perverse, living upon the face of the earth.

[39] We have mentioned above the growing prejudice toward English students who traveled to Italy for further education. Thomas Nashe, in his *Pierce Penilesse His Supplication to the Devil* [1592], in *The Works of Thomas Nashe*, ed. Ronald McKerrow (Oxford: Blackwell, 1966), I, 186, calls Italy the 'Academy of man-slaughter, the sporting place of murder, the Apothecary-shop of poison for all Nations.' He makes the claim that Pope Sixtus V (1585–1590) was poisoned by the King of Spain, whom he had invited to dinner. The following pope, according to Nashe, after his election sent someone a note reading 'Sol, Re, Me, Fa,' which meant Solus Rex me facit: 'the king of Spain made me pope.'

Nashe (1567–1601) is best known as the author of *The Unfortunate Traveller*, which some consider the first English novel.

[40] Robert Greene, in 'A Notable Discovery of Coosnage' [1591], in *The Life and Complete Works of Robert Greene*, X, 6. In most cases, we have modernized the English.

> I'll try new ways and learn to paint my face,
> Use language that is flowery and refined,
> Invent new fashions for my style of dress;
> I'll learn to dance with ease, play instruments,
> Be skilled in horsemanship and use of arms,
> Or make my eyes seem often full of tears
> And languorously turn them heavenward,
> Showing their whites as stricken lovers do;
> And I will seek to hide my evil thoughts
> Behind a mask of wordless suffering.[41]

It is particularly interesting in this regard that we find a passage which deals with teaching the prostitute how to act like a lady. She is taught the proper social manners for an aristocratic home and how to pretend she understands music.

> And don't sit there like a ninny or an owl, but do everything graciously; and if they are playing music or singing, listen attentively to the music and the song, and praise the musicians and singers, even if you take no delight in them and do not understand what they are doing.[42]

If this passage reflects a lack of true appreciation for art music by the prostitute class, at least they could appreciate the value of the instruments themselves. Instead of money, advises the older prostitute, ask them for musical instruments!

> So ask one man for a lute, another for a harpsichord, this man for a viola, the next for a flute, the third for a little organ, and the fourth for a lyre; it's all to the good. You will then get the *maestri* to come and teach you how to play them, and will try to keep them amused, getting them to play for you for nothing, paying them with hopes and promises and a few pecks at it, but at the gallop.[43]

---

[41] Marguerite de Navarre, *The Prisons*, trans. Hilda Dale (Reading: Whiteknight's Press, 1989), II, 328ff. This long poem is fiction and does not describe actual prison life. Marguerite (1496–1549) was a sister to King François I, and mother to an extraordinary woman, Jeanne d'Albret, mother to Henri IV.

[42] Pietro Aretino, *Dialogues*, trans. Raymond Rosenthal (New York: Marsilio, 1971), 181.

[43] Ibid., 223.

In Praise of Women

As mentioned in the previous essays, the first great characteristic of the Renaissance Period is the new emphasis on the individual man, apart from the traditional dogma of the Church and its views of men. For women it would be a longer birth of freedom from the Church, indeed one that is still continuing today. Nevertheless the harbingers of a new role for women in society were a number of distinguished female musicians of the Italian Renaissance. It is only appropriate, then, that we begin our discussion with the sisters, Beatrice and Isabella d'Este, the most remarkable women of the fifteenth century. Beatrice d'Este (1475–1497) married Duke Ludovico Sforza (1481–1499), famed for his building of numerous hospitals and universities in Milan. We have a letter written by her to her husband in which she describes a banquet held in honor of her marriage in Venice.

> MOST EXCELLEENT AND ILLUSTRIOUS LORD,
> MY DEAREST HUSBAND,
> … a hundred lighted torches hung from the ceiling, and a representation was given on the stage, in which two big animals with large horns appeared, ridden by two figures, bearing golden balls and cups wreathed with verdue. These two were followed by a triumphal chariot, in which Justice sat enthroned, holding a drawn sword in her hand inscribed with the motto 'Concordia,' and wreathed with palms and olive. In the same car was an ox with his feet resting on a figure of St. Mark and the adder. This, as your Highness will readily understand, was meant to signify the League … Behind the chariot came two serpents, ridden by two other youths, dressed like the first riders. All these figures mounted the tribunal in the center of the hall, and danced round Justice, and after dancing for a while, their balls exploded, and out of the flames appeared an ox, a lion, an adder, and a Moor's head suddenly appeared …
>
> Then the banquet followed, and the different dishes and confetti were carried in to the sound of trumpets. First came pastry figures of the pope, the doge, and the duke of Milan, with their armorial bearing and those of your Highness; then St. mark, the adder, and the diamond, and many other objects, all colored and gilded sugar, as many as three hundred in all.[1]

But everyone agreed it was Beatrice, vivacious, brilliant and intellectual, who brought the Renaissance to Milan. A contemporary, Bernardino Corio, in his *Historia di Milano* (1500) recalled,

> Here was the learning of Greece, here Latin verse and prose flourished resplendently, here were the poetic Muses; hither the masters of the sculptor's art and those foremost in painting had gathered from distant countries, and here songs and sweet sounds of every kind and such dulcet harmonies were heard, that they seemed to have descended from Heaven itself upon this excelling court.[2]

---

1 Julia Cartwright, *Beatrice d'Este* (Freeport, NY, 1899), 200ff.
2 Bernardino Corio, *Historia di Milano* [ca. 1500], quoted in Ella Noyes, *Story of Milan* (London, 1908), 165.

One of the artists attracted to the court was Leonardo da Vinci and the story is that he, a man with the broadest resume of any man, in the end gained the job by singing to a lyre he had made in the shape of a horse's head. He was soon fulfilling a wide variety of requests for the court, including decorating stables, planning pageants, designing girdles for Beatrice, painting portraits for family members—and when he had some spare time, his masterpiece, *The Last Supper*.

Beatrice herself was an accomplished singer and one eyewitness reports of her that she spent 'day and night in singing and dancing and in all manner of delights.'[3] A letter from Lodovico's son-in-law, Galeazzo, to Isabella d'Este, sister to Beatrice, describes Beatrice singing chansons while traveling.

> I started at ten o'clock with the duchess [Beatrice] and all of her ladies on horseback to go to Cuzzago, and in order to let your Highness enter fully into our pleasures, I must tell you that first of all I had to ride in a chariot with the duchess and Dioda, and as we drove we sang more than twenty-five chansons, arranged for three voices.

In 1493 Beatrice wrote a letter to her sister, Isabella, describing the 'wedding of the century' which had occurred in Milan, the marriage of Maximilian I, emperor-elect of the Holy Roman Empire with Bianca Maria (1472–1510), a daughter to Galeazzo Maria Sforza.

> Within the church, the aisles were hung with brocade as far as the choir, in front of which a triumphal arch had been erected on massive pillars. This was entirely painted, and bore in the center the effigy of Duke Francesco on horseback, in his ducal robes, with the ducal arms and those of the King of the Romans [Maximilian I] above …
>
> In the extreme corners of the choir were two raised stages, one for the singers, the other for the trumpeters, and in the space between were seated the doctors of law and medicine, with their birettas and capes lined with fur, each according to his rank …
>
> The street leading to the Duomo was beautifully decorated … On both sides of the street, the walls were hung with satin, excepting those houses which have lately been adorned with frescoes, and which are no less beautiful than tapestries.
>
> On the morning of the day, at about nine o'clock, her serene Highness the Queen ascended the triumphal car … which was drawn on this occasion by four snow-white horses. The queen wore a vest of crimson satin, embroidered in gold thread and covered with jewels. Her train was immensely long, and the sleeves were made to look like two wings, which had a very fine appearance … The chariot was followed by the ambassadors who have been sent by his Most Christian Majesty of France to honor these nuptials, and after them came the envoys of the different Italian powers, according to their rank …
>
> When we were all in our places, the Most Reverend Archbishop of Milan entered in full vestments, with the priests in ordinary, and began to celebrate mass with the greatest pomp and solemnity, to the sound of trumpets, piffari, and organ music, together with the voices of the chapel choir, who adapted their singing to Monsignore's time …
>
> After mass had been celebrated with the greatest solemnity, the queen rose from her place between the ambassadors of his Most Christian Majesty, and, accompanied by the duke and my husband, Duchess Isabella and myself, and followed by all the princes of the blood, advanced to the alter. The

---

3   Julia Cartwright, *Beatrice d'Este* (London, 1928), 165.

ambassadors of King Maximilian advanced on their side, and we all stood before the alter, where Monsignore the Archbishop pronounced the marriage service, and the Bishop of Brixen first gave the ring to the queen, and then, assisted by the archbishop, placed on her head the crown, which act was accompanied with great blowing of trumpets, ringing of bells, and firing of guns and shells. And the said crown was of gold, enriched with rubies, pearls, and diamonds, set in the form of arches meeting in the shape of a cross, and on top of all was a figure of the globe, crowned with a small imperial cross.[4]

Beatrice, one of the greatest women of the Renaissance, died at age twenty-two.

In Mantua we encounter the sister to Beatrice, Isabella d'Este (1474–1539), who married Gianfrancesco Gonzaga in 1490. As extraordinary as her sister, the poet Niccolo da Correggio called her, 'the first lady of the world.'[5] When an ambassador said of Isabella 'I had heard much of her singular intelligence, yet I would not have believed the extent of it,' she was only six years of age!

By the age of sixteen she was an accomplished singer and performer on the clavichord. The distinguished poet, Pietro Bembo, who heard her sing some years later, left this account of hearing her singing.

> When she sings, especially to the lute, I believe that Orpheus and Amphion, who knew how to bring inanimate objects to life with their song, would be stupefied with wonder on hearing her, and I do not doubt that neither of them would have known how to do as well as she does in keeping the harmony most diligently so that the rhythm never falters, but rather measures the song, now rising, now falling, and keeps the harmony on the lute and at once according her tongue and both hands with the inflections of the song. Thus if you were to hear her sing even a single time, I am certain that you would be like those who heard the Sirens and forgot their native lands and their own homes.

Another eyewitness heard Isabella sing in 1502, reporting that 'with a lute in her hands she sang various canzonette with [beautiful] tunes and utmost sweetness.'[6]

She also continued to maintain her proficiency on the clavichord as we see in an interesting letter she wrote to Lorenzo da Pavia, a maker of keyboard instruments.

> Honored Sir: We remember that when we were in Pavia we saw a very beautiful and flawless clavichord which you made for the illustrious duchess of Milan, our sister. We now wish to own an instrument of such perfection, and hold the view that there is nobody in all Italy who could satisfy us better than you. We therefore ask you to make us a clavichord of such beauty and excellence as would be consonant with your talents and the confidence that we repose in you. We make only one condition: it must be light to the touch. Our hands are weak and we cannot play well if we have to press the keys hard.

---

4   Ibid., 212ff.

5   Julia Cartwright, *Isabella d'Este* (London, 1915), I, 83.

6   Zambotti, 'Diario ferrarese,' 327, in a report by Cagnolo, quoted in Nino Pirrotta and Elena Povoledo, *Music and Theatre from Poliziano to Monteverdi* (Cambridge: Cambridge University Press, 1982), 52.

She was as demanding of all the artists who worked for her, including the singers of the churches of her lands, as we see in a letter she wrote the abbot of one of these.

> Kindly remember that we discussed your improving the singing of the nuns. I find it shameful that the Women's College performs in a disorderly fashion. If they learned to sing, they would not only offer greater glory to God but please me better ... My ears are offended when I hear such discords.

Isabella also maintained a wind band which played sophisticated music[7] and had her own children study the shawm and trombone privately.

Contemporary evidence seems to point to a fertile environment for women musicians in Ferrara in the sixteenth century. First, Giustiniani reports on the remarkable level of singing among the aristocratic ladies of Ferrara:

> The ladies of Mantua and Ferrara were highly competent, and vied with each other not only in regard to the timbre and training of their voices but also in the design of exquisite [improvisation] delivered at opportune points, but not in excess. Furthermore, they moderated or increased their voices, loud or soft, heavy or light, according to the demands of the piece they were singing; now slow, breaking off with sometimes a gentle sigh, now singing long passages legato or detached, now groups, now leaps, now with long trills, now with short, and again with sweet running passages sung softly, to which sometimes one heard an echo answer unexpectedly. They accompanied the music and the sentiment with appropriate facial expressions, glances and gestures, with no awkward movements of the mouth or hands or body which might not express the feeling of the song. They made the words clear in such a way that one could hear even the last syllable of every word, which was never interrupted or suppressed by [improvisation] or other embellishments.[8]

The most famous musical institution in Ferrara was an orchestra of twenty-three Nuns of St. Vito, who are mentioned frequently in contemporary literature and were pictured in several paintings of the period. It is in Bottrigari that we have the most complete description of this famous orchestra, whom he introduces as representing 'the highest degree of perfection.'

> How you would melt away when you see them convene and play together with so much beauty and grace, and such quietness! ...
>
> They are indubitably women; and when you watch them come ... to the place where a long table has been prepared, at one end of which is found a large clavicembalo, you would see them enter one by one, quietly bringing their instruments, either stringed or wind. They all enter quietly and approach the table without making the least noise and place themselves in their proper place, and some sit, who must do so in order to use their instruments, and others remain standing. Finally the Maestra of the concert sits down at one end of the table and with a long, slender and well-polished baton, and when all the other sisters clearly are ready, gives them without noise several signs to begin, and then continues by beating the measure of the time which they must obey in singing and play-

---

7   Iain Fenlon, *Music and Patronage in Sixteenth-Century Mantua* (Cambridge University Press), 15, fn. 13.

8   Vicenzo Giustiniani, *Discorso sopra la Musica* [ca. 1628], trans. Carol MacClintock (American Institute of Musicology, 1962), 67ff.

ing ... And you would certainly hear such harmony that it would seem to you either that you were carried off to Helicona or that Helicona together with all the chorus of the Muses singing and playing had been transported to that place ...

Neither Fiorino nor Luzzasco, though both are held in great honor by them, nor any other musician or living man, has had any part in their work or in advising them; and so it is all the more marvelous, even stupendous, to everyone who delights in music.[9]

Bottrigari, in speaking further of this female orchestra, reveals two very interesting facts. First, that they ordinarily doubled the parts in church music and, second, that they improvised!

> DESIDERIO. But what about the particulars of their learning to sing, and even more, to play instruments, particularly those of wind, which it is almost impossible to learn without maestri. Being women they cannot easily manipulate Cornetti and Trombones, which are the most difficult of musical instruments.
> BENELLI. Those instruments are nearly always used doubled in the music which they play ordinarily on all the Feast days of the year. And they play them with such grace, and with such a nice manner, and such sonorous and just intonation of the notes that even people who are esteemed most excellent in the profession confess that it is incredible to anyone who does not actually see and hear it. And their [improvisation] is not of the kind that is chopped up, furious, and continuous, such that it spoils and distorts the principal air, which the skillful composer worked ingeniously to give to the *cantilena*; but a times and in certain places there are such light, vivacious embellishments that they enhance the music and give it the greatest spirit.
> DESIDERIO. I am stupefied; I am truly amazed. But, after all, who instructed them in the beginning? It must be necessary if one wishes to maintain, if not to increase the bright splendor of musical concerts, that there be someone who looks after it, and is intelligent and expert enough to instruct, so that it may be done so carefully and dexterously.
> BENELLI. That same nun who is the director of the concerto is also Maestra of all the beginners both in singing and in playing; and with such decorum and gravity of bearing has she always proceeded and continued in this office that her equals, as they are, are glad to acknowledge her and esteem her for their superior, loving and obeying her, fearing and honoring her completely.[10]

But there was still more activity among the women of Ferrara. Bottrigari also mentions in passing three noble ladies in the court of the duchess of Ferrara who also joined in performing with her private music. Vessella also mentions that there was correspondence between the court of Ferrara and a lady wind player named Barbara di Brandeburgo of whom we know nothing else.[11]

Finally, perhaps there were even women percussionists at Ferrara. Johannes Cochlaeus, who studied theology at Ferrara, in his *Tetrachordum Musices* (1511) mentions women musicians only under *tympanum*, coining the term for them *tympanistria*.[12]

---

[9] Hercole Bottrigari, *Il Desiderio*, trans. Carol MacClintock (American Institute of Musicology, 1962), 58ff.

[10] Ibid., 59ff.

[11] Alessandro Vessella, *La Banda* (Milan, 1935), 60ff.

[12] Johannes Cochlaeus, *Tetrachordum Musices*, trans. Clement Miller (American Institute of Musicology, 1970).

Giustiniani, above, mentioned the city of Mantua was also noted for women performers. Two of these, daughters of Antonio Pellizzari, an official of the Accademia Olimpica, were performers on cornett and trombone. A particularly interesting record of 1585 speaks in admiration of their performance in the incidental music to Sophocles' *Oedipus Rex*, composed by Andrea Gabrieli.[13] Fenlon believes these women were among those heard when members of the court visited Ferrara in 1589. An eye-witness recalled,

> For entertainments there were ... hours of exquisite music-making ... With the Duke of Mantua came four ladies from Vicenza who sing very well and play the cornetto and other instruments.[14]

The growing recognition of women during the Renaissance is also reflected in fiction. In Aretino's *Il Marescalco* there is a passage which also reflects the fact that there were distinguished women musicians in sixteenth-century Italy. In this comedy, the point is also made that such talent in wives presents a problem for husbands.

> COUNT. Let's change the subject and get back to the bride: she is talented, you know.
> CAVALIER. It's true. She composed the new madrigal everyone's singing to that tune of Marchetto's.
> JACOPO. That's all I ever sing.
> MARESCALCO. So she is accomplished?
> COUNT. Very accomplished.
> MARESCALCO. And a poet?
> CAVALIER. She is, as you've heard.
> MARESCALCO. It's all clear to me. I can feel them; I can see them coming! She composes? The moment women begin composing songs, husbands begin to feel a weight on their foreheads.[15]

This passage reminds us of a place in German literature, Sebastian Brant's influential book, *The Ship of Fools*. In making a point about the importance of planning ahead, he seems to admit that women are superior in this regard.

> But those who plan the while they act
> Must have experience in fact,
> Or must have watched the other sex,
> Who're very shrewd in these respects.[16]

---

[13] Jonathan Glixon, 'Music at the Venetian Scuole Grandi, 1440–1450,' in *Music in Medieval and Early Modern Europe*, ed. Iain Fenlon (Cambridge: Cambridge University Press, 1981), 128. This music is extant, being part of Gabrieli's *Chori*.

[14] Ibid., 132.

[15] Pietro Aretino, *Il Marescalco*, trans. Leonard Sbrocchi (Ottawa: Dovehouse, 1986), V, ii. Aretino (1492–1556) was one of the first authors whose books were placed on the Index of Prohibited Books, a development of the Council of Trent.

[16] Sebastian Brant, *The Ship of Fools*, trans. Edwin Zeydel (New York: Columbia University Press, 1944), 12.

Shakespeare appears to have expected knowledge of music to be among the attributes of a noble lady. In *Much Ado About Nothing*, there is a young noble of Padua, Benedick,[17] who is a confirmed bachelor, determined never to marry. But, on one occasion he does list the qualities a woman must have, should he decide to marry. She must be rich, good-looking, noble and an excellent musician.[18] Also, Othello includes music among the virtues of his wife.

> To say my wife is fair, feeds well, loves company,
> Is free of speech, sings, plays, and dances well.
> Where virtue is, these are more virtuous.[19]

Finally, we must mention that first 'modern woman,' Kate, in Shakespeare's comedy, *The Taming of the Shrew*. There is in this play a private music lesson, but when Kate discovers the teacher is not really a music teacher but a disguised suitor named Hortensio, she hits him over the head with his lute and called him a 'fiddler,' an intended derogatory reference to an instrument still associated with peasants.

> BAPTISTA. How now, my friend! why dost thou look so pale?
> HORTENSIO. For fear, I promise you, if I look pale.
> BAPTISTA. What, will my daughter prove a good musician?
> HORTENSIO. I think she'll sooner prove a soldier.
> Iron may hold with her but never lutes.
> BAPTISTA. Why, then thou canst not break her to the lute?
> HORTENSIO. Why, no; for she hath broke the lute to me.
> I did but tell her she mistook her frets
> And bowed her hand to reach her fingering;
> When, with a most impatient devilish spirit,
> 'Frets, call you these?' quoth she; 'I'll fume with them';
> And, with that word, she stroke me on the head,
> And through the instrument my pate made way.
> And there I stood amazed for a while.
> As on a pillory, looking through the lute,
> While she did call me rascal, fiddler.[20]

---

17 The spelling of the name is a typical example of Shakespeare's humor, like the preacher 'Martext' in *As You Like It*.
18 *Much Ado About Nothing*, II, iii, 26ff.
19 *Othello*, III, iii, 209.
20 *The Taming of the Shrew*, II, i, 145ff.

PART 2
COMMENTARY ON THE NEW RENAISSANCE VALUES

On Music and Society in the Fifteenth Century

BECAUSE OF THE ENTRENCHED CONSERVATIVE VIEWS of the universities and the Church, most of the philosophers and theorists of the fifteenth century can only be called *ars antiqua*. Nevertheless, one does notice that some people were influenced by the Humanism movement and were thinking in a new way about music. It would, however, be the sixteenth century before the full effects of Humanism were manifested in music thought and practice. We will begin by looking at some of the old-fashioned philosophers.

Franchino Gaffurio (1451–1518) having done his duty to *musica speculativa*, with treatises on theory and harmony, in 1496 published an important book on *musica practica*. Although his book is basically a text on composing, it nevertheless offers important first-hand observations on the actual performance of music in Italy in the second-half of the fifteenth century. This influential book was reprinted four more times before 1512 and material was taken from it by such later writers as Zarlino, Glarean and even John Dowland.

Gaffurio begins his book, by way of a dedication to Duke Ludovico Sforza of Milan, with a glowing tribute to the virtues of music. It makes for interesting reading, but unfortunately these are the old values, values that might have been described five hundred years earlier.

> It is readily apparent, illustrious Prince, how much influence the profession of the art of music had and with what veneration it was held among the ancients. We know this both from the example of the greatest philosophers, who, when they were very old, devoted themselves to this discipline as if in it they put the finishing touch to their studies, and from the practice of the strictest governments, which with the utmost diligence saw to it that whatever was harmful to public morals should be eliminated. Not only did these states not banish the art of music; they cultivated it with the utmost zeal as the mother and nurse of morals. In a word, the position of music is firmly established by the unanimous and steadfast conviction of all people and all nations who have held this art in greater honor than any other.
>
> What other discipline has ever been accepted with so much approval? What other discipline has ever been accepted with so much unanimity by people of every age or sex, so that no one, in any condition of life, has yet been found who was not eager to soothe his cares with music.[1]

From the same backward looking perspective, Gaffurio goes on to state that the study of music has very practical benefits, even related to fields outside of music itself. In this regard he hastens to add that by music he means only a certain kind of music.

> Now music is not, like the other learned disciplines, merely a speculative pursuit: it reaches out into practice, and as was said previously, is connected with morality. I would not have fulfilled my duty if I had remained in the field of research only, serving a few without toiling diligently for the public good also.

---

[1] *The Practica musicae of Franchinus Gafurius*, trans. Irwin Young (Madison: University of Wisconsin Press, 1969), 3.

> Thus this field of music theory is valuable not only because of the knowledge it gives music itself, but also because its roots extend very far; it aids other disciplines. This has been verified by the testimony of very influential men who have acknowledged that they learned literature from music above all else. Fabius Quintilian declares, on the authority of Timagenes, that this art 'is the most ancient of all studies in liberal education.'
>
> Now when I talk about music, I do not mean that theatrical and effeminate music which destroys rather than forms public morals, but rather that moderate, manly music celebrated by the ancient heroes, that music which was presented at the tables of kings and festive banquets when the guests, vying with one anther as the cithara circulated among them, sang of famous deeds of famous men, which was certainly a great inducement to kindle their eagerness for brave deeds. Truly this music rose even higher: she penetrates the heavens, and according to the testimony of the most celebrated bards, tells of the labors of the sun and the wandering moon and the titan stars, and as if not content to have filled the spaces of earth with merit, she invades the skies and takes her place among the mysteries of things divine.[2]

Another music theorist who saw the world of music through a rear-view mirror was Johannes Tinctoris (1435–1511). Gustave Reese calls Tinctoris 'very much a man of his own time,' primarily because of the often quoted statement by Tinctoris that in his view only the compositions of the past forty years were worth performing.[3] We acknowledge that the writings of Tinctoris are indeed valuable for his reflections of performance practice and instruments of the fifteenth century. However, when it came to philosophy and discussion of the nature and value of music, Tinctoris still belonged to the old medieval definition of the liberal arts with its designation of music as a branch of mathematics. This should not be surprising, in his case, as he was in fact a mathematician, identifying himself in the Prologue to his treatise, *Concerning the Nature and Propriety of Tones*, as one who professes 'the mathematical sciences.'[4] In this same work, in speaking of Church modes he says these were named,

> according to arithmetic, without which it is obvious no famous musicians escapes.[5]

Indeed one of the most significant hints in the works of Tinctoris that a new way of thinking about music was in the air is his admission that a musician, surely a humanist, threatened to make him eat one of his mathematically based books on music! In the words of Tinctoris, he recalls, in the above-mentioned treatise, that he has previously written a work on proportions, called *Proportionale Musices*, which had been criticized by one of 'the most ridiculous of all singers.' Indeed, he confides this man 'has not been afraid to menace me with a violent meal of this little book if ever I should return to my native land.'

Tinctoris' critic may have reacted to a passage in the earlier book, which both seems to recognize a new style, by way of pointing out that composers such as Okeghem are breaking the old rules, but testifies once again on behalf of a mathematical understanding of music.

---

2   Ibid., 5ff.

3   Gustave Reese, *Music in the Renaissance* (New York: Norton, 1959), 141.

4   *Concerning the Nature and Propriety of Tones*, trans. Albert Seay (Colorado Springs, 1976), 1.

5   Ibid., 3.

> As a result of this tempest, the musical ability of our time has undergone such an increase that it seems to be a new art ...
>
> But alas! I wonder not only at these but even at many other famous composers, for while they compose so subtly and so ingeniously with incomprehensible smoothness, I have known them to ignore entirely musical proportions or to signify incorrectly those which they do know. I do not doubt that this results from a lack of arithmetic, without which no brilliant achievement in music escapes, for proportion is produced from its entrails.[6]

In another place he says again that errors in proportions among composers he knew as being due to their failure in expertise in arithmetic.[7]

Indeed, Tinctoris seems one thousand years behind the times when he makes the point that one can only understand music as a listener if one has the necessary mathematical background.

> Although the Spartans may have said that they could judge without learning about good and bad harmonies, this position has not been completely defended, for as the universal opinion of all philosophers holds, a sense of hearing is too often lacking. If the truth is to be confessed I have known and put to the test many people, not deaf, but experts in the art of music, who, not admiring the size or beauty of the voice, prefer calf-like bellowings to moderate rationalities and, as I say, to angelic songs. I think these people worthy to have their human faces with their stupid ears changed by divine intervention into those of an ass.[8]

In another place, Tinctoris makes the sixth-century argument that if you don't know the 'numbers' you are not a musician, hence a mere beast.

> A musician is one who takes up the metier of singing, having observed its principles by means of study. Hence, someone has set down the difference between a musician and a singer in the following jingle:
>
> *There is a big difference between musicians and singers.*
> *These know, those talk about, what music is.*
> *And he who doesn't know what he talks about is considered an animal.*[9]

It is no wonder someone threatened to make him eat his books!

The one country that was hopelessly bogged down back in the *ars antiqua* frame of mind during the fifteenth century was France. In the history of aesthetics in music, fifteenth-century France is a curious and ironic chapter. In the field of Church music there were some very gifted men, writing important music. But Dufay, Binchois, Dunstable, Ockeghem and the rest were already an anachronism. While the polyphonic style would continue to develop for another century, the humanists, particularly in Italy, who represented the new direction music history would take, were already condemning and abandoning this style. General music history texts still pretend this polyphonic activity was the sole and substance of Western Euro-

---

6   *Proportionale Musices*, trans. Albert Seay in *Journal of Music Theory* 1, no. 1 (1957): 27, http://www.jstor.org/stable/843090

7   Ibid., III, ii.

8   Ibid., 5.

9   *Dictionary of Musical Terms*, trans. Carl Parrish (New York: Free Press of Glencoe, 1963), 45.

pean composition at this time, but the truth is that it was a style driven by scholastic principles of an era whose time had already passed. No matter how effective some of this polyphonic music is, it is music written from a premise of mathematics, and not feeling. Thus, it is no surprise that these composers,

> began to indulge in complicated rhythmic tricks and in the invention of highly involved methods of notating them.[10]

The failure in French thought to participate in the new humanistic ideas was due in part to two rather obvious problems. First, the century was dominated by wars, both with England (1337–1453) and with the Burgundians, creating an intellectual environment inhospitable to the arts. Second, at a time when the arts were still supported primarily by the aristocracy, this society was led by a series of very weak kings. Just before the turn of the century there was Charles V, an idiot who was completely insane by 1392. Charles VI and VII were weak and overwhelmed by war. It was Charles VII who could not prevent the tragedy of Joan of Arc. Next comes Louis XI, a strange man who dressed as an impoverished pilgrim. It would only be Charles VIII (1483–1498), by virtue of his aborted crusade, who would bring the Renaissance back to France from Italy.

Curiously enough, we find some writers in fifteenth-century France who, taken by themselves, appear to reveal no awareness or influence of the great flowering of Humanism during the previous century. There was still love poetry intended to be sung, and indeed Charles VI founded a Court of Love in 1401 in which members wrote poetry and music in the thirteenth-century Trouvère manner. The extant poetry praises love, but it no longer praises the power of music. And far from representing Humanism, some writers appear to have reverted to medieval ideals. It seems incredible that Christine de Pizan (1364–1430) could write,

> The holy doctors of the Church prove it to us, that all the joys that one could want or wish in this world are nothing but mud, filth, and emptiness compared to those of the heavenly glory that those who die well receive at the end.[11]

As we can sense in her choice of words, a certain pessimism hangs over French literature of the fifteenth century and, indeed, the subject of music is rarely mentioned. In Christine de Pizan, it sometimes seems as if she deliberately omits music. For example, in one of her books, she describes, in a vision, visiting 'a noble university.' She finds there 'each separate branch of knowledge,' including grammar, dialectic, arithmetic, geometry, astrology, theology, philosophy, 'and so on with the other forbidden and liberal arts.' Music is conspicuously missing.[12]

---

[10] Gustave Reese, *Music in the Renaissance* (New York: Norton, 1959), 11, quoting Apel.

[11] Christine de Pizan, *The Epistle of the Prison of Human Life*, trans. Josette Wisman (New York: Garland Publishing, 1984), 51. Christine de Pizan was perhaps the most prolific writer of the fifteenth century. Reared as the daughter of Charles V's Italian physician, from the age of five Christine lived in the Louvre and enjoyed an education as good as that available to that of any aristocrat in Paris.

[12] Christine de Pizan, *Christine's Vision*, trans. Glenda McLeod (New York: Garland Publishing, 1993), II, ii.

In another book, she quotes a story of Cyrus, King of Persia (ca. 550 BC), one often retold in early literature, which told of his concern over a conquered people and his decision to have the people instructed in music so that they might become effeminate and thus be unlikely to cause trouble. It is interesting that when Christine de Pizan tells this story, she omits 'music' and substitutes for it 'gambling and accustoming themselves to merchandise.'[13]

A rare glimpse of new values can be found among the poets, such as Pierre de Ronsard. In a letter to his royal patron he promises that music will lighten his cares and allow him to return to his royal burden fresher and better disposed. Then Ronsard makes an interesting observation on the difference between the arts and science, a definite harbinger of the future in its implicit higher recognition of the value of art.

> The divine inspirations of music, poetry, and painting do not arrive at perfection by degrees, like the other sciences, but by starts, and like flashes of lightening, one here, another there, appear in various lands, then suddenly vanish. For that reason, when some excellent worker in this art reveals himself, you should guard him with care, as being something so excellent that it rarely appears.[14]

In the German-speaking lands, during the fourteenth and fifteenth centuries one can see a rapidly accelerating force of intellectual ideas, but they are centered in a contest between Church and State. Several German towns were in open revolt against the Catholic Church during the fifteenth century, among them Madeburg, Passau and Erfurt. The Hussite revolt in Bohemia was having repercussions in Germany.

Germany had its humanists as well, including Jakob Wimpheling, Conradus Celtes, Johann Muller and Johananes Trithemius. The latter, the abbot of Sponheim, wrote in 1496, 'The days of building monasteries are past; the days of their destruction are coming.'[15] These men helped construct the explosive atmosphere which Luther would ignite. It was not an environment likely to produce much philosophic contemplation on the arts.

An important, if old-fashioned, fifteenth-century scholastic German philosopher was Nicholas of Cusa in whom we find some strange notions about the origin of music. The medieval philosophers had kept education alive during the Dark Ages by endorsing the Liberal Arts as useful for helping the Christian understand the Scriptures. Now, Nicholas tells us, God used the Liberal Arts to create the world!

> In creating the world, God used arithmetic, geometry, music, and likewise astronomy. (We ourselves also use these arts when we investigate the comparative relationships of objects, of elements, and of motions.) For through arithmetic God united things. Through geometry He shaped them, in order that they would thereby attain firmness, stability, and mobility in accordance with their conditions. Through music He proportioned things in such a way that there is not more earth in earth than water in water, air in air, and fire in fire, so that no one element is altogether reducible to another. As a result, it happens that the world-machine cannot perish …

---

[13] Christine de Pizan, *The Book of the Body Politic*, trans. Kate Forhan (Cambridge: Cambridge University Press), I, xxviii.

[14] Pierre de Ronsard, *Livre des mélanges* [1560].

[15] James Thompson, *Economic and Social History of Europe in the Later Middle Ages* (New York, 1931), 604.

> And so, God, who created all things in number, weight, and measure, arranged the elements in an admirable order. (Number pertains to arithmetic, weight to music, measure to geometry.)[16]

General music history texts often find a certain lull in fifteenth-century England, after Dunstable, with no significant new composers. For example, Reese characterizes the period as one of 'insular conservatism,' and quotes Tinctoris as commenting that the English 'continue to use one and the same style of composition, which shows a wretched poverty of invention.'[17] Such references to conservatism are not only true, but may well reflect a broader philosophical climate.

In England, as in France, there seems to have been a momentary philosophical swing of the pendulum away from the fourteenth-century gains of the humanists and back to the old dogma of the Church. Indeed, the debates, given below, between Reason and Sensuality, may well be taken as metaphors for the struggle between the Church and the humanists. Unfortunately, in both 'debates' it is the old-fashioned church view which prevails, not the views of humanism and the future.

In the first of these, found in John Lydgate's 'Reson and Sensuallyte,'[18] early in the fifteenth century, Dame Nature begins by stating that man has essentially two choices, two paths, he can follow. We take this as another illustration of early deduction, long before the confirmation of modern clinical research, of the fundamentally different forms of understanding in the twin hemispheres of the brain. This is made more evident when Dame Nature explains that these two paths are the Eastern, the way of Reason, and the Western, the way of Sensuality. This conforms perfectly with the nature of the twin hemispheres of the brain, of course, as 'the Eastern,' that is the direction of the right hand, represents the left hemisphere, which includes all of Reason, and the Western direction, referring to the left hand, is similarly an association with the right hemisphere, which includes music, spatial perception and the emotions. It is particularly interesting here, that Dame Reason associates with the right hemisphere (the Western) those things of a passing and transitory nature, characteristics for which music was often criticized in medieval literature.

> The wey of sensualyte,
> which set his entente in al
> To thinges that be temporal,
> Passynge and transytorie,
> And fulfylled of veyn glorie.[19]

---

[16] Nicholas of Cusa, 'On Learned Ignorance,' trans. Jasper Hopkins (Minneapolis: Banning Press, 1981), II, xiii, 175.

[17] Gustave Reese, *Music in the Renaissance* (New York: Norton, 1959), 763.

[18] The discussion begins with line 644.

[19] *Lydgate's Reson and Sensuallyte*, ed. Ernst Sieper (London: Oxford University Press, 1901), lines 678ff. Lydgate mentions this traditional left hemisphere prejudice again in his *Fall of Princes*, VI, 18ff, where 'a marvelous woman' appears before him covered with summer flowers on the right side of her body and with the left side 'beaten by winter storms.'

Dame Nature now explains that man has been given two Virtues, the Sensitive, by which he perceives things, and Understanding. In contrast to most philosophers by this time, who had agreed that the basis of our understanding comes from information obtained by the senses, Lydgate diminishes the value of sensory information by comparing it with the bark of a tree, which has only doubtful and outward understanding of that which is within. The purpose of intelligence in man, he says, is that he may understand the divine.

Man should be governed only by Reason, 'lest he suffer the great shame of losing his reputation.'[20] Dame Nature acknowledges that man's feelings often conflict with Reason, since sensuality desires only bodily delight. She advises man to set his mind on Heavenly things and hold fast to Reason, whose road leads to Heaven.[21]

The second 'debate,' a lengthy discussion of Reason and Sensuality, is found in the play, *Nature*, by Henry Medwall (b. 1461). The play opens with Nature stating that there is nothing on earth which is not a partner to her influence. Among the examples she offers, are two musical ones:

> Who taught the cock his watch hours to observe,
> And sing with courage, with shrill throat on high? ...
> Who taught the nightingale to record so well
> Her strange tunes, in silence of the night?

Nature introduces the principal discussion with another interesting subconscious deduction of the twin hemispheres of the brain. She tells man that Reason will govern him on his way, but that Sensuality is on *the other side*!

> Address thyself now towards your journey,
> For as of now, you shall no longer here abide.
> Lo, here, Reason, to govern you in your way,
> And Sensuality, upon your other side.
> But Reason I appoint to be your chief guide,
> With Innocence, that is your tender nurse,
> Evermore to win you from the appetite of vice.[22]

Nature responds by warning man once again to 'Let Reason govern you in every situation.'[23]

Now Sensuality enters and protests to Nature that she should have equal status with Reason and Innocence.[24] She contends, 'I am the chief perfection of his nature!' Without me, man would have no feeling, he might as well be made of wood or stone.

---

[20] Ibid., lines 760ff.

[21] Ibid., lines 768, 778, 831 and 844.

[22] Henry Medwall, *Nature*, I, 99ff.

[23] Ibid., I, 159.

[24] Ibid., I, 169ff.

> And now you have put me out of his service,
> And have assigned Reason to be his guide
> With Innocence his nurse; thus am I set aside!
>
> You made him lord of all beasts living,
> And nothing worthy, as far as I can see;
> For if there be in him no manner of feeling
> No lively quickness, what kind of lord is he?
> A lord made of rags! or carved from a tree!
> And fares as an image carved from stone
> That can do nothing but stand alone!

Allow me to have influence with him, Sensuality pleas with Nature, and I will make him governor of the world. But if 'Reason tickles him in the ear,' he will never be able to do earthly good.

No, says Nature, Reason must be preferred, reminding Sensuality, 'You have brought many men to a wretched end.'[25]

Sensuality now becomes agitated,

> By Christ! yet will I not hide my face,
> For as soon as we shall to the world resort
> I have no doubt he will me support.[26]

You should obey me, Reason says to Sensuality, wherever I go. Sensuality answers, 'No, that I shall never do!'[27]

Sensuality now proposes to Reason a bargain, which once again subconsciously reflects the completely separate natures of the twin hemispheres of the brain. It is as if we can hear the right hemisphere speaking to the left,

> Meddle in no point that belongs to me,
> And I promise never to meddle with thee.[28]

At length Man decides to subjugate his Sensuality to Reason.

> Reason, Sir, my chief counselor.
> And this, Innocence, my previous nurse,
> And Sensuality, that other, by whom I have power
> To do as all sensuous beasts do.
> But Reason and Innocence, chiefly these two,
> Have the whole rule and governance of me,
> To whom is subdued my Sensuality.[29]

---

[25] Ibid., I, 211ff.

[26] Ibid., I, 241ff.

[27] Ibid., I, 314.

[28] Ibid., I, 321.

[29] Ibid., I, 533.

Later another character, Pride, suggests that a 'wild worm' has come into man's head if he thinks he will always be led only be Reason. He doubts that Reason will always endure with man, pointing out that, 'Sensuality ... is chief ruler, when Reason is away.'[30]

In spite of all these old-fashioned, scholastic and Church philosophical viewpoints, there was also an increased amount of humanistic activity during the fifteenth century. But this occurred more on the 'practical,' that is to say, performance, side of things, in the increased concert activity in the towns and courts. This we will treat in another place, as well as the growing complaints against polyphonic music. You won't find these complaints in music history texts because we have not yet come to the great masters of this style, Josquin and Palestrina. To tell it like it was would be to diminish considerably their chapters on those composers and rob the Renaissance as they see it of its great climax. In this essay we will confine ourselves to a few literary comments reflecting Humanism.

Nothing so marks the progress of Humanism in Italy, not to mention the distance traveled by the Church since the Middle Ages, than a pronouncement made by Pope Nicholas V (1447–1455) shortly before his death. He urged Church officials to follow his example in supporting the arts and learning for the good of the Church. He even went so far as to proclaim the humanities as an essential part of the education of the clergy.[31] This pope, in fact, not only provided large stipends to leading scholars to make translations of ancient Greek literature, and to scribes to make copies, but he himself had personally made discoveries of important manuscripts.[32] He was a very rare exception, of course, as popes go. Indeed there would soon be a conservative counter-Reformation movement in Rome during which the Church sought refuge in returning to its ancient dogma.

Gradually, however, during the course of the fifteenth century, painting, sculpture and architecture began to be accepted as members of the liberal arts and distinguished from the manual arts. It had taken two thousand years since the ancient Greeks to reach this point and yet to come was the concept of the 'fine arts,' which appears in the sixteenth century in the term *Arti di disegno*. Likewise the purpose of art was becoming more defined. Alberti said the painter should please the crowd [*tutta la moltitudine*], but Leonardo raised the standard to pleasing the higher part of the crowd, speaking scornfully of those painters who aim to please the ignorant.[33]

This increased recognition of music as an art is also reflected in some areas by an increase in pay for the musicians. We can see this interest in creating higher levels of artist among the household musicians in Ferrara. Under the next duke, Ercole I (1471–1505) the musi-

---

30 Ibid., II, 308ff.

31 John D'Amico, *Renaissance Humanism in Papal Rome* (Baltimore: Johns Hopkins University Press, 1983), 122.

32 Charles Stinger, *The Renaissance in Rome* (Bloomington: Indiana University Press, 1985), 283ff. Not all Church officials were so enlightened. The important philosopher, Giovanni Pico della Mirandola, was charged with heresy and had to flee to France in 1486 after he invited fellow scholars to Rome to debate his 'Nine Hundred Theses,' which he had deduced from his study of ancient and medieval philosophy. [Ibid., 301]

33 Anthony Blunt, *Artistic Theory in Italy, 1450–1600* (Oxford: Clarendon Press, 1959), 55ff.

cal establishment grew to include separate ensembles of singers, 'musici, trombeti, piffari,' and 'tromboni.' Early in his reign he established the goal of creating 'a most celebrated cappella,' for which he mentions in a letter the 'excellent musicians, whom we are looking for everywhere.'[34] By 1474, this court, under Galeazzo, had an establishment of forty singers, of which eighteen were designated 'da camera.' The pay records indicate that one of the musicians was paid as much as a physician and all of them nearly twice the pay for court workers such as gardeners.[35]

There began to be a demand for German musicians and the high pay of these particular German musicians, and their status and influence in other countries, in Italy[36] and Spain in particular, are a testimonial to the quality of their music. Reseach by Keith Polk found that in the 1440s Augsburg civic musicians were in the top fifteen percent of the wealth of the city.[37]

From this point forward there is an increased emphasis on communicating the emotions through music. This is the point where most philosophers began to stress how important it is for the music to mirror the emotions of the text in poetry. Vincenzo Calmeta, for example, writes that while pleasure may be experienced from many kinds of music for its own sake, when music is used together with poetry it must give up some of its individuality and take on the primary responsibility of emphasizing the emotions and thought of the text.

> We must praise the good judgment of those, who in singing put all their effort into expressing the words well … and have them accompanied by the music in the manner of masters accompanied by their servants … not making the thoughts and emotions subservient to the music, but the music to the emotions and thoughts.[38]

Similarly, in a note to composers, Gaffurio also emphasizes that the music must emotionally support the words. It is interesting here that he associates love with 'doleful sounds.'

> Let the composer of music strive to adapt the melody in its sweetness to the words of the song, so that when the words concern love or a longing for death or some lamentation, he will articulate and arrange doleful sounds so far as he can, as the Venetians are wont to do.[39]

The end of feelings in music is, of course, to move the listener. Among the treatises on music extant from the University of Padua in the fifteenth century, is one by Prosdocimus de Beldemandis, 'Brevis summula proportionum,' which deals with both *musica speculativa* and

---

34 Quoted in Lewis Lockwood, 'Strategies of Music Patronage in the Fifteenth Century: the Cappella of Ercole I d'Este,' in Iain Fenlon, ed., *Music in Medieval and Early Modern Europe* (Cambridge: Cambridge University Press, 1981), 231.

35 Werner Gundersheimer, *Ferrara* (Princeton, 1973), 293ff.

36 A civic statute of 1445 in Florence said future civic hires must be German, see Keith Polk, 'Instrumental music in the Urban Centres of Renaissance Germany,' in *Early Music History,* VII, 176.

37 Ibid., 179.

38 Quoted in Nino Pirrotta and Elena Povoledo, *Music and Theatre from Poliziano to Monteverdi* (Cambridge: Cambridge University Press, 1982), 28.

39 Young, *The Practica Musicae of Franchinus Gafurius,* 161.

musica practica.⁴⁰ In his 'Tractatus de contrapuncto,' he stresses that one must judge music by the ear as well as the intellect and recognizes the ability of *harmonia delectabilis* to move the listener.⁴¹ As odd as it seems to say so, to listen with the ear, instead of the intellect and to have a purpose of to move the listener are hallmarks of Humanism and were ideas made very secondary for the previous one thousand five hundred years by the Church.

When one begins to understand that music is for the ear, rather than being a manifestation of mathematics, one begins to listen. From this point on one even begins to find an occasional theoretical discussion that bears evidence of how we hear. An example is the music theorist Giorgio Valla, who attempts to discuss tone itself from an aesthetic perspective rather than from a mathematical (overtone series) one.

> Some are straight, others round and reverberant; some rough, others flabby; some harsh, others grating; some are equal, such as unisons, others unequal, such as combinations of high and low pitch. Some are equal sounding, as are the diapason and disdiapason; others consonant, such as the diapente and diatessaron. Some are melodious, such as the tone; others are dissonant and hard, like the tritone; others unmelodious, such as the semitone and ditone. There are transparent, yet not unpleasant, sounds; others are lean, like the voices of infants or sick persons; others are plump and dense, such as voices of men of warm temperament, or thin, as of boys, eunuchs, and women. Or they may be hard and bitter, harsh and violent, like thunder or hammering, or mute and raucous. Of voices some are strong and vigorous and at the same time pleasant, others broken and dissolute, weak and tremulant.⁴²

What we begin to see, then, in the fifteenth century, is a fundamental divide, the humanists who sought to return music to its ancient purpose of expressing feeling moving away from the Church and university's concept as music being a branch of mathematics, containing no more emotion than mathematics itself. One who understood this difference was Marsilio Ficino, the fifteenth-century founder of the Florentine Academy and a philosopher who played the lyre for his own relaxation and for concerts in the Medici palace.⁴³ He symbolized very nicely the new place of music in the life of man when he observed that music served man's 'spirit' in the same way medicine serves the body and theology the soul.

---

40 Nan Cooke Carpenter, *Music in the Medieval and Renaissance Universities* (Norman: University of Oklahoma Press, 1958), 44ff.

41 Ibid., 46.

42 Valla, 'De Musica,' quoted in Claude V. Palisca, 'An Italian Renaissance in Music,' in *Humanism in Italian Renaissance Musical Thought* (New Haven: Yale University Press, 1985, 79ff.

43 Paul Kristeller, 'Music and Learning in the Early Italian Renaissance,' in *The Journal of Renaissance and Baroque Music* 1, no. 4 (1947): 269ff.

Johannes Tinctoris on Music

GUSTAVE REESE CALLS JOHANNES TINCTORIS (1435–1511) 'very much a man of his own time,' primarily because of the often quoted statement by Tinctoris that in his view only the compositions of the past forty years were worth performing.[1]

Be that as it may, and for all his brilliance and skill in observation of the current musical scene, he was nevertheless a theorist of the old Scholastic school. He was, after all, a canon of the church at Nivelles early in his career, which perhaps explains that for him (like some modern musicologists!) music meant Church music, with only token recognition of the wider world of music going on all around him. During his tenure in Naples under Ferdinand I, Tinctoris must have been exposed not only to Italian Humanism, but to a wide variety of secular art music of high quality. Yet he assigns little space to these things in his treatises and concluded Jesus Christ to have been the greatest singer.

Music, to Tinctoris, still belonged to the old medieval definition of the liberal arts, where it resided as a branch of mathematics. Contemporary information makes this association with Tinctoris irrefutably clear. A biographical note of 1495 calls him an outstanding mathematician, as well as a musician of the highest rank,[2] and in the Prologue to his own treatise *Concerning the Nature and Propriety of Tones*, Tinctoris identifies himself as one who professes 'the mathematical sciences.'[3] In this same work, in speaking of Church modes he says these were named,

> according to arithmetic, without which it is obvious no famous musicians escapes.[4]

He also mentions, in this same treatise, that he has previously written a work on proportions, called *Proportionale Musices*, which had been criticized by one of 'the most ridiculous of all singers.' Indeed, he confides this man 'has not been afraid to menace me with a violent meal of this little book if ever I should return to my native land.' We can only assume that it was a musician of more modern humanistic leanings who made this threat. The critic may have reacted to this passage in the earlier book, which both seems to recognize a new style, to the extent that even composers such as Okeghem are breaking the old rules, and testifies once again on behalf of a mathematical understanding of music.

> As a result of this tempest, the musical ability of our time has undergone such an increase that it seems to be a new art.

---

1 Gustave Reese, *Music in the Renaissance* (New York: Norton, 1959), 141.

2 Quoted in Ibid., 138.

3 *Concerning the Nature and Propriety of Tones*, trans. Albert Seay (Colorado Springs, 1976), 1.

4 Ibid., 3.

> But alas! I wonder not only at these but even at many other famous composers, for while they compose so subtly and so ingeniously with incomprehensible smoothness, I have known them to ignore entirely musical proportions or to signify incorrectly those which they do know. I do not doubt that this results from a lack of arithmetic, without which no brilliant achievement in music escapes, for proportion is produced from its entrails.[5]

In another place he accounts for errors in proportions among composers he knew as being due to their failure in expertise in 'arithmetic.'[6]

One frequently discussed topic of the old Scholastic tradition which Tinctoris did not accept was the hypothesis of the 'music of the spheres.' However, because the topic was still being seriously advanced by some in the fifteenth century, he felt compelled to begin his treatise, the *Art of Counterpoint*, with a reference to, and rejection of, this two thousand-year-old notion.

> I unshakably agree with Aristotle …, together with our more recent philosophers, who most clearly prove that there is neither real nor potential sound in the heavens.[7]

Tinctoris gives as the first purpose of music that it delight the listener, adding that he agrees with Boethius that 'consonances rule all the delight of music.'[8] He continues by expressing his feelings very clearly regarding music which offends the ear.

> And, if I may refer to what I have heard and seen, I have held in my hands at one time or another many old songs of unknown authorship which are called *apocrypha* that are so inept and stupidly composed that they offended the ears rather than pleased them.[9]

An additional purpose of music given by Tinctoris is quite interesting for it is something quite similar to Aristotle's original concept of catharsis, a term he invented to describe the effect of Tragedy on the observer. With regard to music, Tinctoris describes the listener as being 'more refreshed and wiser.' He begins this passage with his observation, mentioned above, that he believed no composition more than forty years old was worthy of performance. He then lists composers he considered exemplary, including names familiar to musicians today, such as Dufay, Dunstable, Busnois, Binchois and Okeghem. After admitting he does not know whether the source of their excellence is 'some heavenly influence or to a zeal of constant application,' he gives the aesthetic purpose we have referred to.

---

[5] *Proportionale Musices*, trans. Albert Seay in *Journal of Music Theory* 1, no. 1 (1957): 27, http://www.jstor.org/stable/843090

[6] Ibid., III, ii.

[7] *The Art of Counterpoint*, trans. Albert Seay (American Institute of Musicology, 1961), 14.

[8] Ibid.

[9] Ibid.

> Almost all of these men's works exhale such sweetness, that, in my opinion, they should be considered most worthy, not only for men and heroes, but even for the immortal gods. Certainly I never listen to them or study them without coming away more refreshed and wiser.[10]

Tinctoris acknowledges the effect of music on the listener, but here mostly in the context of rather practical results: music delights God, it excites the soul to piety, it elevates the mind, it makes work easier and it increases convivial pleasures.[11]

But on the other hand, for all his care in associating both the natural sweetness of consonance, and that dissonance which offends, with the musical materials themselves, Tinctoris was not quite willing to accept the position of both the ancient Greeks and the modern humanists that musical materials also affect character. No doubt his beliefs, like those regarding the mathematical nature of music, were conditioned by his adherence to the old Church dogma, which clearly had reserved for itself the role of character formation. At the same time, he seemed to share with the Greeks a genuine respect for the power of music.

> And how great was that melody by whose power the gods, shades, dread spirits, animals, including those capable of reason, and inanimate objects are read to have been moved! For (and this is the unbelievable part) it is not far from a mystery, since poets would not have conceived such things about music unless they had seen its power as something to be marveled at, with, at times, a divine invigoration of the soul.[12]

For Tinctoris any ability musical performance had in reflecting a particular emotional quality was a characteristic not merely of the musical materials themselves, but also of their performance or in the natural emotional makeup of the listener.

> To be sure, it will be possible for a song in one and the same [mode] to be plaintive and cheerful and stern and neutral, not only in regard to composers and singers, but instruments and sound-makers as well. For what person skilled in this art does not know how to compose, to sing and to perform some [melodies] plaintively, others cheerfully, some sternly and others neutrally, although their composition, singing and performance are carried out in the same [mode]?
>
>   Also, certain kinds of voices and instruments are made or are naturally or artificially plaintive, certain cheerful, certain stern and certain neutral …
>
>   Certain of these particular harmonies agree, are fitting and are useful for various ages and customs. There is not the same delight or a similar judgment to all people. A cheerful soul is delighted by cheerful harmonies and conversely stern ones are accepted by a stern soul.[13]

Modern clinical research has proven that Tinctoris is not quite correct, for we know today that emotions are universal and that the emotions communicated by music are also universal, at least on a general level. It follows, from common sense if nothing else, that ordinary listeners would not appreciate music as they do, if it were necessary for them to understand

---

10   Ibid., 14ff.

11   Gustave Reese, *Music in the Renaissance*, 146.

12   *Proportionale Musices*, Prologue.

13   *Concerning the Nature and Propriety of Tones*, 4ff.

the conceptual aspects of it. But Tinctoris returns to the ancient dogma, which followed the Church view that music was about mathematics and not emotion. Only musically educated persons, he declares, can properly hear music.

> Although the Spartans may have said that they could judge without learning about good and bad harmonies, this position has not been completely defended, for as the universal opinion of all philosophers holds, a sense of hearing is too often lacking. If the truth is to be confessed I have known and put to the test many people, not deaf, but experts in the art of music, who, not admiring the size or beauty of the voice, prefer calf-like bellowings to moderate rationalities and, as I say, to angelic songs. I think these people worthy to have their human faces with their stupid ears changed by divine intervention into those of an ass ...
>
> Only musicians judge sounds correctly. Tullius has therefore written this to Hortensius: 'Many things escape us in song; only those trained in this field hear plainly.' Hence, Aristotle comes to this conclusion not uselessly in the eighth book of the *Politics*: 'The young should give themselves to the practice of the art of music so that, as old men, they can judge and enjoy it correctly.'[14]

In another place, Tinctoris extends this view to the performer as well, paraphrasing an old Scholastic idea first advanced by Guido d'Arezzo.

> A musician is one who takes up the metier of singing, having observed its principles by means of study. Hence, someone has set down the difference between a musician and a singer in the following jingle:
>
>> *There is a big difference between musicians and singers.*
>> *These know, those talk about, what music is.*
>> *And he who doesn't know what he talks about is considered an animal.*[15]

Finally, in another treatise, Tinctoris mentions the importance of music in increasing pleasures, observing that,

> singers and all types of instrumentalists—shawms, drummers, organists, lutenists, recorder and trumpet players—add to the magnificence of great banquets.[16]

He points to Obrecht, in his only reference to this composer, as being expert in such music. While never mentioned in general music history texts, Obrecht's father was the leader of a civic band and perhaps Obrecht was therefore more active in secular music than the student would ever guess.

The first interesting comment which Tinctoris makes regarding melody suggests that for him it still had its ancient association with poetry.

> A melodic interval is the immediate connection of one syllable after another.[17]

---

[14] Ibid., 5.

[15] *Dictionary of Musical Terms*, trans. Carl Parrish (New York: Free Press of Glencoe, 1963), 45.

[16] Quoted in Gustave Reese, *Music in the Renaissance*, 146.

[17] *Dictionary of Musical Terms*, 17.

Next he makes two statements which may seem startling to the modern reader.

> Melody is the same as harmony.
> Melos is the same as harmony.[18]

Tinctoris, unfortunately, does not explain what he meant by this, but these statements make much sense in view of modern clinical research. Although in modern music schools melody and harmony are treated as if separate, but equal, elements of music, clinical research clearly demonstrates that melodic patterns have a strong genetic universality. All melody has harmonic character, of course. But beyond this fact, harmony probably has little impact on the listener, even with regard to feeling. The old 'major is happy and minor is sad' cliché is not borne out in either clinical research or in actual practice by composers. Melody communicates happy or sad feelings, but harmony probably contributes primarily to the effect of motion.

In one other place, Tinctoris says 'Harmony is a certain pleasantness caused by an agreeable sound.'[19] Tonality (mode) he associates only with a single line, above all with the tenor, of a polyphonic work. Indeed, in one place he suggests that if one tries to sing a polyphonic work with the tenor part left out,

> the other parts would sound improperly discordant to each other and would bitterly offend our ears.[20]

For the smallest element of time, the single note, Tinctoris quite correctly reminds the reader that notation is only a symbol of the real music.

> A note is the symbol of a sound, and is of either definite or indefinite time value.[21]

Perhaps the most impressive of all the treatises by Tinctoris is the *Proportionale Musices*, an extraordinarily complex exposition of the possibilities of this system of progressive metric changes in the individual line. Reese observes,

> We find him here a musical mathematician, at times explaining proportions that can have had little to do with actual practice, though they may have been studied for purposes of exercise.[22]

We would go further and declare it impossible to imagine that any singer, then or now, could manage much of these abstract potentialities. Tinctoris himself seems to recognize this when he recommends a 'simple method' of approach to proportions in Church music to eliminate 'delay and doubt' in performance, for,

---

[18] Ibid., 41.

[19] Ibid., 9.

[20] *Proportionale Musices*, III, iv.

[21] *Dictionary of Musical Terms*, 47.

[22] Reese, *Music in the Renaissance*, 146.

When any compositions have been brought to a performing group, they ought to be performed without the slightest hesitation.[23]

Nevertheless, here Tinctoris was clearly on home ground and he is very outspoken regarding the errors he finds in even gifted composers. He does this, he says, not from arrogance, but for the purpose of fighting for truth.[24] In various places he criticizes 'the inexcusable error of Okeghem,'[25] a 'bad use' by Dufay[26] (in another place, since he admired Dufay, he says the composer has 'most wonderfully erred'[27]) and with a 'ridiculous' practice by Pasquin, 'lacking in all art and melody.'[28]

Among Tinctoris's observations regarding form, we find the following the most interesting. The reader will notice the suggestion here of improvisation, a topic we are much indebted to Tinctoris for, for his many insightful comments.

> A canon is a rule showing the purpose of the composer behind a certain obscurity.[29]
>
> ......
>
> A cantilena is a small piece which is set to a text on any kind of subject, but more often to an amatory one.[30]
>
> ......
>
> A part-song is one which is produced by the relationship of the notes of one part to those of another in various ways, and which is commonly called 'composed' [written out].[31]
>
> ......
>
> A *cantus ut jacet* [the piece as it lies] is a piece which is sung entirely as it is written, without any improvisation [diminution].[32]
>
> ......
>
> A hymn is the praise of God in song.[33]

The careful attention Tinctoris gives to consonant and dissonant intervals is limited to his principal interest in Church music and his conclusions unfortunately do not reflect the broader world of secular music being performed all around him.[34] Nevertheless, one definition of con-

---

23 *Proportionale Musices*, I, ii.

24 Ibid., Prologue.

25 Ibid., I, iii.

26 Ibid.

27 Ibid., III, vi.

28 Ibid., I, vi.

29 *Dictionary of Musical Terms*, 13.

30 Ibid., 13.

31 Ibid., 13. This appears to be a distinction to a melody with improvised parts.

32 Ibid.

33 Ibid., 37.

34 Reese, *Music in the Renaissance*, 145.

sonance which he offers, in his *Dictionary*, would have been acceptable to all musicians, for he defines it as 'a blending of different pitches, which strikes pleasantly on the ear.'[35] In another treatise, he constantly prefers the simple definition, 'sweet,' but adds an important new insight. Here he clearly associates both consonance and dissonance with *feeling*, and not mathematical ratios. It is a truth almost completely forgotten in today's music theory classroom.

> A concord is the mixture of two pitches, sounding sweetly to our ears by its natural virtue; I think that the word, 'concord,' is derived metaphorically from 'con' and 'cor,' for just as a sweet friendship is brought about from the coming together of two hearts that are in mutual agreement, so is a smooth concord made from a mixture of two pitches that are mutually agreeable.[36]

With regard to the discussion by Tinctoris of the various intervals, we again focus only on those comments which carry aesthetic clues. Among the intervals which he considers, in general, 'concords,' he begins with the unison.

> The unison, because of its temperate sweetness is most carefully to be avoided, except when a composition is begun with it, or, for the sake of its charm.[37]

The intervals of the fifteenth and twenty-second, he finds 'most sonorous, sweet and perfect.'[38]

Both the third and the seventeenth 'has the highest sweetness,' whereas the octave and a third he merely calls 'suave.'[39]

Regarding the fourth, Tinctoris admits this was favored 'by our ancestors,' but for his generation he says it produces 'an intolerable discord.' Here, also, he quotes Cicero as saying that 'learned ears cannot put up with a discordant harmony.'[40] The interval of the eleventh he finds 'intolerably harsh to learned ears.'[41] The eighteenth he finds somewhat more interesting, for it 'offends learned ears in a wonderful way. Hence in counterpoint it is not allowed.' On the other hand, he notes that it is permissible 'if either a third or a fifth, by which it is made sweeter, will be placed beneath it.'[42]

---

35 *Dictionary of Musical Terms*, 15. In the Brussels manuscript of this book, an additional definition is found: 'Symphony is the same as consonance.' [Ibid., 77]

36 *The Art of Counterpoint*, 17.

37 Ibid., 22.

38 Ibid., 60, 80.

39 Ibid., 25, 43, 65.

40 Ibid., 29.

41 Ibid., 48.

42 Ibid., 70.

Interestingly enough, Tinctoris was not quite comfortable in calling the sixth a consonance. His reason, once again, was that, rather than 'sweetness,' for his ears it produced rather 'asperity.'[43] Similarly, the thirteenth he states 'brings to the senses more asperity than suavity,' and in another place he calls it 'harsh,'[44] and the interval of the twentieth he calls 'more of a discord than a concord.'[45]

In his *Dictionary*, Tinctoris defines dissonance as 'a combination of different sounds which by nature is displeasing to the ears.'[46] In another place, using his same analogy above, in which this term is a metaphor for feeling, Tinctoris calls a dissonance that which is,

> a mixture of two pitches naturally offending the ears. And it is called discord metaphorically from 'dis' and 'corde,' for, just as the bitterness of enmity arises from the separation of two hearts from a mutual uniformity of sentiment, so the harshness of a discord is produced from two pitches not agreeing with each other.[47]

One should never, he cautions, think of a dissonance as simply a bad consonance. He reserves his most aesthetically descriptive language for the tritone, which he declares 'is so unfriendly to nature that it not only offends the ears, but also, indeed, is impossible.'[48]

The psychological states of tension and release familiar to the use of dissonance and its resolution in music of the period of functional harmony, and later, was an aesthetic concept not permissible for Tinctoris.

> There are some who approve the introduction of an integral discord for the reason that an immediately following concord would appear more suave, since it has been alleged that one quality placed beside its antithesis gleams forth more brightly. O most invalid reasoning! Never ought any vice be committed by a man of commendable virtue so that his virtue may shine more clearly; never ought any inept ideas be inserted into a distinguished oration so that the other parts may seem more elegant. And which one of our learned painters striving to delight the sight, I ask, has considered introducing some kind of deformity into any lovely form so that the other members may appear more beautiful?[49]

He quotes Cicero as pointing out that the trained listener hears even the most minute discrepancies in intonation in lyres or flutes. Tinctoris, therefore, concludes that such an intentional discord would have the result,

> that the soul of the erudite listener falls into grief, contrary to the intention of music, which Aristotle claims to contain a natural delight within itself.[50]

---

43 Ibid., 34.

44 Ibid., 55ff.

45 Ibid., 76.

46 *Dictionary of Musical Terms*, 25.

47 *The Art of Counterpoint*, 85.

48 Ibid., 88.

49 Ibid., 127.

50 Ibid.

Interestingly enough, he then seems to permit 'small discords,' presumably if they are what we call today passing tones. The most important principle, for Tinctoris, seems to be that the dissonance is not heard at the beginning of a principal tone. This corresponds with some modern research which has suggested that it is the attack, and not the tone itself, which often influences listeners to decide if a given tone quality is good or bad.

> Nevertheless, small discords ... are at times allowed to be used by musicians, just as reasonable figures [of speech] by grammarians, for the sake of ornament and necessity. For a song is ornamented when an ascent or descent is made from one concord to another by compatible means and by syncopations which cannot occasionally be made without discords. These particular small discords, therefore, do not represent themselves so vehemently to the hearing, since they are placed above the last parts of notes, as if they were used above the first [parts of notes]. Musical sounds, to be sure, are made from a violent motion; hence, if violent motion is their nature, so it is abated near the end. The consequence is that the second parts of notes are not of as violent [not as loud] a sound as the first.[51]

Contrary to the view which has captured some university music professors in the United States during our time, Tinctoris correctly and categorically states: Music is Performance!

> Music is that skill consisting of performance in singing and playing, and it is threefold, namely harmonic [voice], organal [instruments], and rhythmical.[52]

As a Church official by training, music performance to Tinctoris meant first and foremost singing. Among the definitions in his *Dictionary* regarding singing, the following are the most interesting from an aesthetic point of view.

> A *jubilus* is a melody delivered with a certain high exuberance.[53]
>
> ……
>
> Pronunciation is the elegant delivery of the voice.[54]
>
> ……
>
> There is also another semitone which is called the chromatic [*Cromaticum*]. It is used when, in singing, some note is raised for the purpose of a beautiful delivery.[55]

In general, Tinctoris says a good singer must have '*ars, mensura, modus, pronunciatio, et vox bona.*'[56]

Among Tinctoris's various discussions of Church singing, no doubt the most surprising topic for the modern reader is his rather frequent reference to improvisation [*super librum*]. But this is not only representative of the most ancient performance of music, but, as Reese

---

[51] Ibid., 127ff.

[52] *Dictionary of Musical Terms*, 43.

[53] Ibid., 37.

[54] Ibid., 49.

[55] Ibid., 57.

[56] Quoted in Reese, *Music in the Renaissance*, 147.

observes 'the prominent role it played in the musical life of the time [of Tinctoris].'⁵⁷ In one of his more explicit references to this, Tinctoris suggests the improvisation was primarily done against the tenor and suggest that some pre-agreement among the singers has a more profitable result.

> But, with two or three, four or many, harmonizing *super librum*, one is not subject to the other, for, indeed, it suffices that each of them make consonances with the tenor with those things that pertain to the law and arrangement of concords. I do not, however, think it disgraceful, but rather most laudable, if, agreeing among themselves on a similarity of assumption and arrangement of concords, they sing prudently, or thus they make of their harmonizing a fuller and more suave [effect].⁵⁸

Later in this same treatise, Tinctoris, seems to suggest *variety in performance* as a primary virtue of improvisation.

> Variety must be most accurately sought for in all counterpoint, for, as Horace says in his *Poetics*: 'One who sings to the kithara is laughed at if he always wanders over the same string.' Wherefore, according to the opinion of Cicero, as a variety in the art of speaking most delights the hearer, so also in music a diversity of harmonies vehemently provokes the souls of listeners into delight; hence Aristotle, in his *Ethics*, does not hesitate to state that variety is a most pleasant thing and human nature in need of it.
>
> Also, any composer or improviser of the greatest genius may achieve this diversity if he either composes or improvises now by one quantity, then by another, now by one perfection, then by another, now by one proportion, then by another, now by one conjunction, then by another, now with syncopations, then without syncopations, now with *fugae*, then without *fugae*, now with pauses, now without pauses, now diminished, now as written. Nevertheless, the highest reason must be adhered to in all these, although I have kept silent about improvisation [*super librum*], which can be diversified by the will of those improvising; nor do so many and such varieties enter into one chanson as so many and such in a motet, nor so many and such in one motet as so many and such in one mass.⁵⁹

In his treatise, *De Inventione et Usu Musicae*, Tinctoris actually points to a tradition, called *cantus regalis*, in which some improvisation was done over plain chant.⁶⁰

Finally, he suggests that the most successful musician is the one who 'composes with constant effort or sings *super librum*.' He concludes this discussion with the interesting observation that he has never known one successful composer or improviser who began his practice after the age of twenty.⁶¹

In his treatise, *De Inventione et Usu Musicae*, Tinctoris writes at length of the principal instruments, as well as the best performers known to him.

---

57   Ibid.,143. Reese also suggests that much of the idioms of later style were first worked out in improvisation.
58   *The Art of Counterpoint*, 105.
59   Ibid., 139.
60   Reese, *Music in the Renaissance*, 147.
61   *The Art of Counterpoint*, 140ff.

In Book III he discusses the history of the early shawm, known first as *tibiae*, and in his time as *celimela*. It is interestingly that he mentions the continued existence of the double shawm [*duplici tibia*], which is surely the ancient aulos, but he calls this instrument the least perfect. The shawm he gives in three sizes, soprano, tenor [*bombarda*] and contratenor, the latter of which might be substituted by the trombone.[62] Together the ensemble is called *alta* [wind band]. The best player of the shawm he knew was Godefridus, a musician of Frederick III.[63]

Book IV and V Tinctoris devotes to a very detailed discussion of the wide variety of string instruments familiar to the Renaissance. The only string instrument he finds disagreeable is the Turkish *tambura*, which he calls a 'miserable and puny instrument which the Turks with their even more miserable and puny ingenuity, have evolved from the lyra.'[64] He later mentions that he heard this instrument in Naples played by Turks in captivity, to console themselves. To the ears of Tinctoris,

> The extravagance and rusticity of these pieces were such as only to emphasize the barbarity of those who played them.[65]

All of the strings he points out can play music in four parts and the lute, in particular, is used at feasts, dances and public and private entertainments. Among the most gifted players of the lute he points to Pietro Bono of Ferrara and Heinrich, a German in the service of Charles the Bold. The Germans, in particular, Tinctoris says 'improvise marvelously upon a treble part with such taste that the performance cannot be rivaled.'[66]

He speaks of the *viola* [viol] as being used in Spain and Italy to accompany the recitation of epic poetry and mentions the musicianship of two Flemish brothers, Charles and Jean Orbus.

> At Bruges, I heard Charles take the treble and Jean the tenor in many songs, playing this kind of viola so expertly and with such charm that the viola has never pleased me so well.[67]

The viol and rebec were clearly the favorite instruments of Tinctoris.

> I am similarly pleased by the rebec, my predilection for which I will not conceal, provided that it is played by a skillful artist, since its strains are very much like those of the viola. Accordingly, the viola and the rebec are my two instruments; I repeat, my chosen instruments, those that induce piety and stir my heart most ardently to the contemplation of heavenly joys. For these reasons I would rather reserve them solely for sacred music and the secret consolations of the soul, than have them sometimes used for profane occasions and public festivities.[68]

---

[62] Anthony Baines, 'Fifteenth-century Instruments in Tinctoris's *De Inventine et Usu Musicae*,' in *The Galpin Society Journal* 3 (1950): 20ff, http://www.jstor.org/stable/841898

[63] Reese, *Music in the Renaissance*, 147ff.

[64] Baines, 'Fifteenth-century Instruments in Tinctoris's *De Inventine et Usu Musicae*,' IV, 23.

[65] Ibid., IV, 25.

[66] Ibid., 24.

[67] Ibid.

[68] Ibid., 24ff.

Gustave Reese emphasizes the importance of this reference by Tinctoris to the use of these instruments in sacred music as valuable 'supplementary evidence that instruments were used' in the performance of Church music.[69]

Finally, Tinctoris mentions the new guitar of Spain and found it played primarily by women to accompany love songs.

---

[69] Reese, *Music in the Renaissance*, 148.

On Music and Society in the Sixteenth Century: The Opposition by the Church

Since Italy led Humanism in music, it should be no surprise that music was highly honored in many courts. One only has to recall Bottrigari's description of the ducal palace in Ferrara, with rooms devoted to housing the instrument collection and for the private practice of the resident musicians. And his charming description of the Duke himself attending rehearsals:

> And the Sig. Duca also comes in person, with most kind and serene bearing and brotherly majesty, and when he has heard them often gives them efficacious advice, with his perfect judgment, and admonitions, encouraging them to bear themselves well and to do themselves honor.[1]

And then there was the minor nobleman, Gesualdo, who performed on the lute, composed and discussed music and did not hesitate to make his views known regarding performances he heard, as Fontanelli describes in a letter of 1594.

> On Monday the prince was invited to dine by the patriarch, and there was music. But in Venice they sing badly, and His Excellency has a taste difficult to satisfy, as Your Highness knows. Thus he could not restrain himself from withdrawing from the room, summoning the director and cembalist and reproving them in such a manner that I felt sorry for them.[2]

Such liberal activity soon came under attack by the Counter-Reformation, which might as well be called 'Counter-Renaissance,' in so far as Humanism was concerned. The Church, faced with the challenge of Luther, retreated to its strong point—medieval dogma. Some of these retrenchments, such as abolishing the right of the individual to act on his own conscience or judgment,[3] are with us still today. We can see the impact of this primarily in Rome, where the Humanist school of painting begins to disappear, to be replaced by a style called Mannerist.[4]

In addition, the Renaissance itself suffered a significant setback in Italy due to invasions. Between 1512 and 1530, Brescia, Genoa, Pavia, Naples and Florence were sacked. In the famous 'Sack of Rome,' in 1527, looters even entered the Sancta Sanctorum of the Lateran and played ball with the relic heads of St. Peter and St. Paul![5] Rome did not become a center of the arts

---

[1] Hercole Bottrigari, *Il Desiderio*, trans. Carol MacClintock (American Institute of Musicology, 1962), 52ff.

[2] Quoted in Glenn Watkins, *Gesualdo, The Man and His Music* (Chapel Hill: The University of North Carolina Press, 1973), 64.

[3] Anthony Blunt, *Artistic Theory in Italy, 1450–1600* (Oxford: Clarendon Press, 1959), 105.

[4] Ibid., 106.

[5] Charles Stinger, *The Renaissance in Rome* (Bloomington: Indiana University Press, 1985), 322.

again until 1600. Stinger finds in Michelangelo's *Last Judgment* an expression of the somber mood in Rome following the sack and believes it was ordered to reflect 'a forceful reassertion of theology over philosophy, of faith over reason, of divine grace over human free will.'[6]

One German philosopher who turned against Humanism was Henry Agrippa (1486–1536). In his earlier *De occulta philosophia* he had discussed the impressive references to the ethos of the various modes by the ancients, but fifteen years later he finds that in his experience music has been degraded in practice by the character of the men who perform it.

> Although men confess that this art has much sweetness, yet the common opinion is, and everyone may see it by experience, that it is the exercise of base men, and of unprofitable and intemperate wit ... For this reason Music has ever been wandering here and there for price and pence and is the servant of the bawdy which no grave, modest, honest or valiant man ever professed ... But in very deed what is more unprofitable, more to be despised, and more to be eschewed, than these pipers, singers, and other sorts of musicians, which with so many and diverse voices of songs, surpassing the chirping of all birds, with a certain venomous sweetness, like the Mermaids, with voices, gestures, and lascivious sounds, do destroy and corrupt men's minds?

Agrippa includes the dance as a branch of music, and again condemns the former with all the enthusiasm of a Puritan.

> To Music, moreover, belongs the Art of Dancing, very acceptable to maidens and lovers, which they learn with great care, and without tediousness do prolong it until midnight, and with great diligence do devise to dance with framed gestures, and with measurable passes to the sound of the cymbal, harp, or flute, and do, as they think very wisely, and subtly, the fondest thing of all and, little differing from madness, which except that it is tempered with the sound of instruments ... There is no sight more ridiculous, taken out of context, than dancing: this is a liberty to wantonness, a friend to wickedness, a provocation to fleshly lust, enemy to chastity, and a pastime unworthy of all honest persons.[7]

In Switzerland we find another curious prohibition of dancing. A civic ordinance in Zürich in 1500 reads, 'In order that God the Lord may protect the harvests which are in the field, and may give us good weather, let no person dance.'[8] Another in 1519 reads,

> Let it be announced in the pulpits of the city and written notice sent into the country that since dancing has been forbidden, it is also forbidden to musicians or anyone else to provide dances in courts or other places, whether it be at public weddings or church festivals.

In England, with respect to the aesthetic and social recognition given music in the English-speaking world, the late sixteenth century must in retrospect be viewed as an unfortunate turning point. In spite of the extraordinary example set by both Henry VIII and Elizabeth I,

---

6   Ibid., 325.

7   Henry Cornelius Agrippa, *Of the Vanitie and Uncertaintie of Arts and Sciences*, ed. Catherine Dunn (Northridge: California State University, Northridge Press, 1974), 69. Interestingly enough, he associates the origin of dance to the movement of the planets and the 'music of the spheres.'

8   Quoted in Jackson, *Huldreich Zwingli* (New York: Putham, 1901), 24.

as members of the highest class who were active musicians, the view that nobles should be performing musicians was clearly changing. There seem to us two significant reasons for this change in attitude.

First, in the view of some, the obvious growth in intellectual self-confidence, so apparent in the development of sixteenth-century literature, led to a certain insular isolation.[9] We will let an anonymous poem of 1600 represent many contemporary references to the general problem.

> A Painter lately with his pencil drew
> The picture of a Frenchman and Italian,
> With whom he placed the Spaniard, Turk, and Jew;
> But by himself he sat the Englishman.[10]

This self-imposed isolation is especially evident in the frequent ridicule of English students going to Italy for further study, for whom there was a commonly used term of contempt, the 'Italianate Englishmen.' Unfortunately this attitude blinded English high society to the most important insights of Humanism.[11] What was sensitive in Italy was called effeminate in England and the active interest demonstrated by Italian nobles in promoting high quality music is only rarely found in England.

Second, the growth in economic power in England during the sixteenth century permitted England to follow the same transition one sees in ancient Rome. That is, music begins in association with the highest levels of society, but as society becomes wealthy, music becomes the activity of hired slaves. We can see this very clearly in Thomas Nashe's *The Anatomie of Absurditie* (1589). In his preface he describes a group of 'extraordinary Gentlemen' discussing the 'qualities required in Castiglione's *Il Cortigiano*' (*The Courtier*). One of the gentlemen mentions the importance of being able to perform on the citterne and lute. But another gentleman, who believed that 'the only adjuncts of a Courtier were scholarship and courage,' dismisses the idea of a noble performing music. Leave it, he says,

> to the birthright of every six-penny slave.[12]

---

[9] Gustave Reese, *Music in the Renaissance* (New York: Norton, 1959), 763, dates this isolation in music even earlier, to the latter part of the fifteenth century. That this was widely recognized, Reese points to Tinctoris' observation regarding the 'wretched poverty of invention' in English music.

[10] Anonymous, 'Tom Tel-Troths Message,' [1600] in F. Furnivall, ed., *Miscellaneous, Series VI, Shakespere's England, Nr. 2* (Vaduz: Kraus Reprint, 1965), 122. We have modernized the English in all these sixteenth-century texts.

[11] One who misunderstood the Italians was Sir Philip Sidney. In a letter to his brother, quoted in *The Prose Works of Sir Philip Sidney*, ed. Albert Feuillerat (Cambridge: Cambridge University Press, 1962), III, 127, he writes,

> And for the men you shall have there, although some indeed be excellently learned, yet they are all given to such counterfeit learning, as a man shall learn of them more false grounds of things, than in any place else that I do know … In certain fine qualities, such as Horsemanship, Weapons, Vaulting, and such like, they are better than in those other countries.

[12] Thomas Nashe, *The Anatomie of Absurditie* [1589], in *The Works of Thomas Nashe*, ed. Ronald McKerrow (Oxford: Blackwell, 1966), I, 7.

Of course, we acknowledge there were fine performers and composers in England at the end of the sixteenth century, but they were not nobles, they were slaves, or if you prefer, servants to high society. In terms of social status, and pay, can anyone pretend that this regrettable model has not remained in place in the English-speaking world until the present day?

Many people tend to think of the 'Renaissance Man' as that well-rounded gentleman who was, among many other things, an amateur musician. Thomas Whythorne, writing about 1575, believed that at this time this was indeed the case in England.

> Those who learn [music] … for the love they have for the science and not to earn a living by … are to be accounted among the number of those who the book called the 'Institution of a Gentleman' doth allow to learn music, and also which the book called 'The Courtier' doth … for they would have the great gentlemen and the courtiers to learn music … Which counsel … the nobility and the worshipful do much follow in these days, for many of those estates have schoolmasters in their houses to teach their children both to sing [counterpoint] and also to play on instruments.[13]

However, by the end of the century a general change had taken place as we see in Thomas Morley, who creates a fictional young gentleman who is embarrassed because he is unable to sight-sing.

> Supper being ended and music books (according to the custom) being brought to the table, the mistress of the house presented me with a part earnestly requesting me to sing; but when, after many excuses, I protested unfeignedly that I could not, everyone began to wonder; yea, some whispered to others demanding how I was brought up.[14]

We believe these two quotations serve to frame a change which had taken place in the manners of the gentleman. What was the philosophy which encouraged this?

The writings of Henry Peacham and Roger Ascham (1515–1568), a tutor to queen Elizabeth, summarize the qualities needed by the ideal noble and are in many ways the English counterparts of Baldassare Castiglione's more famous *Il Cortigiano* (*The Courtier*). In *The Schoolmaster* (1570), Ascham begins by revealing a curious attitude toward intellectual brilliance which we believe may have been shared by many English nobles.[15] He has observed that 'those which be commonly the wisest, the best learned, and best men' when young, seem to lose their 'quickest of wit' when older. The explanation, he believes, must be something like a sharp knife which becomes dull. Thus such brilliant young men tend to be unable to concentrate on a single field and never excel in 'hard sciences.' 'The quickest wits,' he concludes may make the best poets, but not the best orators.

Perhaps of more consequence in Ascham's view was that those with 'quickest wit' lack important characteristics appropriate to noble society.

---

13 Craig Monson, 'Elizabethan London,' in Iain Fenlon, ed., *The Renaissance* (Englewood Cliffs: Prentice Hall, 1989), 333.

14 Thomas Morley, *A Plain and Easy Introduction to Practical Music*, ed. R. Alec Harman (New York: Norton, n.d.), 9.

15 Roger Ascham, *The Schoolmaster* [1570], ed. Lawrence Ryan (Ithaca: Cornell University Press, 1967), 21ff.

> Also, for manners and life, quick wits commonly be in desire [of the] newfangled, in purpose unconstant; light to promise anything, ready to forget everything, both benefit and injury, and thereby neither fast to friend nor fearful to foe; inquisitive of every trifle, not secret in greatest affairs; bold with any person, busy in every matter; soothing such as be present, nipping any that is absent; of nature, also, always flattering their betters, envying their equals, despising their inferiors; and by quickness of wit very quick and ready to like none so well as themselves.

In addition, he finds 'quick wits' tend to be 'overquick, hasty, rash, heady, brainsick,' and with a tendency towards light company.

All of this seems to suggest a perceived danger in extended study and here Ascham specifically points to the ill effects of the extended study of music.

> Some wits, moderate enough by nature, be many times marred by overmuch study and use of some sciences, namely, music, arithmetic and geometry. These sciences, as they sharpen men's wits overmuch, so they change men's manners oversore, if they be not moderately mingled and wisely applied to some good use of life. Notice all mathematical heads which be only and wholly bent to those sciences, how solitary they be themselves, how unfit to live with others, and how unapt to serve in the world.

He quotes the early medical writer, Galen (second century AD), as saying 'Much music marreth men's manners,' and then concludes that 'overmuch quickness of wit,' whether by nature or by study, does not result in the 'greatest learning, best manners, or happiest life.'

In another book, a treatise on long bow shooting called *Toxophilus*, Ascham elaborates on the dangers of music. In this dialog, Toxophilus has been explaining the many virtues of shooting, when Philologus introduces the subject of music by observing that it is a common recreation for scholars. Toxophilus answers,

> I cannot deny that some music is fit for learning, and I trust you cannot choose but grant that shooting is also fit … But as concerning which of them is most fit for learning and scholars to use, you may say what you will for your pleasure; [but] of this I am sure, that Plato and Aristotle … do mention music and all kinds of it; wherein they both agree, that music used amongst the Lydians is very ill for young men which be students for virtue and learning, for a certain nice, soft, and smooth sweetness of it, which would rather entice them to naughtiness than stir them to honesty.
>
> Another kind of music, invented by the Dorians, they both wonderfully praise, allowing it to be very fit for the study of virtue and learning, because of a manly, rough, and stout sound in it, which should encourage young stomachs to attempt manly matters. Now whether [today's] ballads and rounds, these galliards, pavanes, and dances, so nicely fingered, so sweetly tuned, be more like the music of the Lydians or the Dorians, you may judge for yourself.[16]

Toxophilus then quotes the same Galen comment above, that 'Much music marreth men's manners,' and elaborates on its meaning.

---

[16] *Toxophilus*, in *The Whole Works of Roger Ascham*, ed. Rev. Giles (London: John Russell Smith, 1864), II, 25ff. Ascham explains at length why shooting is the ideal exercise for the student—such things as tennis and bowling being too 'vehement.'

Although some men will say that it is not so, but rather recreateth and maketh quick a man's mind; yet, methink, by reason it doth as honey doth to a man's stomach, which at the first receiveth it well, but afterward it maketh it unfit to abide any good strong nourishing meat, or else any wholesome sharp and quick drink. And even so in a manner these instruments make a man's wit so soft and smooth, so tender and queasy, that they be less able to brook strong and tough study. Wits be not sharpened, but rather dulled and made blunt, with such sweet softness, even as good edges be blunter which men whet upon soft chalk stones.

Toxophilus then quotes an often repeated anecdote which maintains that Cyrus, after conquering the Lydians and desiring to keep them peaceful, arranged for,

> every one of them should have a harp or a lute, and learn to play and sing. Which thing if you do … you shall see them quickly of men made women. And thus luting and singing take away a manly stomach, which should enter and pierce deep and hard study.

Toxophilus concludes by questioning whether Aristotle and Plato knew what they were talking about.

> Therefore either Aristotle and Plato know not what was good and evil for learning and virtue, and the example of wise histories be vainly set before us, or else the minstrelsy of lutes, pipes, harps, and all other that standeth by such nice, fine, minikin fingering (such as the most part of scholars whom I know use, if they use any), is far more fit, for the womanishness of it, to dwell in the Court among ladies, than for any great thing in it, which should help good and sad study, to abide in the University among scholars.

Now Philologus agrees 'to say the truth, I never thought myself these kinds of music fit for learning.' Nevertheless he attempts to come to the defense of music, although his arguments, while interesting, are all of secondary values.

> That milk is no fitter or more natural for the bringing up of children than music is, both Galen proveth by authority, and daily use teacheth by experience. For even the little babes lacking the use of reason, are scarce so well stilled in sucking their mother's pap, as in hearing their mother sing. Again, how fit youth is made by learning to sing, for grammar and other sciences, both we daily do see … The godly use of praising God, by singing in the church, needeth not my praise, seeing it is so praised through all the scripture …
>
> Beside all these commodities, truly two degrees of men, which have the highest offices under the King in all this realm, shall greatly lack the use of singing, preachers and lawyers, because they shall not, without this, be able to rule their breasts for every purpose. For where is no distinction in telling glad things and fearful things, gentleness and cruelness, softness and vehementness, and such-like matters, there can be no great persuasion … But when a man is always in one tune, like a humble bee, or else now in the top of the church, now down, that no man knoweth where to have him; or piping like a reed, or roaring like a bull, as some lawyers do, which thing they do best when they cry loudest, these shall never greatly move, as I have known many well-trained have done, because their voice was not stayed afore with learning to sing. For all voices, great and small, base and shrill, weak or soft, may be helped and brought to a good point by learning to sing.

> Whether this be true or not, they that stand most in need can tell best; whereof some I have known, which, because they learned not to sing when they were boys, were fain to take pain in it when they were men ...
>
> TOXOPHILUS. It were pity truly, Philologus, that the thing should be neglected; But I trust it is not as you say.
>
> PHILOLOGUS. The thing is too true; for of them that come daily to the University, where one hath learned to sing, six hath not.

Henry Peacham (1576–1643), in his *The Complete Gentleman*, has similar doubts about the appropriateness of a gentleman becoming too involved in music. He first discusses the general nature of nobility, discussing whether it is affected by loss of faith, unexpected poverty, engagement in commerce, etc. In such conditions he is usually able to explain the circumstances as not changing one's noble status. But, when he comes to issues 'touching mechanical arts and artists,' he is adamant.

> Whosoever labor for their livelihood and gain have no share at all in nobility or gentry, as painters, stageplayers, tumblers, ordinary fiddlers, innkeepers, fencers, jugglers, dancers, mountebanks and bearwards.[17]

Unlike Italy, where nobles continued to take pride in being actual performers of music, we see in Peacham clear evidence of a trend in England which would become more strongly evidenced in the following century, namely that the noble might well study music, but not practice it to the extent that he becomes a 'master' or to the extent that it interferes with important duties.

> I might run into an infinite sea of the praise and use of so excellent an art, but I only [touch on it] because I desire not that any noble or gentleman should, save at his private recreation and leisurable hours, prove a master in the art or neglect his more weighty employments.[18]

Proving that one was 'a master in the art,' presumably included demonstration of technical proficiencies. In sixteenth-century Italy Castiglione gives abundant evidence that the gentleman should appreciate listening to music, and even be able to perform, but being a *skilled* performer was quite another matter. Reflecting what seems to have been a basic attitude of nobles nearly everywhere, Castiglione, as well as Peacham here, believed the gentleman should display a certain nonchalance about all skills and should not be expected to apply himself in any form of hard labor which might result in excellence in any skill. This idea may also have formed the background for a comment by Robert Greene (1560–1592). In his greeting 'To the Gentlemen Readers,' of his *Carde of Fancie* (1587), he begins with an anecdote about the god, Pan, which has no relationship with the Romance which follows.

---

[17] Henry Peacham, *The Complete Gentleman*, ed. Virgil Heltzel (Ithaca: Cornell University Press, 1962), 23.

[18] Ibid., 111.

> Pan blowing upon an oten pipe a little homely music, and hearing no man dispraise his small cunning, began to play so loud, and so long, that [the listeners] were more weary in hearing his music, than he in showing his skill, till at last to claw him and excuse themselves, they said his pipe was out of tune.[19]

In addition, Castiglione had specified that one only performs before private gatherings of friends, never before the common masses. Peacham goes even further, saying that the noble does not perform before anyone else.

> I desire no more in you than to sing your part sure and at the first sight withal to play the same upon your viol or the exercise of the lute, privately, to yourself.[20]

John Lyly has composed a poem which speaks of the education of the nobleman and he includes music among a list of subjects which may not be 'unfit,' but nevertheless have nothing to do with virtue.

> Some teach their youth to pipe, to sing and dance,
> To hawk, to hunt, to choose and kill their game.
> To blow their [hunting] horn, and with their horse to prance,
> To play at tennis, set the lute in frame,
> Run at the ring, and use such other games:
> Which feats although they be not all unfit,
> Yet cannot they the mark of virtue hit.[21]

In the second half of the sixteenth century, one finds a number of hostile and negative characterizations of music written by men who were harbingers of the conservative religious right, which was rapidly moving toward the extreme Puritan beliefs of the seventeenth century. The first of these books was written immediately after the first professional theater opened in London, in 1576, and published the following year. This was *A Treatise Against Dicing, Dancing, Plays, and Interludes with other Idle Pastimes*, by a minister named John Northbrooke. Northbrooke admits that some recreation is appropriate, but his initial premise is that there are two inherent dangers. The first is that we abuse recreation 'through too great pleasure which we take in them.'[22] The second danger is that recreation might be used for purposes other than true recreation, as we see in this dialog between 'Youth' and 'Age.'

> YOUTH. Then, I perceive by you that honest recreations, pastimes, and plays are tolerable unto men, and that they may use and frequent it without fault, or offending God, or hurt to the profession of a true, faithful Christian.

---

[19] Robert Greene, *Carde of Fancie* [1587], Prologue, in *The Life and Complete Works of Robert Greene*, ed. Alexander Grosart (New York: Russell & Russell, 1964), IV, 8 His romance, *Pandosto* [1588] was the source of Shakespeare's *Winter's Tale*.

[20] Peacham, *The Complete Gentleman*, 112.

[21] John Lyly, in *The complete Works of John Lyly*, ed. Warwick Bond (Oxford: Clarendone Press, 1967), III, 449ff.

[22] John Northbrooke, *A Treatise Against Dicing, Dancing, Plays, and Interludes* [1577] (London: The Shakespeare Society, 1843), 52.

> AGE. If it be, as I have said, moderately taken, after some weighty business, to make one more fresh and agile, to prosecute his good and godly affairs, and lawful business.[23]

The antithesis of this proper recreation of the Christian was, for Northbrooke, idleness, which for him included musicians. Idleness leads to sin and Northbrooke complains that the laws already on the books were not being upheld.

> If these and such like laws were executed justly, truly, and severely (as they ought to be), without any respect of persons, favor, or friendship, this dung and filth of idleness would easily be rejected and cast out of this commonwealth; there would not be so many loitering, idle persons, so many ruffians, blasphemers, and swing bucklers, so many drunkards, tossepots, whoremasters, dancers, fiddlers, and minstrels, dice players and maskers, fencers, thieves, interlude players, cutpurses, cosiners, masterless servants, jugglers, rouges, beggars, counterfeit Egyptians, etc., as there are.[24]

Having given us his general perspective, Northbrooke now turns to a discussion of music.

> YOUTH. What say you to music, and playing upon instruments? Is not that a good exercise?
> AGE. Music is very good, if it be lawfully used, and not unlawfully abused.[25]

Northbrooke begins his discussion by defining what 'lawful' music is, and this consists of examples of the use of music in the Bible. He praises the examples found there of music for the praise of God, for the praise of the good deeds of nobles, the celebration of joy and for weddings.

> And undoubtedly poetry had its beginning here, and it cannot be denied that it is an excellent gift of God; yet this ought to be kept pure and chaste among men, because certain lascivious men have and do filthily defile it, applying it to wantonness, wicked lusts, and every filthy thing.

Now the question is raised, how does one explain the power of music? Northbrooke's answer, as we would say today, is that music satisfies both the left and right hemispheres of the brain.

> YOUTH. Why doth music so rapt and ravish men in a manner wholly?
> AGE. The reason is plain: for there are certain pleasures which only fill the outward senses, and there are others also which pertain only to the mind or reason; but music is a delectation so put in the middle, that both by the sweetness of the sounds it moveth the senses, and by the artfulness of the number and proportions it delighth reason itself: and that happens then chiefly, when such words are added unto it whose sense is both excellent and learned.

---

[23] Ibid.
[24] Ibid., 76.
[25] Ibid., 108ff.

Northbrooke here reviews several of the anecdotes of music in ancient literature and then turns to Church music. He reviews some early Christian music practice and especially focuses on St. Augustine's concept that it is the words, not the music, which is important in church music. Thus, one 'when he sang he should but little alter his voice, so that he should be like rather unto one that readeth, than unto one that singeth.'

> YOUTH. Let me hear, then, what is to be done and observed, to the end music may lawfully and fruitfully be used in the church.
>
> AGE. First we must take heed that in music be not put the whole sum and effect of godliness, and of the worshiping of God, which among the papists they do almost everywhere think, that they have fully worshiped God, when they have long and much sung and piped. Further, we must take heed that in it be not put merit or remission of sins. Thirdly, that singing be not so much used and occupied in the church, that there be no time, in a manner, left to preach the word of God and holy doctrine; whereby it comes to pass that the people depart out of church full of music and harmony, but yet hungering and fasting for heavenly food and doctrine. Fourthly, that rich and large stipends be not so appointed for musicians, that either very little, or in a manner nothing, is provided for the ministers … Fifthly, neither may that broken and quavering music be used, wherewith the listeners are so [overwhelmed], that they cannot understand the words … Lastly, we must take heed, that in the church nothing be sung without choice, but only those things which are contained in the holy scriptures, or which are by just reason gathered out of them, and do exactly agree with the word of God.

Northbrooke concludes by correctly noting that there is no mention of music in the church service in the New Testament and therefore if some church elects not to have music it should not be criticized. Now a final topic is addressed.

> YOUTH. What say you of minstrels, that go and range abroad, and thrust themselves into every man's presence and company, to play some mirth unto them.
>
> AGE. These sort of people are not sufferable, because they are loiterers and idle fellows; and are, therefore, by the laws and statues of this realm, forbidden to range and roam abroad, counting them in the number of rouges, and, to say the truth, they are but defacers of music.

Northbrooke mentions music again with respect to dancing. As the reader can no doubt guess, Northbrooke considers dancing a fundamental evil, calling it, among other things, wicked and filthy.[26]

> Concupiscence is inflamed by dancing with the fire of lust and sensuality; it gives occasion to whoredom and adultery; it makes men forget and neglect their duties and services …
>
> We now in Christian counties have schools of dancing, howbeit that is no wonder, seeing also we have houses of bawdy. So much the Pagans were better and more sad than we be, they never knew this new fashion of dancing of ours; and unclean handlings, gropings, and kissings, and a very kindling of lechery, whereto serveth all that bussing, as it were, pigeons, the birds of Venus …

---

[26] Ibid., 145ff.

> Yea, and further, the ballads that they sing be such, that they would kindle up the courage of the old … And when the minstrels do make a sign to [stop], then, if you do not kiss her that you are leading by the hand and did dance with, then you are taken for a peasant and one without good manners and nurture.

Music by itself, he says, cannot be condemned. It is the abuse of music through its association with dancing which renders it objectionable.

> Music of itself cannot be condemned; for as much as the world doth almost always abuse it, we ought to be so much the more circumspect: we see at this day that they which use music do swell with poison against God; they become hard hearted; they will have their songs, yea, and what manner of songs? Full of villainy and ribaldry; and afterward they fall to dancing, which is the chief mischief of all, for there is always such unchaste behavior in dancing, that of itself, as they abuse it (to speak the truth in one word) it is nothing but an enticement to whoredom …
>
> To music belongs the art of dancing, very acceptable to maidens and lovers; which they learn with great care, and without deviousness do prolong it until midnight, and with great diligence do devise to dance with framed gestures, and with measurable paces to the sound of the cymbal, harp, or flute, and do, as they think, very wisely, and subtly, the fondest thing of all other, and little differing from madness; which, except it were tempered with the sound of instruments … there would be no sight more ridiculous … than dancing.[27]

We find it rather charming that Northbrooke concludes his book by revealing that no one is paying much attention to such strong condemnation as we have read.

> There was never more preaching and worse listening, never more talking and less following …

The most influential of the radical religious books which attacked music was Stephen Gosson's *The Schoole of Abuse* of 1579. He begins his discussion of music with a few references to the commendable uses of music by the ancient Greeks, but finds these virtues are unobtainable in contemporary music.

> Do you think those miracles could be wrought with the playing of dances, *Dumpes*, Pavanes, Galliards, *Measures Fancyes*, or new strains? They never came where this grew, nor knew what it meant.[28]

At this point, we must remind the reader that for a thousand years formal education had stressed the so-called 'speculative' form of music, the theoretical, with very little reference to the 'practical,' or performance. Only in the sixteenth century did most universities begin giving performance more respectability. Thus, in the following, Gosson's point is that the student must forget performance and return to the study of 'speculative' music and to the concept of

---

[27] This last paragraph is taken almost word for word from the German philosopher, Henry Agrippa's *On the Vanitie and Uncertaintie of Arts and Sciences*, quoted above. See Catherine Dunn (Northridge: California State University, Northridge Press, 1974), 69.

[28] Stephen Gosson, *The Schoole of Abuse* [1579], ed. Edward Arber (London, 1868), 26.

Harmony used by the Greeks to represent the order of the world. First, he quotes Pythagoras, in something the philosopher surely never said, as 'condemning as fools, anyone who judges Music by sound and by ear.' Then, to the point he wishes to make,

> If you wish to be good Scholars, and to profit from the Art of Music, shut your fiddle cases, and look up to heaven: the order of the Spheres, the infallible motion of the Planets, the just course of the year, and variety of seasons, the concord of the elements and their qualities, Fire, Water, Air, Earth, Heat, Cold, Moisture and Drought concurring together to the constitution of earthly bodies and sustenance of every creature.[29]

Furthermore, instead of those distinguished poet-musicians of ancient Greece, today most musicians are beggars.

> We have infinite Poets, and Pipers, and such peevish chattel among us in England, that live by merry begging, maintained by alms, and privately encroach on every man's purse.

And, assuming that music of his time was more complicated, he wonders instead of those noble and simple instruments of antiquity, what would Pythagoras say, if he were alive today, and saw,

> how many frets, how many strings, how many stops, how many keys, how many clefs, how many modes, how many flats, how many sharps, how many [lines], how many spaces, how many notes, how many rests, how many quirks, how many corners, what chopping, what changing, what tossing, what turning, what wresting and wringing is among our Musicians?[30]

Gosson also condemns music for its role in the theater, noting that as poetry and music are 'German cousins,' so music and acting have great affinity, and all three are 'chained links of abuse.'[31] Indeed, he quotes Maximus Tyrius as saying that the introduction of musical instruments to theaters and drama 'was the first cup that poisoned the commonwealth.' He now makes the very interesting observation that music is more dangerous than painting, because it reaches the heart. A number of earlier philosophers had feared music for this same reason.

> Cooks have never shown more craft in their junkets to vanquish the taste, nor Painters in shadows to allure the eye, than Poets in Theaters to wound the conscience.
> There set they abroache strange consorts of melody, to tickle the ear; costly apparel, to flatter the sight; effeminate gesture, to ravish the sense; and wanton speech, to whet desire to inordinate lust. Therefore of both barrels, I judge Cooks and Painters the better hearing, for the one extendeth his art no farther than to the tongue, palate, and nose, the other to the eye; and both are ended in outward

---

[29] Ibid., 26

[30] Ibid., 28.

[31] Ibid., 28ff.

sense, which is common to us and the brute beasts. But these by the private entries of the ear, slip down into the heart, and with gunshot of affection gall the mind, where reason and virtue should rule the roost.[32]

Music, in Gosson's view, is largely responsible for the decay of the English man, from that strong, naked man who ate roots and bark and could suffer any hardship. Early English man found his recreation in shooting, running, wrestling, etc.,

> But the exercise that is now among us, is banqueting, acting, music and dancing, and all such delights as may win us to pleasure, or rock us asleep.
>
> Oh what a wonderful change is this? Our wrestling at arms, is turned to wallowing in Ladies laps, our courage to cowardice, our running to riot … We have robbed Greece of gluttony, Italy of wantonness, Spain of pride, France of deceit and Germany of drinking.[33]

As one can imagine, there was considerable reaction to this conservative religious attack on the arts. Soon Gosson published 'An Apologie of the Schoole of Abuse,' in answer to some of his critics. It is interesting in this passage that he twice uses the word 'wanton,' a word that the *ars antiqua* used to describe the early Renaissance music. Some musicians had responded by saying that both the instruments and the music today are better than they had ever been before, but Gosson simply answers, 'who is to judge?'[34] Then he challenges the musicians further.

> Because I would have Dionysius followed, let them not think I abhor Music: if they put on their spectacles, or take their eyes in their hands, and look better in the *Schoole of Abuse*, they shall find that with Plutarch I accuse them for bringing their cunning into theaters: that I say, they have willfully left, or with ignorance lost, those warlike tunes which were used in ancient times, to stir up in us a manly motion, and sound out new descant with the dancers of Sybaris, to rock us to sleep in all ungodliness. If they had any wit, any learning, or experience, they might know that *Excellens fensible laedit fensum*, their dainty consorts will make us wantons. Aristonicus the musician, for his memory with all posterity, had a brazen idol erected to him by Alexander the Great, and was wonderfully honored for his art. This was not done for playing 'Les guanto Spagniola,' or inventing sweet measures, or coining new dances, but for kindling his soldiers courage, and heartening them all to take armor … Which of our musicians that are so perfect, is able with his instrument to make a fresh water soldier run to his weapons, or force dolphins in the sea to save his life, if he suffer shipwreck? Which of all their instruments that are so absolute, can perform that which others have done before? If ancient musicians have gone beyond us, where is our cunning? If their instruments have passed ours, where is the perfectness that our Pipers imagine? …
>
> Yet I do not forbid our new found instruments, so long as we handle them as David did, to praise God; nor bring them any more into public theaters, to please wantons.

---

32 Ibid., 32.

33 Ibid., 34.

34 Stephen Gosson, 'An Apologie of the Schoole of Abuse,' in *The Schoole of Abuse* [1579], ed. Edward Arber (London, 1868), 68ff.

One of the many books inspired by Gosson was the *Anatomy of the Abuses in England* (1583) by Philip Stubbs, written in support of Gosson. Stubbs, in fact, begins his lengthy condemnation of the abuses of music by plagiarizing much of Gosson's work. Then, proceeding on his own in a dialog between Spudeus and Philoponus, Stubbs writes, in the final paragraph, the strongest language we have seen used against music.

> SPUDEUS. I have heard it said (and I thought it very true) that Music dooth delight both man and beast, reuniteth the spirits, comforteth the heart, and maketh it apter to the service of God.
>
> PHILOPONUS. I grant Music is a good gift of God, and that it delighteth both man and beast, reuniteth the spirits, conforteth the heart and maketh it readier to serve God; and therefore did David both use music himself and also commend the use of it to his posterity (and being used to that end, for man's private recreation, music is very laudable).
>
> But being used in public assemblies and private conuenticles as directories to filthy dancing, through the sweet harmony and smooth melody thereof, it estrangeth the mind, stireth up filthy lust, womannisheth the mind, ravisheth the heart, enflameth concupiscence and bringeth in uncleanness. But if music openly were used (as I have said) to the praise and glory of God, as our Fathers used it, and as was intended by it at the first, or privately in a man's secret chamber or house, for his own solace or comfort to drive away the fantasies of idle thoughts, solicitude, care, sorrow, and such other perturbations and molestations of the mind, the only ends whereto true music tends, it were very commendable and tolerable. If music were thus used it would comfort man wonderfully, and move his heart to serve God the better; but being used as it is, it corrupteth good minds, maketh them womanish, and inclined to all kinds of whordom and mischief ...
>
> Wherefore, if you would have your son become womanish, unclean, smooth mouthed, affected to bawdy, scurrility, filthy thymes, and unseemly talking; briefly, if you would have him, as it were, transformed into a woman, or worse, and inclined to all kinds of whordom and abomination, send him to dancing school, and to learn music, and than shall you not fail of your purpose. And if you would have your daughter whorish, bawdy, and unclean and a filthy speaker, and such like, bring her up in music and dancing, and, my life for your's, you have won the goal.[35]

During the Middle Ages there were traditions involving civic dancing in the church yard, in part because it was the largest open space in the small villages. Church officials issued many edicts against this practice during the later Middle Ages, but apparently the practice continued.[36] Stubbs, in particular, was alarmed to see minstrels playing for the 'devil's dance.'

> Then they have their hobbyhorses, dragons and other Antiques, together with their bawdy Pipers and thundering Drummers to strike up the devil's dance. Then march these heathens toward the Church and Church-yard, their pipers piping, their drummers thundering, their stumps dancing, their bells ringing, their handkerchiefs swinging about their heads like madmen, their hobbyhorses and other monsters skirmishing along the route. And in this sort they go to the Church (I say) and into the Church (though the minister be at prayer or preaching), dancing and swinging their handkchiefs

---

[35] Philip Stubbs, *The Anatomy of the Abuses in England* [1583], ed. Frederick Furnivall (London: The New Shakespeare Society, n.d.), 169ff.

[36] A sermon preached by John Stockwood in 1578 included the following observation.

> Insomuch that in some places [the actors] shame not in the time of divine service to come and dance [in] the church, and without, to have naked men dancing in nets, which is most filthy. [Quoted in Northbrooke, *A Treatise Against Dicing, Dancing, Plays, and Interludes*, xiv.]

over their heads in the Church, like devils incarnate, with such a confused noise that no man can hear his own voice. Then, the foolish people they look, they stare, they laugh, they leer & mount upon pews to see these goodly pageants solemnized in this sort. Then, after this, about the Church they go again and again and so forth into the church-yard, where they have commonly their Summer halls, their bowers, arbors and banqueting houses set up, wherein they feast, banquet and dance all that day and all the night too.[37]

There were also important publications in opposition to Gosson and in support of music and the arts. One of the most important of these was Thomas Lodge's (1558–1625) *A Defence of Poetry, Music and Stage-plays* (1580). Lodge, obviously a very well-read scholar, quotes extensively and to the point from ancient Greek and Roman literature as he separately defends poetry, music and the theater. His own personal comments, like those of the opposition, are passionate. We present here only his own observations on music, which begin with the ancient Greek notion that the universe, in its perfect organization, must be somehow related with music.[38]

But another matter calls me and I must not stay upon [poetry] only; there is an easier task in hand for me, and that which if I may speak my conscience, fits my vein best, your Second Abuse Gosson, your dispraise of Music, which you misadvisedly call Piping: that is it well most by you, what so is an overstay of life, is displeasant to your person: Music may not stand in your presence, whereas all the learned philosophers have always had it in reverence ... Look upon the harmony of the Heavens? Hang they not by music? Do not the spheres move? Be not they *inferiora corpora* affected *quadam sympathia* and agreement? How can we measure the debility of the patient but by the disordered motion of the pulse? Is not man worse accounted of when he is most out of tune? Is there anything that more affects the sense? Doth there any pleasure more *acuat* our understanding? ... O Lord! how it maketh a man to remember heavenly things, to wonder at the works of the Creator. Eloquence can stop the soldier's sword from slaying an orator, and shall not Music be magnified which not only saves the body but is a comfort to the soul? ...

Are not the strains in Music to tickle and delight the ear? Are not our warlike instruments to move men to valor? You confess they move us, but yet they delight not our ears, I pray you whence grew that point of Philosophy? It is more than ever my Master taught me, that a thing of sound should not delight the ear. Perhaps you suppose that men are monsters, without ears, or else I think you will say they hear with their heels: it may be so, for indeed when we are delighted with Music, it maketh our heart to skip of joy, and it maybe perhaps by ascending from the heel to the higher parts, it may move us. Good policy in sooth, this was of your own coining; your mother never taught it you: but I will not deal by reason of philosophy with you for that confound your senses, but I can assure you this one thing, that this principle will make the wiser to mislike your invention. It had been a fitter jest for your howlet in your Play, than an ornament in your book: but since you wrote of Abuses we may license you to lie a little, so the abuse will be more manifest ...

But you can not be content to err, but you must maintain it too. Pythagoras, you say, allows not that Music is discerned by ears, but he wishes us to ascend unto the sky, and mark that harmony. Surely this is but one [professor's] opinion (yet I dislike not of it) but to speak my conscience, I think Music best pleases me when I hear it, for otherwise the catterwalling of Cats, were it not for

---

37 Phillip Stubbs, *The Anatomy of the Abuses in England*, 147. Stubbs was opposed to dancing in general, calling it an 'introduction to whordom, a preparation to wantonness.' [Ibid., 154ff.]

38 Thomas Lodge, *A Defence of Poetry, Music and Stage-plays* (London: Shakespeare Society, 1853), 17ff.

harmony, should more delight my eyes than the tunable voices of men. But these things are not the chief points you shout at, there is somewhat else sticking in your stomach, God grant it hurt you not! From the dance you run to the pipe … Our pleasant consorts do discomfort you much, and because you like not thereof, they are discommendable. I have heard it is good to take sure footing when we travel to unknown countries; for when we wade above our shoe latchet, Appelles will reprehend us for cobblers; if you had been a father in Music and could have discerned of tunes I would perhaps have liked your opinion somewhat where now I abhor it; if you were a professor of that practice I would quickly persuade you that the adding of strings to our instrument makes the sound more harmonious, and that the mixture of Music maketh a better concent. But to preach to unskillful is to persuade the brute beasts. I will not stand long in this point although the dignity thereof require a volume, but how learned men have esteemed this heavenly gift, if you please to read you shall see … The matter is so plentiful that I cannot find where to end, as for beginnings they be infinite, but these shall suffice, I like not to long circumstance where less do serve, only I wish you to account well of this heavenly concent, which is full of perfection proceeding from above, drawing his original from the motion of the stars, from the agreement of the planets, from the whistling winds, and from all those celestial circles, where is either perfect agreement or any *Sumphonia*.

But as I like Music, so admit I am not of those that deprave the same: your Pipers are so odious to me as yourself, neither allow I your harping merry beggars; although I knew you myself a professed play maker, and a paltry actor, since which the windmill of your wit hath been turned so long with the wind of folly, that I fear me we shall see the dog return to his vomit, and the cleansed sow to her mire, and the reformed schoolmaster to his old teaching of folly. Beware it be not so, let not your book be a blemish to your own profession. Correct not Music therefore when it is praiseworthy, lest your worthless misliking betray your madness; weigh the abuse.

These attacks on music became official policy when the Puritans took control of the government in the seventeenth century. Instrumental music was removed from the church and the organs were destroyed under a government order. And, because of the Puritans and their arguments, there are American churches today which have no instrumental music. They point out that you do not find the word 'piano' in the New Testament.

Polyphony, the Child of Mathematics, is Left on the Steps of the Church

AFTER ONE THOUSAND YEARS of talking about the subservience of music to mathematics the Church's proud achievement was sixteenth-century polyphony. Several decades ago courses in sixteenth-century counterpoint were foundational courses in every music department (and you can't teach that course without talking about numbers). Undergraduate music texts dealing with the Renaissance focused almost entirely on Church polyphony, with a small wave of the hand at madrigals. For all these reasons, those of us who were undergraduate students in music in the 1950s were told that the sixteenth century was 'the polyphonic era.' But that is a misnomer. The sixteenth century might better be called the century in which polyphony died.

But before we speak of the death of polyphony, let us first consider its life in its time. We believe that if the reader could somehow be transported back to the sixteenth century he would hear performances of Palestrina, let us say, which were musically far more interesting than those heard today.

First, taking all evidence in contemporary treatises under consideration, it seems pretty clear that you would hear the addition of dynamics. Of course, generally there were not yet written dynamic markings but it is clear the performers were adding them in the sixteenth century. Consider, for example, this description of ordinary lute performance by Galilei. The discussion concerns how much more expressive the lute is than the organ. The organ cannot match the lute, says Galilei, because,

> by the nature of the instrument, [organ players] have not been able, cannot, and never will be able to express the harmonies for *affetti* like *durezza, mollezza, asprezza, dolcezza*—consequently the cries, laments, shrieks, tears, and finally quietude and rage—with so much grace and skill as excellent players do on the lute.[1]

Now think of the lute players you have known, or classical guitar players for that matter. Now think of singers you have known. Can anyone believe, if lute players and other musicians were adding the dynamics needed for performance as expressive as that described above, the singers would be standing there singing only in a plain, dull, non-varying *mezzopiano* which has been the tradition for most of the twentieth century for singing sixteenth-century Church polyphony? Why are their performances so boring, dynamically? Because almost no choral conductor feels entitled to pick up a pen and add dynamics to a score of Palestrina.

Second, we think the odds are that you would hear wind instruments doubling the vocal parts. There is so much evidence for this in the seventeenth century, and in the ecclesiastical concerti style which began in the sixteenth century, it is difficult to believe there was not some tradition for this in the performance of sixteenth-century polyphony. The reader will

---

[1] Vincenzo Galilei, *Fronimo* [1584], trans. Carol MacClintock (Neuhasen-Stuttgart: Hanssler-Verlag, 1985), 87.

see below that the famous sixteenth-century theorist, Zarlino, refers to polyphonic music as, 'a jumbled din of voices *and diverse instrumental sounds.*' And consider the Sistine Chapel in the Vatican. It has no organ. But the papal pay records for the sixteenth century document regular payment to the members of the pope's wind band to perform there during the service. What were they doing? They were participating in the services of the Sistine Chapel, according to the diary of the Papal Master of Ceremonies, Paris de Grassis.[2]

Third, given the numerous references to improvisation in church music in the sixteenth century (and before), we are inclined to believe you would also hear in contemporary performances of Palestrina some improvisation. There appears to have been a long tradition for improvisation over chant in the church. Perhaps this was the origin of the idea behind polyphony, with its elaboration in individual voices written, one by one, against the chant.

But even if the actual sixteenth-century performances of church polyphony had all these elements, making the performance far more effective than anything heard today, sixteenth-century Church polyphony still had a fatal flaw. For one thousand years, beginning with St. Augustine, the Church had been stressing the requirement that in church music the words must be more important than the music. But in polyphony, you can't hear the words! That is because at any given moment in time you hear four or more words sung simultaneously.

Music based on mathematics left the Church with nothing to compete against the more interesting music being heard outside the church. Polyphony was dead as a creative force. Needless to say, Catholic composers continued to write in this style well into the Baroque, but their numbers were small and they produced not a single work which is performed today. The battle for the hearts and minds of musicians and listeners alike was finished. Mathematics lost; feeling won.

Actually, far from the sixteenth century being the 'polyphonic era,' the death of polyphony had clearly begun in the fifteenth century, long before the masterworks of its last stage, those by Josquin and Palestrina. In the view of Pirrotta, the association of this old style with the Scholastic dogma of the Church was the first problem for the humanists.

> To humanists the *ars musicae* appeared irremediably tied to scholastic traditions, so they tended to reject it as something too close to medieval sophistry, outmoded, and far from the classicism and simplicity which they aspired to reestablish.[3]

One fifteenth-century writer, whom Pirrotta quotes, criticized the Northern polyphony, in particular the music of Issac, Brumel, Compere and others, for being 'so florid that it more than satiates the ordinary capacity of the ear.'[4] The severe preacher, Savonarola, made a similar objection late in the fifteenth century. He wanted to eliminate the counterpoint and return to simple chant.

---

[2] Dr. John Shearman, 'Leo X and the Sistine Chapel,' London, BBC Radio 3, August 20, 1971.

[3] Nino Pirrotta, in *Music and Culture in Italy from the Middle Ages to the Baroque* (Cambridge: Harvard University Press, 1984), 75.

[4] Paolo Cortese, 'De cardinalatu libri tres,' quoted in Ibid.

> These princes have their cappelle of singers which are a great confusion, because there stands one singer with a big voice who sounds like a calf, and the others howl around him like dogs, and no one understands what they are saying. So let these *canti figurati* go and sing instead the *canti fermi* ordered by the church.[5]

Some of the fifteenth-century composers seem, in retrospect, more involved in the mathematical challenges and,

> began to indulge in complicated rhythmic tricks and in the invention of highly involved methods of notating them.[6]

It was this period of artificial mathematical complexities that is referred to by Girolamo Cardano (1501–1576). We must first point out that his own predilection for mathematics did not lead him to a preference to the polyphonic style, a fact he mentions several times. His preference for the music of his own humanistic generation can be seen in a comment he made after discussing Ockeghem.

> But the music of our day is as much more elegant as it was more elaborate in earlier times.[7]

But, speaking of complexities, Cardano mentions here a composition unknown today, a canon by Ockeghem for thirty-six voices!

By the sixteenth century many complaints about polyphony began to be voiced by distinguished critics and composers. For Mei, the general confusion caused by a number of equal voices prevented the listener from experiencing the kind of catharsis discussed by Aristotle. In Mei's view, music should aspire to the same aesthetic end as that expressed in Aristotle's *Poetics*: music should purge men of their passions not by soothing them but by arousing in them those very passions.[8] He, as others,[9] felt sixteenth-century music failed to do this, that polyphony, in particular, all sounded the same. Polyphony reminded him of men pulling with all their forces on ropes from opposite directions. With its separate parts, polyphony,

> conveys to the soul of the listener at the same time diverse and contrary affections as it mixes indistinctly together melodies and Tones that are completely dissimilar and of natures contrary to each other.[10]

---

5   Quoted in Lewis Lockwood, 'Strategies of Music Patronage in the Fifteenth Century: the Cappella of Ercole I d'Este,' in Iain Fenlon, ed., *Music in Medieval and Early Modern Europe* (Cambridge: Cambridge University Press, 1981), 243.
6   Gustave Reese, *Music in the Renaissance* (New York: Norton, 1959), 11, quoting Apel.
7   Quoted in Clement Miller, *Hieronymus Cardanus, Writings on Music* (American Institute of Musicology, 1973), 153.
8   Quoted in Claude Palisca, *Letters on Ancient and Modern Music* (American Institute of Musicology, 1960), 70.
9   Ibid., 72, mentions similar views by Cirillo Franco (1549) and Don Nicola Vincentino (1551).
10 Ibid., 73.

Bardi, with whom we associate the famous Camerata, in a letter to Caccini in 1578, begins somewhat sarcastically, observing that the composer of Church polyphony considers it a sin if the various parts play together.

> It would seem, I say, a mortal sin if all the parts were heard to beat at the same time with the same notes, with the same syllables of the verse, and with the same [rhythm]; the more they make the parts move, the more artful they think they are.[11]

The Italian composer, Agostino Agazzari (1578–1640), makes a similar objection:

> If someone told me that the bass is not sufficient in the case of the old motets and pieces which are full of imitations and counterpoints I would reply that we no longer make use of such compositions of their kind, because of the confusion and the garbling of the text and words which result from the long and interwoven fugues. Besides, they really give no pleasure and lack charm, for when all voices are sung one hears neither sentence nor sense, since everything is interrupted by frequent imitations and all voices sing different words at the same time, which displeases discerning listeners who pay attention to this ... For while such compositions may be good according to the rules of counterpoint, they are not good according to the precepts of good and true music.[12]

Bardi admitted that the polyphonic style was not so objectionable in instrumental music, as you did not have the problem of the confusion of the words. But in general, he foresaw the need to plea for composers to abandon this style and find a new one.

> [One should] endeavor not to spoil the verse, not imitating the [polyphonic] musicians of today, who think nothing of spoiling it to pursue their ideas or of cutting it to bits to make nonsense of the words ...
>
> In composing, then, you will make it your chief aim to arrange the verse well and to declaim the words as intelligibly as you can, not letting yourself be led astray to the counterpoint like a bad swimmer who lets himself be carried out of the course by the current and comes to shore beyond the mark that he had set, for you will consider it self-evident that, just as the soul is nobler than the body, so the words are nobler than the counterpoint. Would it not seem ridiculous if, walking in the public square, you saw a servant followed by his master and commanding him?

Galilei, writing in 1581, concluded that no sacred or secular polyphony of the Renaissance had ever succeeded in achieving the ethical impact of the music of the ancient Greeks.

---

[11] Giovanni de' Bardi, 'Discourse on Ancient Music and Good Singing,' in Oliver Strunk, *Source Readings in Music History* (New York: Norton, 1950), 294ff. Bardi (b. 1534) was a gentleman vitally interested in the arts. It was in his home, in Florence, where the male 'salon' known as the 'Camerata' met to discuss Greek tragedy. Their discussions were an important step toward opera.

[12] Quoted in Michael Praetorius, *Syntagma Musicum*, facsimile of the original German publication by Barrenreiter Kassel, 1958, 150.

> For all the height of excellence of the practical music of the moderns, there is not heard or seen today the slightest sign of its accomplishing what ancient music accomplished, nor do we read that it accomplished it fifty or a hundred years ago ... Thus neither its novelty nor its excellence has ever had the power, with our modern musicians, of producing any of the virtuous, infinitely beneficial and comforting effects that ancient music produced.[13]

He clearly found it odd, if not unacceptable, that polyphonic composers made the 'rules' more important than the judgment made by the ear.

> [It is clear] that the rules observed by the modern contrapuntists as inviolable laws, as well as those they often use from choice and to show their learning, [are] directly opposed to the perfection of the true and best harmonies and melodies.

We can sense one of the important forces which lead to the Classical Period when Galilei notes that the ear tells us that high tones have a particular nature, as do low tones, and when they are mixed in multi-part music this automatically causes a conflict in the nature of the music itself. Only by writing simple melodies can the emotions of the words be communicated.

> Using few notes is natural both in speaking and singing, since the end of one and the other is solely the expression of the affections of the soul by means of words, which, when well expressed and understood by the listeners, generate in them whatever emotions the musician cares to treat through this medium.[14]

The explanation which Galilei finds for the failure of the sixteenth-century polyphonic composers to understand the importance of the communication of the emotions is that they are simply satisfied by the superficial pleasing of the ear through sound itself,

> Consider each rule of the modern contrapuntists by itself, or, if you wish, consider them all together. They aim at nothing but the delight of the ear, if it can truly be called delight ... And in truth the last thing the modern [church composers] think of is the expression of the words with the passion that these require ... And if it were permitted me, I should like to show you, with several examples of authority, that among the most famous contrapuntists of this century there are some who do not even know how to read, let alone understand. Their ignorance and lack of consideration is one of the most potent reasons why the music of today does not cause in the listeners any of those virtuous and wonderful effects that ancient music caused.[15]

The famous sixteenth-century theorist, Zarlino found that in solo vocal performances one saw a power over the emotions of the listener which he did not find in performances of polyphonic music, which he calls 'a jumbled din of voices.'

---

[13] Galilei, in Strunk, *Source Readings in Music History*, 306ff.

[14] 'Dubbi intorno a quanto io ho detto dell'uso dell'enharmonio,' quoted in Claude V. Palisca, *Humanism in Italian Renaissance Musical Thought* (New Haven: Yale University Press, 1985), 393.

[15] Galilei, in Strunk, *Source Readings in Music History*, 312ff.

> Even in our times we see that music induces in us various passions in the way that it did in antiquity. For occasionally, it is observed, when some beautiful, learned, and elegant poem is recited by someone to the sound of some instrument, the listeners are greatly stirred and moved to do different things, such as to laugh, weep, or to similar actions ... If such effects were wrought by music in antiquity, it was recited as described above and not in the way that is used at present, with a multitude of parts and so many singers and instruments that at times nothing is heard but a jumbled din of voices and diverse instrumental sounds, singing without taste or discretion, and an unseemly pronunciation of words, so that he hears only a tumult and uproar. Music practiced in this way cannot have any effect on us worth remembering ... Those songs in which brief matters are related in a few words, as is customary today in certain canzonets called madrigals, truly are able to move the soul but little. Although these delight us greatly, they do not have the force alluded to above. That it is true that music universally pleases more when it is simple than when fashioned with much artifice and sung by many parts may be understood from this: that we listen to a solo singer accompanied by the sound of an organ, lyre, lute, or similar instrument with greater pleasure than to many. Although many singing together stir the soul, there is no doubt that songs in which the singers pronounce the words together are generally heard with greater pleasure than the learned compositions in which the words are interrupted by many voices.[16]

A similar opinion regarding the clarity of the emotions in a solo singer than when hearing a number of singers, as in polyphonic music, is given by Baldassare Castiglione in his famous book on the art of the courtier. In an extraordinary and extensive discussion of aesthetics in art music, introduced by Gaspare, we read,

> 'There exist many different kinds of music, both vocal and instrumental. So I would be gratified to hear which is the best of all and on what occasion the courtier should perform.'
> 'Truly beautiful music,' answered Federico, 'consists, in my opinion, in fine singing, in reading accurately from the score and in an attractive personal style, and still more in singing to the accompaniment of the viol. I say this because the solo voice contains all the purity of music, and style and melody are studied and appreciated more carefully when our ears are not distracted by more than one voice, and every little fault, too, is more clearly apparent, something which does not happen when a group is singing, because then one singer covers up for the other.'[17]

The various objections to polyphony which we have seen above by the Italians were also shared by important persons in other countries. In France, Pontus de Tyard, the chief theorist of the Pléiade, an association of poets in Paris, also writes of his preference for the emotions in the solo voice, as opposed to ensemble polyphony. This is an important point for the preference for the solo voice was an important harbinger for the birth of opera.

---

[16] 'Istitutioni,' II, 9, p. 75, quoted in Claude V. Palisca, *Humanism in Italian Renaissance Musical Thought*, 371ff.
[17] Baldassare Castiglione, *The Courtier*, trans. George Bull (New York: Penguin Books, 1967), II, 120ff

> Music's purpose seems to be that of setting the word in such a fashion that anyone listening to it will become impassioned and carried away by the mood of the poet. The musician who knows how to deploy the solo voice to this end best attains his goal, in my opinion. Contrapuntal music most often brings to the ears only a lot of noise, from which you feel no vivid effect.[18]

As regards Germany, we first must mention Johannes Cochlaeus (1479–1552, who would be only a footnote but for the fact that he was the teacher of Glarean), *Magister Artium* at the University of Köln. Later he studied theology at Ferrara and eventually became rector at St. Lorenz school, in Nürnberg. In a letter of dedication to the prior of the school, Cochlaeus reveals that he was hired with three areas of responsibility. The first was 'the education of our youth in literature and morals' (which also included grammar) and the second was 'ecclesiastical song.' The third is the one most interesting, for it reflects the fact that polyphony was already considered by normal people to have become something of the past. He was to see that,

> polyphonic music (which is very pleasing to our people) should not be neglected entirely.

'Our people,' meant the Church community, for this was a school which trained boys destined for the clergy.[19]

Cochlaeus' student, Heinrich Glarean (1488–1563) of Switzerland was the author of a famous book, his *Dodecachordon* of 1547. In some ways he was the last of the *ars antiqua*, for he was defending a number of ideas which were already, or very nearly, dead. The book is almost a metaphor of the sixteenth-century Church's problems. It is *the* masterwork treatise on the Church modes, but written at a time the old modal system was rapidly being abandoned and being reinvented as the modern tonal system. It is a great book on modes, written too late to have been of value to anyone except historians.

Although a mathematician, Glarean recognizes the problems with polyphony. He finds some symbols, such as the maxima, no longer in use and seems uncomfortable that the entire system of mensuration has no example in antiquity and is a matter 'almost dependent on the decision of ordinary singers.'[20] He also finds the whole question of the beat and tempo a practice which varies from country to country.[21] In this regard the reason he gives for the alla breve symbol is interesting.

> Whenever musicians wish to accelerate the *tactus*, which they consider should be done when they believe the hearing is fatigued, namely, in order to remove weariness, they draw a line downwards through the circle or semicircle.[22]

---

[18] *Les Discours philosophiques* [Paris, 1587], quoted in Daniel Heartz, 'The Chanson in the Humanist Era,' in *Current Thought in Musicology* (Austin: University of Texas Press, 1976), 227.

[19] Johannes Cochlaeus, *Tetrachordum Musices*, trans. Clement Miller (American Institute of Musicology, 1970), 17.

[20] See Glarean, *Dodecachordon*, trans. Clement Miller (American Institute of Musicology, 1965), II, 230.

[21] Ibid., II, 232.

[22] Ibid., II, 234.

It is also interesting that he finds the idea of proportions largely ignored in practice. This practice, of course, was one of the absurd paths traveled by composers forced by the Church to think of music as mathematics. He admits there have been learned and complex treatises explaining this metrical system, but he says,

> Art ought to be transmitted as the art exists. But even the subject now proclaims that the observance of so many proportions is superfluous; no one, however much he is trained in song, can bear these in mind, and none of the most learned musicians of our time has deigned to adopt them, excepting a very few, in a composition, since there is greater trouble in learning them than there is sweetness or grace in singing them.[23]

Glarean then presents the core theme of his book, an extensive discussion of the Church modes. But before he presents this, once again he expresses his own doubts about polyphony, especially music in more than four-parts, which he believes was composed,

> not so much for aural pleasure as for the ostentation of the talented. For it could scarcely be possible that the human intellect, distracted by so many and varied sounds, could follow carefully all voices simultaneously … Indeed, in my opinion, a distinguished [composer] can show the vigor of his talent no less in writing two or three voices than in the accumulation and chattering of many voices.[24]

It is interesting that he was under the impression that polyphony began only about seventy years earlier (he seems unaware of Palestrina).

> But unfortunately, this art has now reached such unrestraint that learned men are almost wearied of it, and this has many causes, but especially, since it is ashamed to follow in the footsteps of predecessors who observed the relations of modes exactly, because we have fallen into a certain other distorted song which is in no way pleasing, unless because it is new.[25]

The one composer of polyphony whom Glarean praises above all others was Josquin, especially because he 'has never brought forth anything which was not pleasant to the ears.' But even Josquin was not above criticism.

> But in many instances he lacked a proper measure and a judgment based on knowledge and thus in some places in his songs he did not fully restrain as he ought to have, the impetuosity of a lively talent, although this ordinary fault may be condoned because of the otherwise incomparable gifts of the man.[26]

Finally, as Glarean looks over the entire field of polyphonic composers, he finds, apart from the question of following his modal rules, a diversity of purpose.

---

[23] Ibid., II, 242.

[24] Ibid., II, 248. Interestingly, he says he omits from his collection a five-part 'Stabat mater' by Josquin, because everyone owns a copy of it.

[25] Ibid., II, 248.

[26] Ibid., II, 264.

> Of these then there have been some (for such a kind must be mentioned briefly) who have composed solely for the ostentation of their own ability, and these are by far the largest crowd; others have composed in order to please the many and some to train the youth. Some have composed in order to support the majesty of ecclesiastical song. One also finds some who compose in this art in order to relieve their own compulsion and there are very many of these.[27]

His last sentence means he finds very few composers who still compose polyphony as art music. And here he was a careful observer, for polyphony was dying and it was killed by Humanism.

It is the nature of our art that the theorists usually follow sometime later the lead of the composers and performers. Therefore it is important that we acknowledge the first music treatise in one thousand years which does not base itself on mathematics. Adrian Coclico, a Flemish theorist who taught at Wittenberg in 1545, wrote a treatise, *Compendium Musices,* in 1552, in which he constantly recommends ignoring the old mathematician-musicians. For example, no sooner has he begun writing of scales, than he stops and observes that this can only be understood in performance.

> I have wished to train this boyish industry in music through but few words and precepts on that account, so that no youth running to the books of musician-mathematicians will waste his life in reading them and never arrive at the goal of singing well.[28]

There is also a very interesting comment in this book by Coclico about his own teacher, the famous Josquin. Even though Josquin is widely considered today to have represented, together with Palestrina, the culmination of the polyphonic period, as a teacher it would seem that he was perhaps already going in a different direction,

> My teacher, Josquin des Pres, never rehearsed or wrote out any musical procedures, yet in a short time made perfect musicians, since he did not hold his students back in long and frivolous precepts, but taught precepts in a few words at the same time as singing through exercise and practice.[29]

---

[27] Ibid., II, 271.

[28] In Adrian Coclico, *Musical Compendium*, trans. Albert Seay (Colorado Springs: Colorado College Music Press, 1973), 10.

[29] Ibid., 16.

On Music and Society in the Sixteenth Century: The Spread of Italian Humanism

> *The time may come when music is embraced by some noble spirit*
> *whose goal will not be the mechanical one of gain*
> *but honor and immortal glory.*[1]
>
> Gioseffo Zarlino, Italian theorist (1517–1590)

TODAY WHEN WE THINK of the sixteenth-century Italian madrigal composers, in particular the passionate works by de Rore and Gesualdo, the free improvisation in the repertoire of Dalla Casa and the new church music by Gabrieli one is tempted to declare the final victory of Humanism over the Church with its dogma of mathematics-based music. It was not an easy victory, even though the educated and aristocratic class enthusiastically adopted Humanism. Lurking behind the scenes there was still a very powerful Church which would soon institute a Counter-reformation movement in which it would argue for a return to the old dogma. The Church's composers, including Josquin and Palestrina, were still writing under the old mathematics rules. The works they produced, polyphonic church music, are given center stage in most music history texts, but some of the musicians who actually heard this music in the sixteenth century considered it old-fashioned and of little interest. It was music with no real future; the future lay with the crowning achievement of Italian humanism, opera—a new form created specifically to communicate emotion. This emotional music laid down aesthetic concepts which made possible the enormous musical achievements of the Classical and Romantic Periods.

In the German-speaking lands the victory of Humanism was retarded by the civic strife which came in the wake of Luther. It was an atmosphere not conducive to the encouragement of the arts, as one can see in these two contemporary views,

> You know the times. No one really looks for a rebirth of the arts. They are so silent and neglected, it may well be feared that dolts will stamp them out. God alone can preserve them by inspiring the leaders of the city to water the seeds and nurture the plants.
>   John Schöner, 1533[2]

> No wonder that music is so utterly despised and rejected at this time, seeing that other arts, which after all we should and must possess, are so lamentably regarded by everyone as altogether worthless.
>   Johann Walter, 1537[3]

---

[1] Gioseffo Zarlino, *The Art of Counterpoint*, trans. Guy Marco and Claude Palisca (New Haven: Yale University Press, 1968). 290.

[2] John Schöner, dedication in the 1533 publication of Johann Müller's *On Triangles* [1464], quoted in Barnabas Hughes, trans., *Regiomontanus on Triangles* (Madison: The University of Wisconsin Press, 1967), 25.

[3] Johann Walter, *Wittenberg Gesängbuch* [1537], Foreword, quoted in Oliver Strunk, *Source Readings in Music History* (New York: Norton, 1950), 343.

Otherwise, opposition to Humanism in these lands came from the universities, but they and their old mathematics-based ideas lost and Humanism won. There are two interesting statements by important German composers which come at the end of the Renaissance. Michael Praetorius, having studied in Italy with Gabrieli and having argued for the introduction of the new Italian style in Germany, was pleased by the new musical style. As late as 1619 he could see no evidence of what we call the Baroque appearing on the horizon. He said, 'music has developed as far as it can.'

On the other hand, the great composer of the Munich court, Orlando de Lassus, seemed to sense something was in the air, that change was yet to come. He saw the Baroque. In 1593, in the dedication of his *Cantiones sacrae*, he wrote,

> In this age of annually renewed fertility, abounding in *cantiones* of every kind and in rival composers who daily come forward with the desire of pleasing, nay of winning for themselves the foremost place, it seems not easy to determine whether this divine art has attained its full growth, not to say the peak, the summit of its perfection, or whether it is decking itself with flowers after a new birth.[4]

Were those Baroque Germans aware of this struggle and that Humanism had won? In Johann Mattheson's biographical work, *Ehrenpforte* (Hamburg, 1740), in reference to a person who had claimed both a goal of making 'music a scientific or scholarly pursuit' and an implied association with Bach, Mattheson responded that Bach certainly did not teach this man 'the supposed mathematical basis of composition.' 'This,' Johann Mattheson testifies, 'I can guarantee.'

France too was late in coming to Humanism, in spite of the efforts of the academy, although in the instrumental dance music there was an important harbinger. But with the eventual arrival of Rameau and his vivid emotional writing real feeling finally came to France. Lully was soon forgotten.

England in the sixteenth century had the great advantage of the leadership of Henry VIII and Elizabeth I, both of whom were very active musicians. But a sinister and rapidly growing movement on the religious right destroyed aesthetic music just as it was reaching a climax. The poison these far right religious men injected into the aesthetics of music so affected how society viewed music that even today the English-speaking world has not yet completely recovered from it. Only after the disillusion with the government run by these narrow-minded religious men did an atmosphere return to England which eventually made possible Purcell and Handel.

In summary, in the sixteenth century Humanism and music based on emotions made great strides, but only against the strongest opposition by both Church and Scholasticism. As a result the following period, the Baroque, would be a period devoted to the pursuit of emotions in music.

---

4   Strunk, *Source Readings in Music History*, 325.

Let us now look at some of the themes of sixteenth-century Italian Humanism. First, for a very brief period toward the end of the sixteenth century the understanding and performance of music became an expected part of the upper class man. Music became important in a way that it has never been since. Music's place in the 'well-rounded' young man is discussed at length in the famous book, *Il Cortigiano* (*The Courtier*), by Baldassare Castiglione (1478–1529). Aretino, in one of his letters, mentions overhearing a young man state that he has the necessary qualities to be a courtier: 'I am a good musician, have some learning, and I love the chase.'[5] The importance of being a well-rounded man can also be seen in a comment by Guicciardini, who regretted that he had failed to develop these skills.

> When I was young, I used to scoff at knowing how to play [an instrument], dance, and sing, and other such frivolities. I even made light of good penmanship, knowing how to ride, to dress well, and all those things that seem more decorative than substantial in a man. But later, I wished I had not done so. For although it is not wise to spend too much time cultivating the young toward the perfection of these arts, I have nevertheless seen from experience that these ornaments and accomplishments lend dignity and reputation even to men of good rank. It may even be said that whoever lacks them lacks something important. Moreover skill in this sort of entertainment opens the way to the favor of princes, and sometimes becomes the beginning or the reason for great profit and high honors. For the world and princes are no longer made as they should be, but as they are.[6]

Machiavelli, also, recommends in his *The Prince*, that the wise prince will also show himself to be a lover of the arts by rewarding accomplished men.[7]

From the perspective of philosophy the great achievement was the restoration of music to its most fundamental purpose, the expression of feelings. Intelligent men arrived at this purpose from their study of the ancient Greek treatises which discussed music. Vincenzo Galilei (1533–1591) in his 'Dialog on Ancient and Modern Music' recalled the disappearance of the Greek ideals in music during the Dark Ages, a period which he characterizes 'as if all men had been overcome by a heavy lethargy of ignorance, they lived without any desire for learning and took as little notice of music as of the western Indies.'[8] Although this treatise is largely an attack on the ideas of Zarlino, Galilei credits him, together with Glarean and Gafurius, as being responsible for the renewal of Greek ideals. He found they did not completely succeed, which 'may have been owing to the rudeness of the times, the difficulty of the subject, and the scarcity of good interpreters.'

---

5   Letter to Ambrogio degli Eusebii, in Thomas Chubb, *The Letters of Pietro Aretino* (New Haven: Shoe String Press [Archon Books], 1967), 103.

6   Francesco Guicciardini, *Maxims and Reflections*, trans. Mario Domandi (New York: Harper Torchbooks, 1965), C, 179. Guicciardini (1483–1540) as a young man served as an ambassador of Florence to the court of the King of Aragon.

7   Machiavelli, *The Chief Works*, trans. Allan Gilbert (Durham: Duke University Press, 1965), I, 84.

8   Vincenzo Galilei, 'Dialogo della musica antica e della moderna,' in Strunk, *Source Readings in Music History*, 303. His famous son, Galileo Galilei, was the first to point out the mathematical and physical impossibility of the account of Pythagoras' discovery of the overtone series by listening to a blacksmith—a story which had been unchallenged for two thousand years!

When Galilei speaks of the 'renewal of Greek ideals,' everything he meant by this was related to feelings. The humanists constantly write of the importance of music expressing the emotions of the words in music. It was because of this that they were so critical of polyphonic music, which presents to the listener different words at any given time. Bardi, with whom we associate the famous Camerata, in a letter to Caccini in 1578, begins somewhat sarcastically, observing that the composer of Church polyphony considers it a sin if the various parts play together.

> It would seem, I say, a mortal sin if all the parts were heard to beat at the same time with the same notes, with the same syllables of the verse, and with the same [rhythm]; the more they make the parts move, the more artful they think they are.[9]

Galilei, writing in 1581, concludes that no sacred or secular polyphony of the Renaissance had ever succeeded in achieving the ethical impact of the music of the ancient Greeks.

> For all the height of excellence of the practical music of the moderns, there is not heard or seen today the slightest sign of its accomplishing what ancient music accomplished, nor do we read that it accomplished it fifty or a hundred years ago ... Thus neither its novelty nor its excellence has ever had the power, with our modern musicians, of producing any of the virtuous, infinitely beneficial and comforting effects that ancient music produced.[10]

He finds the reason for this in the elements of music itself, reasons which the polyphonic composers ignore.

> [It is clear] that the rules observed by the modern contrapuntists as inviolable laws, as well as those they often use from choice and to show their learning, [are] directly opposed to the perfection of the true and best harmonies and melodies.

He finds, for example, that high tones have a particular nature, as do low tones, and when they are mixed in multi-part music this automatically causes a conflict in the nature of the music itself. Only by writing simple melodies can the emotions of the words be communicated.

> Using few notes is natural both in speaking and singing, since the end of one and the other is solely the expression of the affections of the soul by means of words, which, when well expressed and understood by the listeners, generate in them whatever emotions the musician cares to treat through this medium.[11]

---

9   Giovanni de' Bardi, 'Discourse on Ancient Music and Good Singing,' in Strunk, *Source Readings in Music History*, 294ff. Bardi (b. 1534) was a gentleman vitally interested in the arts. It was in his home, in Florence, where the male 'salon' known as the 'Camerata' met to discuss Greek tragedy. Their discussions were an important step toward opera..

10 Galilei, in Strunk, *Source Readings in Music History*, 306ff.

11 'Dubbi intorno a quanto io ho detto dell'uso dell'enharmonio,' quoted in Claude V. Palisca, *Humanism in Italian Renaissance Musical Thought* (New Haven: Yale University Press, 1985), 393.

The explanation which Galilei finds for the failure of the sixteenth-century polyphonic composers to understand the importance of the communication of the emotions (through words) is that they simply concentrated on pleasing the ear through sound itself, without consideration of emotion.

> Consider each rule of the modern contrapuntists by itself, or, if you wish, consider them all together. They aim at nothing but the delight of the ear, if it can truly be called delight … And in truth the last thing the moderns think of is the expression of the words with the passion that these require … And if it were permitted me, I should like to show you, with several examples of authority, that among the most famous contrapuntists of this century there are some who do not even know how to read, let alone understand. Their ignorance and lack of consideration is one of the most potent reasons why the music of today does not cause in the listeners any of those virtuous and wonderful effects that ancient music caused.[12]

As we have mentioned above, the crowning achievement of sixteenth-century Italian Humanism was the discussions by the group of men known as the Camerata which led to the creation of opera, a new medium centered in using music to communicate the emotions of the plot. Actually, this movement can be seen even earlier than the meetings of the Camerata. An anonymous chronicler of a performance of the tragedy *Alidoro*, given in Reggio in 1568, includes the following description:

> An infinite number of singers and instrumentalists started performing together in a truly divine manner; you could hear at once from the gravity of the sound, which was by turns terrible and sad, that the play that was being performed could not be other than tragic … Not only the music of the opening but all the music heard later [was made] to reflect the terrible and sad qualities of the tragedy and to point to every change of mood.[13]

Pirrotta agrees that the whole idea of the *stile recitativo* and *stile rappresentativo* lay not 'so much in the adherence to recitation of the text … as in the vivid immediacy with which a character's inner affective reactions were to be presented live to the audience.'[14]

Since the musical goals of the humanists were so centered in the ideals which they found in ancient Greek literature, it is no surprise that the purpose of music most discussed was relative to its potential to affect character. Thus, in the *De harmonic* (1518) of Gaffurio, and in an anonymous treatise of 1525, we find lists of very specific emotions which it is contended will be aroused by the various Church modes.[15] Galilei also began his *Fronimo* by reflecting in admiration on the views of the ancient civilizations on the virtues of music with respect to character development.

---

[12] Galilei, in Strunk, *Source Readings in Music History*, 312ff.

[13] Ibid., 230ff.

[14] Ibid., 280.

[15] Quoted in Palisca, *Humanism in Italian Renaissance Musical Thought*, 345.

> Music was esteemed to be of such power and virtue by the ancients that it was their opinion that our very souls were harmony, and that sweet and suave harmonies were in this manner inspired to temper uncontrolled emotions so that they should not be discordant with one another. Therefore they took care to introduce good professors of that science, and to honor them with every kind of honor as being useful in their Republics; for the Egyptians never allowed their system of music to be changed by even one note, and just as they had established it, so they continued to accept it for more than ten thousand years, according to their calendar, because they were sure that they could not change the rules and laws of music without serious damage to the body politic.[16]

Galilei was one of the first to come to understand that the Greeks were talking about an entirely different 'Dorian' than the one known to these sixteenth-century writers.[17] Because they were not so confident about the actual fundamentals of Greek music, some were perhaps hesitant to predict precise influences on character for specific types of sixteenth-century music. It was safer to speak more generally and, above all, to emphasize the importance of the character of the performer himself. Thus, for Galilei character was a necessary element of the definition of the most esteemed musician. After a few observations on deficient performers, those with no imagination or poor technique, he says those most esteemed are those who teach us something, meaning affect our character in the manner of the ancient Greeks. It follows, he says, that the character of the musician is an inseparable component.

> For those who teach us a virtue are much more to be esteemed, and the rarer and more excellent they are the more so, than those who merely delight us with their buffooneries; first because it is a greater and a higher thing to know what another does than to do what he does,[18] and then because every purely sensual pleasure ends by satiating us and never makes us thirst for any knowledge. And I say that they are even more deserving when that knowledge of theirs is combined with the highest character, as these are the things chiefly to be desired in the perfect musician and in every follower of the arts, in order that with his learning and his character he may make those who frequent him and listen to him men of learning and good character. In addition I say that it is impossible to find a man who is truly a musician and is vicious, and that if a man has a vicious nature, it will be difficult, or rather impossible for him to be virtuous and to make others virtuous.[19]

However much the courtier may have appreciated the arts, the genuine artists themselves often lived on the edge of poverty. It was the beginning of the aristocratic patronage system which would remain in place well into the nineteenth century. On advising a correspondent on the life led by poets, Pietro Aretino notes that they are all so poor that a nobleman of Milan once saw a fellow in a ragged cloak and said, 'The man must be a poet.'[20] He continues,

---

[16] Vincenzo Galilei, *Fronimo* [1584], trans. Carol MacClintock (Neuhasen-Stuttgart: Hanssler-Verlag, 1985), Preface to the Readers, 27.

[17] Palisca, *Humanism in Italian Renaissance Musical Thought*, 345ff.

[18] A frequently read prejudice among the Scholastic music theorists of the Middle Ages.

[19] Galilei, 'Dialogo della musica antica e della moderna,' in Strunk, *Source Readings in Music History*, 320ff.

[20] Letter to Giovan Gragoncino, in Chubb, *The Letters of Pietro Aretino*, 95. According to Aretino, in Pietro Aretino, *Dialogues*, trans. Raymond Rosenthal (New York: Marsilio, 1971), 255, scholars had the same reputation. He mentions that a scholar flung his purse at someone and it 'hardly made a sound when it hit the floor.'

But we live in this world, praise God, nor must we despair because our lot is cruel. After all, it is a fine thing to have our name hawked at every fair, and to hear what we have written sung by the mountebanks. It makes us lose our fear of Death, for poets, he admits, are not food for his teeth. Long before he gets them they will have been devoured by cold and heat …

So if you want to go barefoot and naked, turn yourself into an air-eating chameleon and become a singer of rhymes.

For a writer, Aretino points out, one means for survival was to attempt to publish one's own works for profit, although he personally found this offensive.

As for having printed at one's own expense and one's own urging the books that a man has drawn forth from his imagination, that seems to me to be like feasting on one's own limbs, and he who every evening visits the bookstore to pick up the money earned by the day's sales, to be like a pimp who empties the purse of his woman before he retires to bed.

For that reason, I hope God will grant that the courtesy of princes rewards me for the labor of writing, and not the small change of book buyers; for I would rather endure every hardship than to prostitute my genius by making it a day laborer of the liberal arts.

It is obvious that those who write for money become hosts to, and even porters of their own infamy, and so if you want the advantage of profit, become a merchant. Frankly call yourself a book peddler, and lay the name of poet aside.²¹

While Aretino prays for a generous prince, his descriptions of such service are not flattering. In a letter of October 1545, to an ambassador, he writes,

Tell your master that as far as barking goes, poets are like dogs. Unbearable hunger is the evil friend which makes the latter bare their teeth and the former wag their tongues. But the pleasant aftereffects of bread set before them at the right hour and time, will quiet the rabies of one and smother the anger of the other. So if His Excellency would only have as much liberality as he has gold, it would be very little trouble for him so to act that the howling of wolves was changed into the sweet singing of swans.²²

Aretino makes a passing reference to the great danger which has always tempted artists, the fact that by selling out and becoming an entertainer their life becomes in many ways easier. He makes this comment as his fame grew and he began to take revenge in his writings. He liked to think that in so doing he had improved the lot of artists at court.

But I for my part have written what I have written for the sake of sacred Genius. Up to now she had been hidden in a dark corner by the avarice of the great lords. Indeed, before I began to lash out and to paint these fellows in their true colors, men of ability had to become beggars for the ordinary needs of life. If any one of them was able to stave off want and misery, he did so by being a clown and not because he was a man of talents. By my pen, armed with its terrors, wrought in such a manner that these mighty folk, aware of its powers, were obliged to receive men of intellect and enforced courtesy even though they hated this worse than some deadly disease.²³

---

21   Letter to Francesco Marcolini, in Chubb, *The Letters of Pietro Aretino*, 66.
22   Quoted in Ibid., 215.
23   Letter to Giantonio da Foligno, in Ibid., 52.

In France, it was the humanists and the 'practical' musicians who were carrying the art of music forward. It was the latter who created the demand leading to important developments in the publishing of music, and for whom Attaingnant alone published in Paris more than two thousand chansons and nine hundred instrumental dances between 1528 and 1555. And, as Freedman points out, the fact that the publications of Attaingnant were widely exported and reprinted by other French publishers invites the conclusion that they had a strong influence on taste.[24]

In spite of all of this activity, the average working musician had to search in every possible direction to make a living. Cunningham's description of Jean d'Estrée no doubt represents many. She points out that he was not only,

> a member of the king's *musicque de l'Ecurie* as *joueur de hautbois du roi*, but he could further augment his salary as a royal musician by playing in small dance-bands for non-court functions, and by making perhaps even more money in editing and arranging the *Danseries* for Nicolas du Chemin. Sixteenth century Paris was a small place, and the boundaries between the activities of musician, courtier, printer and composer were evidently not as great as we might think.[25]

Even the outstanding composer, Janequin, the first to hold the title 'composer in ordinary' to the king (1559), speaks in one publication of his poverty.[26]

We also find French composers beginning to extend their search for expressivity. According to Lesure, under the influence of Italy, French composers made their music become more and more a literal rendition of the texts. Many set Ronsard's poems to music and one notable example was Anthoine de Bertrand, who in his setting of a sonnet set the word 'death' to quarter tones in an attempt to make the music more expressive. However, he hastens to add the note,

> Those who find this singing difficult may sing as though the signs had no meaning.[27]

In the preface to some of his songs published by Le Roy and Ballard in 1576, Bertrand makes reference to an Italian publication by Nicola Vincentino, *L'antica musica ridotta alla moderna prattica*, which was set for a quarter-tone harpsichord.[28]

Certainly one aesthetic objective was the communication of feeling in music and we see this in particular in the chanson. Jean-Antoine de Baïf, in a sonnet praising Janequin, speaks of the composer,

---

[24] Richard Freedman, 'Paris and the French Court under Francois I,' in *The Renaissance* (Englewood Cliffs: Prentice Hall, 1989), 187. Daniel Heartz, in his study, *Pierre Attaingnant Royal Printer of Music* (Berkeley, 1969), 91, establishes that the dance music had its origin in the court.

[25] Caroline Cunningham, *Estienne du Tertre, 'Scavant Musicien,' Jean d'Estree, 'Joueur de Hautbois du Roy,' and the Mid-Sixteenth Century Franco-Flemish Chanson and Ensemble Dance* (Dissertation, Bryn Mawr, 1969), 191.

[26] Reese, *Music in the Renaissance*, 296.

[27] Quoted in Francois Lesure, *Musicians and Poets of the French Renaissance*, trans. Elio Gianturco (New York: Merlin Press, 1955), 71ff.

[28] Heartz, *Pierre Attaingnant Royal Printer of Music*, 212.

> For where does one not hear the sound, the plea,
> Of this voice-weaver, this musician, who,
> Drugging his hearer's with a nectar brew,
> Compels their souls the body's cage to flee?[29]

One of the great men of the Low Countries was Tielman Susato (d. 1561), trombonist,[30] leader of the town wind band in Antwerp and an important publisher. In the 'Apology' to Susato's 1551 publication of the first music in the Flemish tongue, we find a touching statement on the purpose of music.

> Music is a remarkable gift, instituted by order of God and offered to man to be used not for dishonest or thoughtless ends but, above all, to render thanks and praise to the Lord, to shun idleness and make good use of his time, to drive out melancholy and dark thoughts, and in order to restore joy to hearts sorely tried.

We have mentioned above the civil strife in sixteenth-century Germany which had the consequence of greatly retarding the recognition of the studies of the humanists. Humanism becomes prominent in Germany somewhat later than in France or Italy, although it apparently began under Italian influence. By the beginning of the sixteenth century it had begun to depart from Italian models, such as concentration on uniting Humanism and the Church, to seek its own direction, which tended toward interest in poetry, philosophy and German history. One can see, from this alone, traces of those inevitable currents which were leading to the Reformation.

While Humanism in Italy had strong support from the courts, in Germany the movement was centered in the universities where poets, in particular, were challenging traditional studies. These two forces, the humanist poets and the professors, were drawn together in the aftermath of a controversy which began in 1508 with the publication of books by Johannes Pfefferkorn, a converted Jew, which called for the destruction of all Hebrew books. The one person who spoke out strongly against this proposal was Johannes Reuchlin, a lawyer in Württemberg and a Hebrew scholar. After he himself came under attack by the faculty of the University of Köln and the Dominican Order, humanists began to support him. It became a battle of the freedom of knowledge against the old Catholic Scholastic dogma, another obvious harbinger of the Reformation and much of Europe was drawn into the debate.

While Pfefferkorn and Reuchlin were being debated on all sides, a book of satire called *Letters of Obscure Men* was published by Crotus Rubeanus, a teacher, and Ulrich von Hutten, a man of noble lineage who concerned himself with poetry and Humanism. The debate was the focus of this book of fictitious letters, but much of the text ridicules the Catholic clergy, who are often characterized as being men of rather earthly interests. One letter, for example, describes a group of university students surprising a monk who was sleeping with a woman,

---

[29] Quoted in Daniel Heartz, 'The Chanson in the Humanist Era,' in *Current Thought in Musicology* (Austin: University of Texas Press, 1976), 296.

[30] Reese, *Music in the Renaissance*, 290, incorrectly identifies Susato as a trumpeter.

causing him to flee naked into the night.[31] Another letter describes a Churchman visiting a woman and having to flee when the husband comes home.[32] One clergyman is described as being so much in love that he is blinded to the actual physical appearance of his lover. A writer informs him that in fact the lady has,

> a wart on her forehead, long red shanks, and clumsy brown hands, and her breath savoureth because of her foul teeth ... But you are so blinded by that devil-begotten passion that you perceive not her faults.[33]

Another letter claims that the monks of a monastery in Strasburg,

> brought women-folk to their cells by way of the river beneath their walls; and they trimmed their hair, so that for a long while they passed for monks.[34]

Finally, one letter suggests the Church did not worry much over such behavior.

> He hath been preaching too, of late, that priests should in no wise maintain concubines, and he declared that bishops are guilty of mortal sin when they take milktithes, and wink at priests consorting with their handmaidens, whereas they ought to drive them forth one and all.
> Be this as it may, we must sometimes be merry and have to do with a wench, when nobody is the wiser; after, we can make confession; and the Lord is merciful, wherefore we hope for forgiveness.[35]

Such openly satirical portraits of the clergy are found elsewhere and, again, their contribution toward preparing the climate for the coming Reformation can hardly be minimized. Already in 1503, Christopher, Bishop of Basel, had addressed the synod of his diocese on the subject of the immorality of the clergy as follows:

> Since we have learned with the greatest chagrin that the greater part of the priests of our city and diocese when they are called to conduct the funeral services of nobles and other persons, give themselves up to gaming and drunkenness, so that many of them at times sit the whole night at play; others exhaust themselves with swilling and drunkenness and sleep the whole night on the benches, and by other extraordinary excesses bring scandal, disgrace, and derision upon the clerical profession: Therefore, we command that all clergymen who are so invited, and all others, shall not give up themselves to dicing and card-playing, nor to other irregular and disgraceful actions at any time whatever, and especially in taverns ...

---

[31] Letter of 'Johann Kannegieszerr to Ortwin Gratius,' in Francis Stokes, trans., *On the Eve of the Reformation* (New York: Harper & Row, 1909), 12.

[32] Letter of 'Magister Conrad of Zwickau to Ortwin Gratius,' in Ibid., 43.

[33] Letter of 'Magister Ortwin Gratius to Ortwin Gratius,' in Ibid., 69.

[34] Letter of 'Wendelin Tuchscherer, Choir member at Strasburg, to Ortwin Gratius,' in Ibid., 97.

[35] Letter of 'Magister Conrad of Zwickau to Ortwin Gratius,' in Ibid., 21.

> The clergy shall see to it that during the worship in the church they do not walk up and down with laymen ... nor shall they go out upon the market in choir dress during worship to buy eggs, cheese, or anything else.[36]

The *Letters of Obscure Men* also satirized professors, who were for the most part Churchmen. In the very first letter a dinner of 'Doctors, Licentiates and Magisters' is described, during which they eat and drink abundantly while arguing whether 'magister nostrandus' or 'noster magistrandus' is the more appropriate for a candidate of the Doctor in Divinity degree.[37] Especially attractive, regarding the majesty of the professors, is a letter which tells of a student who made the mistake of addressing the Rector of a university in the familiar form of German and who was consequently imprisoned![38]

The University of Paris is attacked in several letters, one calling it 'the mother of all foolishness' and accusing it of broadcasting 'superstition and folly' and calling its students numskulls.[39] One letter says of the university professors of the arts that they,

> decoy youths and take their money, and make Bachelors and Doctors of them though they know nothing. And they have brought it about that students no longer desire to graduate even in Arts, but all wish to become Poets.[40]

There is little literature in sixteenth-century England which openly supports Humanism, but we wish to mention two writers. First, in Philip Sidney (1554–1586) in his *The Defence of Poesie* (1595) has left two passages which caught our attention. He seeks to make the argument that 'neither Philosophy nor History could at the first have entered into the gates of popular judgments, if they had not taken the passport of poetry.' He speaks of the contemporary importance of poets in countries held in little esteem by the English (Turkey and Ireland), and then makes an interesting reference to the New World.

> Even among the most barbarous and simple Indians, where no writing is, yet they have their poets who make and sing songs which they call *Arentos*, both of their ancestors deeds and praises of their Gods.[41]

In the second passage, Sidney recalls his personal introduction to the style of the ancient epic singer, the ancient Greek singer who sings of the heroic deeds of the great.

---

36 Samuel Jackson, *Huldreich Zwingli* (New York: Putham, 1901), 26. Zwingli (1484–1531) was born, educated and served the Reformation in Switzerland.

37 Letter of 'Thomas Langschneider to Ortwin Gratius,' in Stokes, *On the Eve of the Reformation*, 5ff.

38 Letter of 'Magister Johann Krabacius to Ortwin Gratius,' in Ibid., 31.

39 Letter of 'Gerhard Schirrugel to Ortwin Gratius,' in Ibid., 46.

40 Letter of 'Anton Rubenstadt to Ortwin Gratius,' in Ibid., 53.

41 Sir Philip Sidney, 'The Defence of Poesie,' [1595] in *The Prose Works of Sir Philip Sidney*, ed. Albert Feuillerat (Cambridge: Cambridge University Press, 1962), 5.

> Certainly I must confess my own barbarousness [then], for I never heard the old song of 'Percy and Douglas,' but that I found not my heart moved more than with a trumpet; and yet it is sung by some blind Crowder, with no rougher voice, than rude style: which being so evil appareled in the dust and cobwebs of that uncivil age, what would it work, trimmed in the gorgeous eloquence of Pindar? In Hungary I have seen it the manner at all Feasts, and other such meetings, to have songs of their ancestors valor, which that right soldierly nation thinks one of the chief kindlers of brave courage. The incomparable Lacedemonians did not only carry that kind of Music ever with them into the field, but even at home, as such songs were made, so were they all content to be singers of them.[42]

The English Church philosopher, Richard Hooker (1553–1600), who was one of the important rational voices which tried to counter the arguments of the radical Puritans, begins his discussion of Church music with an eloquent testimonial to music. It is a remarkable and courageous statement during the dark and dangerous atmosphere created by the Puritans.

> Touching musical harmony whether by instrument or by voice, it being but of high and low in sounds a due proportionable disposition, such notwithstanding is the force thereof, and so pleasing effects it hath in that very part of man which is most divine, that some have been thereby induced to think that the soul itself by nature is or hath in it harmony. A thing which delighteth all ages and beseemeth all states; a thing as seasonable in grief as in joy; as decent being added unto actions of greatest weight and solemnity, as being used when men most sequester themselves from action. The reason hereof is an admirable facility which music hath to express and represent to the mind, more inwardly than any other sensible means, the very standing, rising, and falling, the very steps and inflections every way, the turns and varieties of all passions whereunto the mind is subject; yea so to imitate them, that whether it resemble unto us the same state wherein our minds already are, or a clean contrary, we are not more contentedly by the one confirmed, than changed and led away by the other. In [music] the very image and character even of virtue and vice is perceived, the mind delighted with their resemblances, and brought by having them often iterated into a love of the things themselves. For which cause there is nothing more contagious and pestilent than some kinds of [music]; then some nothing more strong and potent unto good. And that there is such a difference of one kind from another we need no proof but our own experience, inasmuch as we are at the hearing of some more inclined unto sorrow and heaviness; of some, more mollified and softened in mind; one kind more apt to stay and settle us, another to move and stir our emotions; there is that draweth to a marvelous grave and sober mediocrity, there is also that carrieth as it were into ecstasies, filling the mind with an heavenly joy and for the time in a manner severing it from the body. So that although we lay altogether aside the consideration of the text of a ditty and substance [matter], the very harmony of sounds being framed in due sort and carried from the ear to the spiritual faculties of our souls, is by a native puissance and efficacy greatly available to bring to a perfect temper whatsoever is there troubled, apt as well to quicken the spirits as to allay that which is too eager, sovereign against melancholy and despair, forcible to draw forth tears of devotion if the mind be such as can yield them, able both to move and to moderate all affections.[43]

---

[42] Ibid., 24.

[43] Richard Hooker, *On the Laws of Ecclesiastical Polity*, V, xxxviii, in *The Works of Mr. Richard Hooker* (Oxford: Clarendon Press, 1888), II, 159.

Erasmus on Humanism

> His health was always delicate, and thus he was often attacked by fevers, especially in Lent on account of the eating of fish, the mere smell of which used to upset him. His character was straightforward, and his dislike of falsehood such that even as a child he hated other boys who told lies, and in old age even the sight of such people affected him physically. Among his friends he spoke freely—too freely sometimes, and though often deceived he never learned not to trust them. Having a touch of pedantry, he never wrote anything with which he was satisfied; he even disliked his own appearance.... For high office and for wealth he had a permanent contempt, and thought nothing more precious than leisure and liberty. A charitable judge of other men's learning, he would have been a supreme [teacher] of gifted minds had his resources run to it. In promoting the study of the humanities no one did more, and great was the unpopularity he had to suffer in return for this from barbarians and monks.[1]
>
> Erasmus, describing himself

DESIDERIUS ERASMUS (1469–1536) was one of the great writers of prose of the sixteenth century. He was born near Rotterdam and left an orphan while still a teenager. The executor of his parent's estate, in order to obtain everything for himself, gave Erasmus over to a monastic career. Erasmus in time became an ordained priest and, although he studied at the University of Paris, his viewpoints always reflected to a surprising degree his background in Church dogma.

His fame was such that he was constantly being offered the protection of various kings, as well as high office in the Church, but he foresaw that he could not write freely unless he was independent. Thus he supported himself through his publications as well as through gifts which resulted from his frequent travels. He made a lasting impression on everyone he met in these travels and we will let one famous acquaintance, Sir Thomas More (1478–1536), speak for them all:

> I cannot get rid of a prurient feeling of vanity ... when it occurs to my mind that I shall be commended to a distant posterity by the friendship of Erasmus.[2]

Erasmus was a man whose intellectual brilliance was so astonishing and whose knowledge of ancient Greek and Latin literature seems almost incredible. His overpowering knowledge and the scope of his writings made him one of the most widely known persons of his time and certainly the most influential scholar. This international respect which Erasmus enjoyed made it impossible to enjoy a quiet life as a humanist scholar, for he lived at one of the pivotal

---

[1] Letter to Conradus Goclenius [1524], quoted in *The Collected Works of Erasmus* (Toronto: University of Toronto Press, 1992), IV, 409.

[2] Erasmus, *Epistles* (London, 1901), III, 94.

moments of history. Against his desire, he was thrust into the greatest drama of the sixteenth century, the rise of the Protestant movement and its impact on the Church and states of Europe.

As the Lutheran movement gained support there was tremendous pressure on Erasmus by Catholic leaders for him to write and speak out against Luther. In 1522 even Pope Adrian VI pleaded in a letter to Erasmus to write against 'the heresies, as stupid and boorish as they are godless … Can you then refuse to sharpen the weapon of your pen against the madness of these men?'[3]

Erasmus went to great lengths to attempt to remove himself from the fight, often pleading that he did not know Luther and had not read his books. Putting him in the best light, one can say that he preferred to encourage the fight against Luther, but not participate in it. Indeed, he once compared himself to 'those who sound the trumpet on the battlefield while remaining themselves outside the fray.'[4]

But a less genuine side of Erasmus is often seen in his correspondence, where he attempted to tailor his views to please the reader. For example, in a letter to Albert of Brandenburg, in 1519,[5] he could untruthfully say that he had attempted to prevent the publication of Luther's works. On the other hand, to the Luther supporter, Philippus Melanchthon, he could seem almost sympathetic.

> Luther's supporters—and they include almost all men of good will—would wish that some of what he has written were more courteously and moderately expressed. But it is too late to tell him so now. I can see that things are heading towards civil strife.[6]

In the correspondence of Erasmus we can follow the progress of the Lutheran movement, step by step. By 1520 he had become fully aware of the impact of Luther's views. A correspondent at this time writes of Luther's publications, 'You would hardly believe their universal popularity.'[7] Erasmus, who first thought the Church should simply ignore Luther, now saw the Church beginning to blame everything on the humanist movement. Erasmus, reflecting on the failure of the Church leaders to properly confront Luther, was becoming alarmed.

> I saw that the business took its rise in hatred of the classical languages and what they call liberal studies. I saw that it was carried on with bitter strife and seditious clamor in public, the only result of which was to make Luther's works famous and arouse the common run of men to read them eagerly. Had they first refuted Luther and taken him out of men's minds, and then burnt his books, they might have done away with the whole of Luther without setting the world by the ears.[8]

---

3 Letter of Pope Adrian VI to Erasmus [1522], in *The Collected Works of Erasmus*, IX, 206ff.

4 Letter to Duke George of Saxony [1520], in Ibid., VIII, 5. Curiously, in another letter he referred to Luther as a trumpet, 'like a great trumpet for proclaiming the gospel truth.' [Ibid., 42]

5 Quoted in Ibid., VII, 110.

6 Letter to Philippus Melanchthon [1520], in Ibid., VII, 313.

7 Letter of Arkleb of Boskovice to Erasmus [1520], in Ibid., VIII, 76.

8 Letter to Leo X [1520], in Ibid., VIII, 52.

By 1524 he concludes it is already too late to stop the new movement—too late to simply burn Luther at the stake!

> This business of Luther is very widely spread, and pushes further every day. And so I fear that the common remedies of public recantation, prison, and faggot will not get us very far.[9]

At the same time his strong traditional faith made him wonder if this were not all the work of God.

> Has it pleased God to use Luther, as once he used the Pharaohs, the Philistines, the Romans, and men like Nebuchadnezzar? For Luther's successes can hardly have come about without God's help, especially since many of the actors in the play are vile creatures of extraordinary depravity and stupidity.[10]

By the following year events had become so dramatic that even Erasmus' faith could not sustain his optimism.

> What began with theological argument and noisy protestations soon turned into a matter for papal bulls; then it came to the burning of books and finally to the burning of men. What, I should like to know, has been gained by all this? Here at this moment a bloody drama is being played out … How it will end I do not know.[11]

Already in 1523, Erasmus had found himself becoming the object of attacks by the followers of Luther and by 1524 Erasmus was becoming worried about the impact of the religious strife on humanistic studies.

> Thanks to these new gospellers of ours the humanities are out in the cold more or less everywhere, and we must use every effort to assist them.[12]

The following year he observed,

> Throughout Germany, not just the humanities, but almost every form of learning has crumbled into ruin.[13]

In 1525, as well, Erasmus was becoming alarmed at the general civil unrest.

---

[9] Letter to Archduke Ferdinand [1524], in Ibid., X, 423.

[10] Letter to Duke George of Saxony [1524], in Ibid., X, 457ff.

[11] Letter to Noel Buda [1525], in Ibid., XI, 150.

[12] Letter to Caspar Velius [1524], in Ibid., X, 420.

[13] Letter to Adrianus Barlandus [1525], in Ibid., XI, 177.

> I had fair success in Germany in arousing interest in languages and polite letters, and the applause which greeted my efforts was not entirely grudging; but then there was this sudden and disastrous upheaval, which, with its controversies and senseless disputes, began to throw everything into confusion, and has now reached the point where human blood flows in torrents.[14]
>
> ......
>
> Here considerably more than 100,000 peasants have been killed, and every day priests are arrested, tortured, hanged, decapitated, or burnt at the stake.[15]

As if all these concerns did not weigh heavily enough on Erasmus, he was astonished at the actions of his own Catholic brothers. The thought among the Catholic conservatives was that the new heresies had sprung from the humanities.[16]

> Nothing is so brazen, so pig-headed, as ignorance. These are the men who conspire with such zeal against the humanities. Their aim is to count for something in the councils of the theologians, and they fear that if there is a renaissance of the humanities, and if the world sees the error of its ways, it may become clear that they know nothing, although in the old days they were commonly supposed to know everything ... It is they who run this conspiracy against the devotees of liberal subjects.[17]

Indeed, in 1522 Erasmus had written that the Pope, Adrian VI, 'is entirely a scholastic, and not wholly well disposed to the humanities.'[18]

As the Lutheran movement gained momentum, Erasmus was shocked to find inquisitors in the Low Countries 'astonishingly hostile to the humanities. They start by putting men in jail and only then look for something to accuse them of.'[19] In 1525 a correspondent, Christoph Truchsess, writes to Erasmus of the extent of the hostility of the conservatives toward the humanities.

> Recently a well-known lawyer stood up in a crowded [university] hall in Bologna and without a blush made an attack upon the Muses (I quote his actual words): 'Keep away, gentlemen, from the humane arts, as you would from a painted harlot.'[20]

One can see Erasmus becoming increasingly alarmed. He remarks that certain men ('if such creatures deserve the name of *men*') are conspiring in deadly earnest to destroy the humanities. To combat this, he says, what is needed is,

---

[14] Letter to Benedetto Giovio [1525], in Ibid., XI, 341.
[15] Letter to Erasmus Schets [1525], in Ibid., XI, 393
[16] Erasmus mentions this specifically in a letter of 1519 to Petrus Mosellanus, in Ibid., VI, 313.
[17] Letter to Maarten van Dorp [1515], in Ibid., III, 122.
[18] Letter to John Fisher [1522], in Ibid., IX, 176.
[19] Letter to Willibald Pirckheimer [1524], in Ibid., X, 173.
[20] Quoted in Ibid., XI, 379.

a whole host of champions whose intelligence, virtue, and influence will match the folly, villainy, and insolence of our enemies, these being the qualities in which they indisputably excel. If studies of this sort are snuffed out, how, I wonder, will our life differ from that of cattle or fish or creatures of the wild?[21]

At this time he loses one of his few soul-mates, with the death of Maarten van Dorp.

He stood almost alone in his support of the humanities, which some are now desperately trying to destroy. I do not think they realize what effect this will have upon their own studies, whose success alone interests them; for, as events will prove, once the gentler forms of learning have been destroyed, the things which they are defending with more zeal than wisdom will perish also. Everything would turn out better if the doyens of the old learning graciously welcomed the humanities into a friendly partnership, like exiles returning home to resume their rightful place.[22]

By 1525, Erasmus complains he is being attacked by both the Lutherans and the Catholics. Regarding the latter, he writes,

I am the target of persistent and mindless attacks from monks and theologians whose implacable hostility I have brought upon myself through my support of the humanities, for these swine detest the humanities more than they detest Luther himself.[23]

......

There are some [Catholic clergy], especially among the older generation, who can accept nothing that has the slightest odor of the humanities about it or departs at all from the preferences they acquired as children. They don't realize that times change and that we must change with them.[24]

......

Even the theologians' dogs piss on me as they pass.[25]

During this period of personal attacks by important figures of his own Church, we find Erasmus fighting back with stronger and stronger language. In a letter of 1519 to Pope Leo X, Erasmus characterizes the Catholic scholars who have criticized him for attempting a new translation of the New Testament.

With astonishing unanimity it won the approbation of all save very few, some of whom were too stupid to be convinced by sound arguments, others too proud to be willing to learn, others too obstinate not to feel shame if they showed lack of firmness in pursuing the wrong course ... some too anxious for their own reputation to let it be thought that there was anything they had not known before.[26]

---

[21] Letter to Alexius Thurzo [1525], in Ibid., XI, 103.
[22] Letter to Adrianus Barlandus [1525], in Ibid., XI, 176ff.
[23] Letter to Celio Calcagnini [1525], in Ibid., XI, 112.
[24] Letter to Noel Buda [1525], in Ibid., XI, 148.
[25] Letter to Claudius Cantiuncula [1525], in Ibid., XI, 288.
[26] Letter to Leo X [1519], in Ibid., VII, 57.

Another letter of the same year is more outspoken.

> There are gangs of conspirators who have consigned themselves on oath to the infernal powers if they do not utterly destroy the humanities and classical theology; and they have sworn to hold forth against Erasmus everywhere: at drinking-parties, in markets, in committees, in druggists' shops, in carriages, at the barber's, in the brothels, in public and private classrooms, in university lectures and in sermons, in confidential conversations, in the privacy of the confessional, in bookshops, in the taverns of the poor, in the courts of the rich … There is no place they cannot penetrate, no lie they will not tell, to make me, a general benefactor, into an object of general hatred.[27]

The following year, after an attack by the English scholar, Edward Lee, the language of Erasmus becomes very personal.

> The English viper has burst out at last! Before us stands Edward Lee, an eternal blot on that isle so highly thought of. For eighteen months now he has been boasting of his 'pious annotations.' The whole world awaited a work of scholarship; and here before us is a book running over, raving mad I would say, with brawling and fishwives' abuse. Strip this from the book, and heavens! how worthless, how tedious is what remains! I would describe the monster for you, but I fear posterity will not believe that such a beast was ever born in human shape. No harlot was ever so brazen, no pimp a more abandoned liar.[28]

And in 1521, Erasmus actually writes an extraordinary personal letter to a critic.

> My own feeling for you is pity rather than resentment, and I pity you the more if you have still no pity for yourself. A large element of health lies in diagnosing one's disease. If nature has denied you the brains to become a great scholar, the eloquence to be an effective preacher, the skill to write so that you might publish books for the general good, you must at least try to become a good man. And he begins to become a good man who has ceased to be a bad one. He is a bad man who speaks ill of his neighbor; doubly bad if he speaks ill of one who has done him some good. If you cannot do good to others for want of brains, eloquence, learning, common sense, and judgment, do what you can at least to do them no harm.[29]

From the above, most readers will form the opinion that this great scholar, Erasmus, was a dedicated humanist. Indeed he was, but only from a limited perspective. His definition of humanism was centered in the great books of ancient Greece and Rome. Other than that, in some ways he reflected his Church education and its philosophical positions.

We find it curious, for example, that as a dedicated humanist, he had no strong feelings regarding the importance of the emotions. When this subject comes up, he repeats the old dogma that Reason must rule man. A striking example of his thought is found in his advice to a young prince. God, he tells us, has no emotions. Here we also see an example of the low regard Erasmus held for the common people.

---

[27] Letter to Thomas Lupset [1519], in Ibid., VII, 159.

[28] Letter to Wolfgang Capito [1520], in Ibid., VII, 216.

[29] Letter to Vincentius Theoderici [1521], in Ibid., VIII, 194.

> Although God is swayed by no emotions, he nevertheless orders the world with the greatest good judgment. Following his example in all his actions, the prince must disregard emotional reactions and use only reason and judgment.
>
> Nothing is higher than God, and similarly the prince should be removed as far as possible from the low concerns and sordid emotions of the common people.[30]

In another place, he observes,

> Correct judgment has no use for any kind of emotion, least of all for excessive, uncontrollable, and overwhelming joy, which is wont not only to eradicate all judgment but often also to rob us of our senses entirely.[31]

Erasmus also repeated the old long-held Church position dismissing the importance of the senses, that all the senses distort the truth and thus only Reason can be depended upon.

> What we apprehend with our senses does not really exist, for it is not perpetual, nor does it always take the same form. Those things alone really exist which are apprehended by the contemplation of the mind ... Now although the philosopher, withdrawing from sensible things, practices the contemplation of things intelligible, yet he does not perfectly enjoy them except when the spirit, liberated from the material organs through which it operates now, exercises all its force.[32]

To support this view that the senses distort, Erasmus presents a long discussion of the Greek proverb, 'The Sileni of Alcibiades,' which meant something which appears other than it is. He gives as an example, by the way, a carved figure of wood which appears like a 'caricature of a hideous flute player,' but opens to reveal a deity.

> The real truth of things is always most profoundly concealed, and cannot be detected easily or by many people. The stupid multitude, judging things as they do upside down, and using of course as their criteria for every purpose what is most clearly obvious to the bodily senses, constantly make mistakes and go astray.[33]

Erasmus also appears to share the Church's doubts about the value of personal experience. One phrase certainly echoes the old Church,

> Those who spend their whole lives on gentile literature end up as pagans.[34]

---

[30] 'The Education of a Christian Prince,' [1516] in Ibid., XXVII, 221. In his 'A Complaint of Peace Spurned and Rejected by the Whole World,' [Ibid., XXVII, 296], Erasmus again mentions 'the common people, who are swayed by their passions like a stormy sea.' See also his autobiographical essay, ca. 1525, quoted in Ibid., X, 218 and his letter to Francois I [1523], in Ibid., X, 116.

[31] 'The Tyrannicide,' [1506] in Ibid., XXIX, 77.

[32] Letter to Joris van Halewijn [1520], in Ibid., VII, 317.

[33] 'Adages,' in Ibid., XXXII, 267.

[34] Ibid., XXXII, 268.

In the same way the humanism of Erasmus is shot through with occasional dogma of the Church, his attitude toward education is somewhat complex. Erasmus, who would have been welcome at any sixteenth-century university, was clearly uncomfortable in that environment. While he shared many of the Church viewpoints with the professors, he was clearly bothered by their rigid approach to knowledge, a remnant of medieval Scholasticism. He mentions this in a letter of 1525, where he notes that he has tried to inspire a renewed interest in the liberal arts, both to bring them into religious discussion and to introduce languages and fine literature into the schools. But Erasmus takes pains to disassociate himself from Scholasticism.

> With regard to the teaching of the scholastics, I have always kept away from it as much as possible, for I am very conscious that a person of my modest abilities should not enter this difficult field of dogmatic theology.[35]

In a letter to Henry VIII, Erasmus is less modest. He wonders who would have been willing to face martyrdom for the early Greek philosophies and 'Who gives a fig for those puzzling precepts of Pythagoras?' In a remarkable distortion of the truth, he claims that even Aristotle would be unknown were it not for the Christians.[36]

He takes the opportunity to again attack the world of the professor in discussing the above mentioned proverb, 'The Sileni of Alcibiades,' which deals with appearances versus realities.

> Anyone who looked thoroughly into the driving force of things and their true nature would find none so far removed from real wisdom as those whose honorific titles, learned bonnets, resplendent belts, and bejeweled rings advertise wisdom in perfection. So true is this that you may not seldom find more real and native wisdom in one single ordinary man, who in the world's judgment is an ignoramus and a simple-minded fool, more or less, whose mind has been educated not by the subtle Scotus but by the heavenly spirit of Christ, than in many of our pompous theologians, Professors three and four times over, stuffed with their favorite Aristotle and swollen with a plethora of doctoral definitions, conclusions and propositions.[37]

This condemnation of the world of the professor was due in part to the fact that these same university scholars were constantly attacking his writings. In his 'Complaint of Peace,' Erasmus has Peace bemoan this characteristic of the academic community.

> I shall seek refuge in the company of scholars, for good learning makes men, philosophy makes superior men, theology makes holy men. Surely I shall be allowed to settle down amongst them after all my wanderings. But woe is me! Here too there is warfare, another kind and not so bloody, but just as insane … The heat of the debate mounts from argument to insult, from insults to fisticuffs, and if they don't settle the matter by daggers or spears they take to stabbing with poisoned pens, tear one another with barbed wit, and attack each other's reputation with the deadly darts of their tongues.[38]

---

35   Letter to Noel Buda [1525], in Ibid., XI, 135.
36   Letter to Henry VIII [1523], in Ibid., X, 70.
37   'Adages,' in Ibid., XXXIV, 265ff.
38   'A Complaint of Peace Spurned and Rejected by the Whole World,' [1516] in Ibid., XXVII, 297.

Preferring not to be part of this environment, Erasmus was resigned to the solitary life. In his 'Praise of Folly,' the narrator, Folly, proposes to compare the lot of a wise man to that of a fool. One cannot help but feel this passage is to some degree autobiographical, composed in some moment of self-pity.

> Imagine some paragon of wisdom to set up against him, a man who has frittered away all his boyhood and youth in acquiring learning, has lost the happiest part of his life in endless wakeful nights, toil, and care, and never tastes a drop of pleasure even in what's left to him. He's always thrifty, impoverished, miserable, grumpy, harsh and unjust to himself, disagreeable and unpopular with his fellows, pale and thin, sickly and bleary-eyed, prematurely white-haired and senile, worn-out and dying before his time. Though what difference does it make when a man like that does die? He's never been alive. There you have a splendid picture of a wise man.[39]

Erasmus also wrote at length on the education of younger children. To begin with, his ideal for the teacher of children he expresses in a letter to Johann von Vlatten,

> To this end it will be a great help to have in charge of the school a man of good character no less than good education ... Once he has laid the first foundations of both Greek and Latin, he should read all the best authors with the boys; and this means Cicero, and the others in proportion as they approach him. Among the poets he must choose those who are respectable; and in any case those who are worth reading for the amount they can tell us but are objectionable for their obscenity, of whom Martial is one, must in my view be presented in excerpts which can safely be read with the boys.[40]

In general, however, he seems to have found quite another kind of teacher. In his treatise, 'On the Writing of Letters,' he calls them 'this untaught race of experts, this illiterate horde of literates.'[41]

Erasmus was especially concerned with the treatment of children in school and he often lashes out at the cruel teacher.

> He flogs and tortures the poor creatures, and deafens them with shouting and abuse ...
> You may see this whip-cracking and untaught breed of elementary schoolmasters in power everywhere nowadays, and the caverns where they babble away reverberate on all sides with piteous howling like the realm of the Furies.[42]

And in another place,

> ... schoolmasters, always shouting and clouting and flogging the boys' skin off their backs, and can teach nothing for all that except bad grammar, which they will soon have to unlearn.[43]

---

39 'Praise of Folly,' [1503] in Ibid., XXVII, 110.

40 Letter to Johann von Vlatten [1523], in Ibid., X, 100.

41 'On the Writing of Letters,' [1522] in Ibid., XXV, 12. Erasmus, in 'The Right Way of Speaking Latin and Greek,' [1528] in Ibid., XXVI, 381, says that the word 'bachelor,' in the academic sense comes from *baculus*, or 'rod,' referring to the beating of students.

42 'On the Writing of Letters,' [1522] in Ibid., XXV, 41.

43 Letter to Maarten Lips [1518], in Ibid., VI, 4.

This having been his experience, he is astonished at how casually teachers are hired.

> Nobody commissions a statue from a sculptor without having seen other statues from his workshop, yet we happily hand over our children to a stranger without having seen any example of what he has done.[44]

Erasmus found it curious that of all persons, the highest nobles were the least carefully educated.

> If anyone is to be a coachman, he learns the art, spends care and practice; but for anyone to be a king, we think it is enough for him to be born …
>
> What actually happens is that no kind of man is more corruptly or carelessly brought up than those whose education is of such importance to so many people. The baby who is to rule the world is handed over to the stupidest of womenkind who are so far from instilling anything in his mind worthy of a prince, that they discourage whatever the tutor rightly advises, or whatever inclination to gentleness the child may have in himself—and they teach him to act like a prince, that is like a tyrant. Then no one fails to fawn and flatter. The courtiers applaud, the servants obey his every whim, even the tutor is obsequious; and he is not doing this to make the prince more beneficial to his country, but to ensure a splendid future for himself.[45]

The most famous discussion by Erasmus on the subject of the education of nobles is found in his 'The Education of a Christian Prince.' He begins by stressing that the proper teacher is one who has learned 'by long practical experience and not just by petty maxims.'[46] Oddly enough, Erasmus does not, in this treatise, outline a specific plan of studies for the prince, nor even mention the basic subjects by name. He does recommend the reading of books in general, however with some stipulations.

> Demetrius Phalereus [fourth century BC] shrewdly recommends the prince to read books, because very often he may learn from these what his friends have not dared to bring to his attention. But in this matter he must be equipped in advance with an antidote, as it were, along these lines: 'This writer whom you are reading is a pagan[47] and you are a Christian reader; although he has many excellent things to say, he nevertheless does not depict the ideal of a Christian prince quite accurately, and you must take care not to think that whatever you come across at any point is to be imitated straight away, but instead test everything against the standard of Christ.'[48]

---

44 'The Right Way of Speaking Latin and Greek,' [1528] in Ibid., XXVI, 374.

45 'Adages,' in Ibid., XXXI, 232, 234.

46 'The Education of a Christian Prince,' [1516] in Ibid., XXVII, 208.

47 No doubt Erasmus was thinking of Aristotle, whom he frequently attacks.

48 'The Education of a Christian Prince,' [1516] in Ibid., XXVII, 250.

On Music and Society in the Sixteenth Century: The Growing Irrelevance of the Universities

AT THE BEGINNING OF THE CHRISTIAN ERA the Church fathers engaged in much philosophical discussion on the general topic of the description of the new Christian. One of their foremost concerns was the emotions because the emotions seemed to refuse the control of Reason and because, in their frequently expressed view, the emotions were the first step toward sin. Music was an obvious problem for common observation made the relationship between the emotions and music evident.

After the Church closed the schools, and then reopened them, they made a place for music, but only as a branch of mathematics. We would guess that the Church fathers must have thought, in part, that music was less dangerous if governed thus by a science. But this did not work because there were always musicians on the streets making music even though they were completely uneducated and knew nothing about the scholastic theories of music (as is still true today, of course). To account for this, in the sixth century the Church began to distinguish between 'speculative music' and 'practical music,' that is theory versus performance. Speculative music (theory), they said, is what would be taught in schools and the 'practical music' would be left to the musicians in the streets.

This division, which was unquestioned for the better part of one thousand years, soon took on layers of scholastic prejudice. Soon the Church philosophers were writing that only someone who was educated in 'speculative music' (theory) could be called a 'musician.' Those people playing in the streets, without 'knowledge' of what they were doing, were no better than animals. And so for one thousand years (sixth to sixteenth century) all music treatises were written by scholastic mathematicians while for the same one thousand years the 'animals' were gradually becoming very skilled and very musical as players and increasingly competent as composers and were performing for the enjoyment of the public and the courts as well. In daily life it was being demonstrated before all that the old scholastic dogma was a completely academic and artificial set of definitions which could not last.

In the sixteenth century we begin to see humanist philosophers attacking the foundations of the old dogma, with the result of gaining recognition for 'practical music.' It would take a while and perhaps one can say that the entire subject really only began to make sense after the findings of modern clinical brain research. Today we know that the performance of music is all about expressing emotion and that the very word 'music' must be synonymous only with live performance. Music theory, including notation, although we call it 'music,' is really not music at all. It is, and deals, with a written symbolic language much like the English language and is only a description of music, not music itself. And, of course, we understand that the rational data of theory and notation is processed in completely different parts of the brain than the emotional experience we have in listening to music. While today universities still teach much of theory in the manner of the old medieval Scholastic dogma,[1] in one respect things have reversed. Today a composer writes music and then sometime later someone writes a book on the theory of his music. The music comes first, the theory later. That is quite different from the old medieval Scholastic view of theory, but it is the only kind of contemporary theory that makes musical sense.

As Carpenter clearly documents, in the Italian universities of the sixteenth century music remained bound in its old Scholastic association with mathematics. Thus when, for example, Ludovico Ferrari wished to defend Cardano against Niccolo Tartaglia, he offered to debate the latter 'on any mathematical discipline, including music.'[2] These universities, therefore, continued to grind out music treatises in the old Scholastic mathematics-based perspective.

On the other hand, there were Italian philosophers who had come under the influence of Humanism who found it necessary to begin to chip away at the foundations of the old dogma and to move musical thinking away from the old Scholastic mathematics-based definition of music toward a more valid understanding of an art based on the communication of feelings. In the following passage by Girolamo Mei, we can see an important first step in this process, the recognition that theory and practice are just different processes but are both worthy of respect. This separating of art from science was a distinctly Renaissance attitude.

> The true end of science is altogether different from that of art, since the end and proper aim of science is to consider every contingency of its subject and the causes and qualities of these purely for the sake of knowing truth from falsehood, without caring further how the arts will use this knowledge as an instrument or material or for otherwise gaining their ends ... The science of music goes about diligently investigating and considering all the qualities and properties of the existing constitution and ordering of musical tones, whether these are simple qualities or comparative, like the consonances, and this for no other aim than to come to know the truth itself, the perfect goal of all speculation, and as a by-product the false. It then lets art exploit as it sees fit without any limitation those tones about which science has learned the truth.[3]

In a letter to Galilei, Mei expands this argument, now suggesting that the artist works in the realm of the senses and does not need 'the judgment of the intellect.'

Five centuries before the findings of modern brain research, Mei clearly seems to intuitively understand the difference between the rational and the experiential man.

> You ask me in yours of 17 August how it happens that the practitioner does not follow at all the designs of the theorist, as he should, since the theorist gives the reason why. My answer to you is that considering and understanding are one thing and putting into operation another. The former belongs to the intellect and the latter to the sense. However, the sense of hearing is not as perfect as the judgment of the intellect because of the material and other circumstances that always necessarily accompany the former. Thus the practitioner, having simply to satisfy the sense, does not need as

---

[1] One does not hear much about the emotions in an undergraduate harmony class.

[2] Nan Cooke Carpenter, *Music in the Medieval and Renaissance Universities* (Norman: University of Oklahoma Press, 1958), 129.

[3] Quoted in Claude Palisca, *Letters on Ancient and Modern Music* (American Institute of Musicology, 1960), 65.

much refinement and punctiliousness, so to speak, as the theorist requires. He does not esteem reason as much as the theorist and is content whenever his art succeeds in satisfying the sense without going any further, his end being none other than this.[4]

In Germany, following the civic disruptions in the wake of Luther and his Reformation, writers within and without the university are much more outspoken, which no doubt reflects the new sense of freedom which the Reformation provided. While Humanism in Italy had strong support from the courts, in Germany the movement was centered in the universities where poets, in particular, were challenging traditional studies. These two forces, the humanist poets and the professors, were drawn together in the aftermath of a controversy which began in 1508 with the publication of books by Johannes Pfefferkorn, a converted Jew, which called for the destruction of all Hebrew books. The one person who spoke out strongly against this proposal was Johannes Reuchlin, a lawyer in Württemberg and a Hebrew scholar. After he himself came under attack by the faculty of the University of Köln and the Dominican Order, humanists began to support him. It became a battle of the freedom of knowledge against the old Catholic Scholastic dogma, another obvious harbinger of the Reformation and much of Europe was drawn into the debate.

While Pfefferkorn and Reuchlin were being debated on all sides, a book of satire called *Letters of Obscure Men* was published by Crotus Rubeanus, a teacher, and Ulrich von Hutten, a man of noble lineage who concerned himself with poetry and humanism. The debate was the focus of this book of fictitious letters, but much of the text ridicules the Catholic clergy, who are often characterized as being men of rather earthly interests.

Some Catholic leaders of the university arguing against poetry, 'for it containeth falsehoods ... [and] from an evil root springeth an evil plant.'[5] One Churchman accuses the professors of being not 'Masters of the Seven Liberal Arts, but of the Seven Deadly Sins.'[6] One of the 'Letters of Obscure Men' which attacks poetry is quite interesting in its detail of the state of the German universities and of humanism at this time.

> The old Magister furthermore told me that in his time there were full two thousand students at [the University of] Leipzig, and a like number at Erfurt; four thousand at Vienna and as many at Köln. Nowadays there are not as many students at all the universities put together as there were then in one or two. The Magisters at Leipzig bitterly lament the scarcity of scholars. It is the Poets that do them this hurt. Even when students are sent by their parents to hostels and colleges they will not stay there, but are off to the Poets to learn stuff and nonsense ... Among twenty students you will scarce find one with a mind to graduate. Yet all of them are eager to study the humanities.[7]

---

4 Quoted in Ibid., 66.

5 Letter of 'Petrus Hafenmusius to Ortwin Gratius,' in Francis Stokes, trans., *On the Eve of the Reformation* (New York: Harper & Row, 1909), 16ff.

6 Letter of 'Magister Johann Hipp to Ortwin Gratius,' in Ibid., 36.

7 Letter of 'Magister Konrad Unckebunck to Ortwin Gratius,' in Ibid., 197ff.

Another letter accuses such students of being 'uncivil in the streets, or having consorted with harlots.'[8]

A viewpoint by a German philosopher representing the old university perspective can be seen in the example of a curious, and extremely negative, book by Henry Agrippa (1486–1636), called *Of the Vanities and Uncertaintie of Arts and Sciences*. This book, one of his later works, written in 1527 but not published until after his death, apparently stems from his disillusionment by his treatment by the French court, after which he began to doubt most humanistic studies. His greatest concern, which can be seen early in his book, is that Humanism is ruining men as Christians.

> I see many were proud in Humane learning and knowledge, that therefore do despise and loath the Sacred and Canonical Scriptures of the Holy Ghost as rude and rustic, because they have no ornaments of words, force of syllogisms, and effective persuasions, nor the strange doctrine of the philosophers: but are simply grounded upon the operation of virtue.[9]

He returns to this theme at the end of the book when he observes,

> For they are so stiff and obstinate in their opinions that they leave no place for the Holy Ghost, and are so sure of themselves, and trust in their own strength and proper wit, that they allow no truth which they cannot prove with syllogistical reasons. They despise those things which they cannot search out or understand by their own strength and industry.[10]

And in another place, under the heading, 'Of Science in general,' he observes that regarding 'the salvation of our souls, nothing is more hurtful and pestilent that the arts and sciences.'[11]

Martin Luther had quite a different perspective, believing the problem was not the arts and sciences, but the professors! By 1524, in the process of pleading for the foundation of public schools, even though he was attacking the universities for not being Christian enough, Luther's language in attacking the universities is extraordinary.

> We have today the finest and most learned group of men, adorned with languages and all the arts, who could also render real service if only we would make use of them as instructors of the young people. Is it not evident that we are now able to prepare a boy in three years, so that at the age of fifteen or eighteen he will know more than all the universities and monasteries have known before? Indeed, what have men been learning till now in the universities and monasteries except to become asses, blockheads, and numskulls? For twenty, even forty, years they pored over their books, and still failed to master either Latin or German, to say nothing of the scandalous and immoral life there in which many a fine young fellow was shameful corrupted.
> ......

---

8   Letter of 'Thomas Langschneider Magister Irus Perlirus to Ortwin Gratius,' in Ibid., 221.

9   Henry Cornelius Agrippa, *Of the Vanitie and Uncertaintie of Arts and Sciences*, ed. Catherine Dunn (Northridge: California State University, Northridge Press, 1974), 9.

10 Ibid., 380.

11 Ibid., 11ff.

> We have taken upon ourselves the support of a host of doctors, preaching friars, masters, priests, and monks; that is to say, great, coarse, fat asses decked out in red and brown birettas, looking like a sow bedecked with a gold chain and jewels. They taught us nothing good, but only made us all the more blind and stupid. In return, they devoured all our goods and filled every monastery, indeed every nook and cranny, with the filth and dung of their foul and poisonous books, until it is appalling to think of it.[12]

As in the rest of Europe, exciting new intellectual and musical ideas were transforming the course of music in France. But these ideas were not coming from the Church or from the universities. The University of Paris, for all its importance, was still locked into the medieval misconception of music being but a branch of mathematics. Carpenter documents this extensively and lists numerous sixteenth-century treatises which link music and mathematics.[13] It seems odd to the modern reader that a professor such as Oronce Fine, professor of mathematics in the College de France and himself an outstanding performer on the lute, did not perceive that to speak of mathematics is to miss the point in music. Only seldom do we see the influence of the humanists, as in the example of Anthoine de Bertrand (b. 1545), when publishing some of his music in 1587, felt the necessity to add the observation that 'music should appeal to the senses and not be bound by mathematical subtleties.'[14]

One of the most curious, though interesting, Scholastic philosophers of the sixteenth century was the Frenchman, Jean Bodin, who advanced the notion that the basic nature of the earth's various peoples is formed primarily by climate. This is of interest to us because he includes the emotional development under this influence. In his book on *The Easy Comprehension of History*, Bodin discusses this theory at length.[15] Basically, he believed that people inhabiting northern regions excel in physical strength and stature (which, he says, is why England could never conquer Scotland!), while in warmer climates the people are more subtle of mind and exhibit nervous sensitivity. He found these characteristics to a lesser degree even within the same country and believed these considerations were reflected in both society and government. A typical passage reads,

> Let us therefore adopt this theory, that all who inhabit the area from the forty-fifth parallel to the seventy-fifth toward the north grow increasingly warmer within, while the southerners, since they have more warmth from the sun, have less from themselves. In winter the heat is collected within, but in summer it flows out. Whereby it happens that in winter we are more animated and robust, in summer more languid. The same reason usually makes us hungrier in winter so that we eat more in summer, especially when the north wind blows. The south wind has the opposite effect, that is to say, living things are less hungry. So it comes to pass that when the Germans visit Italy, or the French, Spain, we observe that they eat more frugally.

---

[12] 'To the Councilmen of All Cities in Germany That They Establish and Maintain Christian Schools' [1524], in *Luther's Works* (St. Louis: Concordia, 1961), XLV, 351, 375.

[13] Nan Cooke Carpenter, *Music in the Medieval and Renaissance Universities*, 140ff.

[14] Quoted in Gustave Reese, *Music in the Renaissance* (New York: Norton, 1959), 389.

[15] Jean Bodin, *Method for the Easy Comprehension of History*, trans. Beatrice Reynolds (New York: Columbia University Press, 1945), 85ff. Boden (1530–1596) was educated in Paris and served as a counselor of Henry IV.

As regards physical appearance, Bodin found,

> The Mediterranean peoples, then, as far as concerns the form of the body, are cold, dry, hard, bald, weak, swarthy, small in body, crisp of hair, black-eyed, and clear-voiced. The Baltic peoples, on the other hand, are warm, wet, hairy, robust, white, large-bodied, soft-fleshed, with scanty beards, bluish gray eyes, and deep voices. Those who live between the two show moderation in all respects.

Similarly,

> Since the body and the mind are swayed in opposite directions, the more strength the latter has, the less has the former; and the more effective a man is intellectually, the less strength of body he has, provided the senses are functioning.

Bodin extends these remarks to include the 'humors,' in particular the influence of blood and black bile. In this context he makes a specific reference to music therapy.

> In Lower Germany there are almost none who are mad from black bile, but rather from blood; this type of lunacy the common man calls the disease of St. Vitus, which impels them to exultation and senseless dancing. Musicians imitate this on the lyre; afterwards they make use of more serious rhythms and modes, doing this gradually until by the gravity of the mode and the rhythm the madmen are clearly soothed.[16]

Later he provides a more extended discussion on the relationship of geography and musical preference.

> A similar elegance of manner is found in the Persian posture and action. They also accomplish dulcet harmonies and use the Lydian mode on the lyre. The Scythians, however, dislike mellifluent speech and charming diction, as we understand from their language and their consonants striking together harshly without vowels. They cannot endure the Lydian mode, but the cultivate roughness of voice; as Tacitus wrote, with a battle cry they kindle their spirits, making a noise with their shields brought up to their lips so that the voice may swell to a fuller and heavier note. They listen gladly to trumpets and drums, but care nothing for the lyre …
>
> The southerners seek the solitude and prefer to hide away in the woods rather than to move about in plain sight. Men of the middle region there is no need to describe, if one understands the extremes, since from these the means are easily understood. For instance, Scythians use the Phrygian mode more often; southerners, the Lydian; those in the intervening region become fiercer to the sound of the Dorian and stir up Mars with song, as [Virgil] says. The Lydian makes the southerners even more languorous. The Dorian, in harmony with nature, directs the strivings of souls toward valor and honor. This mode is therefore praised by Plato and vigorously approved by Aristotle in his books about the commonwealth. When the Christian religion was accepted by the Romans, the Dorian form was adopted with so much enthusiasm that a warning was issued lest anyone should use any other mode than the Dorian in the rites. On the other hand, the Spartans used the flute [aulos], the

---

[16] Ibid., 103.

> Cretans the lute in warfare—not to restrain their wrath, as Thycydides and Plutarch wrote (for in the opinion of Plato and Aristotle it was given to men as helpful for purposes of revenge), but to suit their own nature, since in Europe there is no race more southerly than the Cretans and the Spartans.[17]

Bodin returns to this subject in another book, his *Six Books of the Commonwealth*. Here, in particular, he dwells on emotional character as it reflects geography.

> The southern peoples are cruel and vindictive in consequence of their melancholy, which engenders extreme violence in the passions and impels men to take vengeance for what they suffer.[18]

Later, however, he says of melancholy,

> This is the privilege of the melancholy temperament which is composed in spirit, and given to contemplation.[19]

Finally he also makes some curious broad generalizations, in this book, regarding the nature of society and climate.

> If one considers carefully the natures of the peoples of the northern, southern, and temperate zones, one finds that they can be compared to the three ages of man, youth, age and maturity, and the qualities characteristic of these ages ... Northerners rely on force, those in the middle regions on justice, and southerners on religion.[20]

When Bodin turns to the subject of music he returns to the old medieval Scholastic and Church view that the only value of the senses is to supply information to the mind. The goal, he contends, must be for the knowledge acquired by the senses to carry man on to the higher knowledge of the mind and ultimately to divine understanding.[21] In this regard he divides man's occupations into three categories: the highest being those 'relating to the protection of men's lives,' including such things as medicine, cattle breeding and agriculture. The next category is occupations of mechanical arts, such as piloting and weaving. The lowest category is occupations which provide mere delight, among which is music. Here he adds what appears to be a startling observation on the affect of improvisation in music.

---

[17] Ibid., 129ff.

[18] Jean Bodin, *Six Books of the Commonwealth*, trans. M.J. Tooley (New York: Macmillian, 1955), 150. By way of example, he mentions that the Persians stuff the skin of the victim and mount it on an ass.

[19] Ibid., 153.

[20] Ibid., 151.

[21] Bodin, *Method for the Easy Comprehension of History*, 30ff.

> Harmony weakened and overdone by excessive elaboration exerts an influence, for while one both simple and natural is wont to cure serious illness of the mind, on the contrary one contrived from a medley of sounds and rapid rhythms usually drives a mind insane. This happens to men too anxious to please their ears, who dislike the Doric mode and dignified measures. They affect the Ionian, so that it ought not to seem remarkable if many become insane.[22]

One finds much interesting commentary among the prose writers relative to the place of music in society. Bodin gave considerable thought to whether 'harmony' in society, so frequently mentioned by ancient Greek writers, was merely a figure of speech or could be attributed to some natural mathematics ratio found in nature, and most clearly illustrated in music. In his *Method for the Easy Comprehension of History* he takes the position that this is nonsense.

> Let us see whether changes in empires can be calculated from the Pythagorean numbers. The fact that Plato measures the vicissitudes and the collapse of states by mathematical sequences alone seems to me clearly absurd …
>
> The interpreters of Plato record that the fall of the state would occur at the point where the harmony of numbers fails. In that case, if the state were going to fall by an internal weakness or loss of equilibrium, it would not be that best form of government which Socrates had in mind. That this should have a mathematical origin would seem absurd, for even if numbers which fit together badly do create a disagreeable discord, because the sounds produced from these cannot mingle and, striking each other with some jangling, try to enter the ear, yet when the symphony of sounds is mingled harmoniously, that is, when they are arranged properly in numbers according to proportion, there can be no discord. A state thus tempered and blended in constantly pleasing concord, where there is no disagreement, no clashing of sounds, and from hypothesis cannot be—I do not see in what way it can totter.[23]

Later in this same book, however, he seems more comfortable with the idea of equating the internal organization of government with the ratios found in music.

> In this way, then, is royal power constituted, the most excellent of all, as indeed it seems to me, especially helpful for the citizen body and, like harmony, tempered by sweet concord. As for the fact that Plato wished his state to be governed according to geometric ratio, Aristotle decided subtly and cleverly said that this concerned rewards only. Arithmetic ratio he related to honoring pledges and to penalties … Therefore if we should follow our investigation through a perpetual series it becomes plain that the division of authority among several is as abhorrent to nature as is harmony among many numbers. Moreover, that characteristic peculiar to a musical proportion—that is, that the interval is more important than the separate notes and if the ratio were reversed the notes would harmonize well among themselves—is fitted to a monarchy alone, in which authority is carried down gradually to the magistrates. As they govern the lower classes, so in turn they obey their superiors, until unity is achieved in the prince, from whom, like a fountain perennial, flows the majesty of the entire kingdom.[24]

---

[22] Ibid., 31.

[23] Ibid., 223.

[24] Ibid., 286ff.

Nothing symbolizes the distance between Scholastic philosophy and our modern understanding of music based on clinical research than Bodin's comment here that the interval is more important than the separate notes. For the medieval Scholastic and Church philosopher who was thinking of music as mathematics, the interval, in its relationship to the overtone series, was the foundation of the entire structure of music. But modern clinical studies all suggest it is melody, not harmony, that communicates to the listener. Music would have never been called the 'International Language' if every listener had to understand intervals.

The development of sixteenth-century music in Spain was influenced in some degree by Italy, through the Spanish singers who had participated in the Papal Choir and returned, and by France through the intermarriage of the aristocracy. As a result, Spain is represented by those who reflect the conservatism caused by its geographical isolation and those who were introduced to more liberal ideas in other countries.

This mixture was evident at the important Spanish university at Salamanca, known for its humanistic tendencies, it was in some ways very liberal. The statutes of 1538, for example, allow teaching of music in Spanish, rather than Latin, and specifies equal emphasis on speculative and practical music.[25] There seems to have been a close association between the music and medical faculties and students elected candidates to fill vacant chairs in music.

On the other hand, some of the sixteenth-century music treatises, such as one by Pedro Ciruelo, the most important mathematician of the century, remain in the old medieval tradition of consigning music to a branch of mathematics. The most dogmatic of these old style philosophers was Juan Espinosa, who in one treatise attacked a colleague for basing his conclusions on music on the basis of judgments of the ear![26]

In Spain, Vives, in his *On Education*, continues in the Church Scholastic tradition of classifying music as a branch of mathematics. However, whereas he finds geometry and arithmetic as vital instruments for the search of Truth, he assigns music a lesser value, 'for relaxation and recreation of the mind through the harmony of sounds.'[27] Interestingly enough, he then classifies all poetry under the heading of music. When discussing the appropriate subject matter for schools, Vives again defines Music as 'arithmetic applied to sounds.'

In the Low Countries, the university created by papal bull in Louvain in 1425 had become a vital humanistic center until the turmoil following Luther somewhat derailed it. In any case we can see by its statutes that it closely followed the model of Paris, with music still firmly tied to mathematics. Further, Erasmus frequently complained that the Catholic conservatives were seeking to diminish the humanities taught in this university.

> But in Louvain the trouble has been that the leading men prevent anyone from giving instruction in any humane subject, even without a fee! I cannot tell you how they conspired against something which would be a great benefit and a great credit, not only to the university but to the whole region.

---

[25] Nan Cooke Carpenter, *Music in the Medieval and Renaissance Universities*, 210ff.

[26] Ibid., 219.

[27] *Vives: On Education*, trans. Foster Watson (Cambridge: University Press, 1913), l, v.

> An ancient regulation was produced that no one had ever heard of. The authority of the whole university was brought to bear; the protection of the king's court was invoked; lay magistrates were summoned to give aid; finally the police were called in. No stone was left unturned, no expedient untried.[28]

He returns to this topic again in a letter to Cardinal Wolsey in England, in which he mentions that two of the theologians at Louvain 'hate me for the sake of the humanities, of which they are more terrified than of dog or snake.'[29] The same pessimism is mentioned in another place by Erasmus.

> Only in my own country are we still backward, and barbarism, defeated elsewhere, seems to have fled to us as its last refuge. The reason is partly that the court here has not yet learnt to treat good literature with respect; partly the personal pretensions of a few men, who are convinced that humane studies will interfere with the distinction they have hitherto enjoyed among the common herd.[30]

But, speaking of 'treating good literature with respect,' Erasmus himself quotes the great testimonials of music found in ancient literature, but sometimes he seems to miss their true meaning and sometimes he distorts them. Take for example one of the most famous Greek myths, the story of Orpheus taming stones and trees with music. The purpose of the myth was to illustrate that music can affect and improve the nature of man. Erasmus, who surely knew better, offers two outrageously false explanations:

> Take those wild men sprung from hard rocks and oak trees—what power brought them together into a civilized society if not flattery? This is all that's meant by the lyre of Amphion and Orpheus.[31]
>
> ……
>
> The same poets record that Orpheus, poet and lute player, moved the hardest of stones with his singing. What did they mean? They meant to show that men as unfeeling as stone, who were living after the manner of wild beasts, were rescued from promiscuity by this wise and eloquent hero and initiated into the holy ways of marriage.[32]

That he thought he could get away with this only illustrates once again how far removed the Scholastic philosophers were from real life.

---

[28] Letter to Juan Vives [1520], in Ibid., VII, 308.
[29] Letter to Thomas Wolsey [1522], in *The Collected Works of Erasmus* (Toronto: University of Toronto Press, 1992), IX, 40.
[30] Letter of Erasmus to Louis Ruze, Mechelen, 1519, in Ibid., VI, 273.
[31] 'Praise of Folly,' [1503] in Ibid., XXVII, 101.
[32] 'On the Writing of Letters,' [1522] in Ibid., XXV, 135.

On Sixteenth-Century German Music Treatises

BEFORE THE DRAMATIC NEW WAVE OF FREEDOM OF THOUGHT which was the essence of the Luther revolution, most early German music treatises remained locked in the old medieval Scholastic notion that music belonged to mathematics. Thus, in 1505, the University of Leipzig appointed Sebastianus Muchelon as '*lector musicae et aritmetice*,'[1] a document of the University of Köln in 1515 specifies the teaching of 'the books on mathematics, that is geometry, arithmetic, music and astronomy' and in 1558 the University of Heidelberg employed a lecturer in mathematics who was expected to include music in his teaching.

Of course, at the beginning of the sixteenth century the universities had close ties with the Church and so even the exciting discussions of the humanists appear to have had little influence. A rare exception was the University of Vienna, where Maximilian I, in 1501, added to the arts faculty a '*Collegium poetarum et mathematicorum*,' bringing poetry and oratory into the curriculum.[2]

While most early sixteenth-century university treatises were still locked into the old Church dogma, as the century progressed one can find real movement in a new direction. The influence of Humanism, especially the acknowledgement of the importance of emotions in music, becomes stronger and stronger. Indeed, by mid-century it is now Germany who leads the way, which is why we devote a chapter to these works. In revisiting the most influential of these sixteenth-century German treatises, we skip over the usual mathematical discussion of theory, etc., and for this reason we acknowledge, but do not discuss, two valuable books devoted to musical instruments, the Virdung's *Musica getutscht* (1511) and Agricola's *Musica Instrumentalis Deutsch* (1528). The most important German treatise dealing with sixteenth-century performance practice, the *Syntagma Musicus* of Praetorius, we have discussed in another book.

Here follows a brief survey of the most important of the German music treatises which were the harbingers of a new world of music.

JOHANNES COCHLAEUS, *TETRACHORDUM MUSICES* (1511)

Johannes Cochlaeus, who would be only a footnote but for the fact that he was the teacher of Glarean, was *Magister Artium* at the University of Köln. Hired at the St. Lorenz School in Nürnberg, in a letter of dedication to the prior of the school, Cochlaeus reveals that he was hired with three areas of responsibility. The first was 'the education of our youth in litera-

---

[1] Nan Cooke Carpenter, *Music in the Medieval and Renaissance Universities* (Norman: University of Oklahoma Press, 1958), 251. Carpenter documents the association with mathematics extensively.

[2] Ibid., 228.

ture and morals' (which also included grammar) and the second was 'ecclesiastical song.'[3] The third is quite interesting, for he was to see that 'polyphonic music (which is very pleasing to our people) should not be neglected entirely.' 'Our people,' meant the Church community, for this was a school which trained boys destined for the clergy. The phrase mentioning that polyphony should not be 'neglected entirely' reflects the fact, quite contrary to the impression given by modern music history texts, that polyphony had become considered by many musicians actually living in the sixteenth century as having become archaic and irrelevant.

Cochlaeus follows the medieval categorization of music into three divisions: Mundane, Human and Instrumental, although he greatly expands these fields. Mundane music now includes not only the 'music of the spheres,' but the calendar, the seasons and the phases of the moon as well. Human music concerns the soul and its relationship with Reason and the body. Instrumental music includes both instruments and the voice. He follows this with another general division, the Natural and Artificial. In the latter, dealing essentially with notation, we see the relationship with mathematics.

> Indeed, all four mathematical sciences are concerned with quantity, for arithmetic is concerned with absolute numerals, music with numerals related to each other, geometry with magnitudes individually and without motion, and astronomy with mobile magnitudes.[4]

His final division is Theoretical Music and Practical Music ('the practical application of sounds and consonances').

We find his most interesting chapter, called 'Four Kinds of Musicians,' one which does reflect the influence of Humanism, for it recalls that the ancient Greeks considered both poetry and dance as types of music. Cochlaeus defines his four categories of musicians as follows:

1. Those who are concerned with prose, and who express their thoughts in words rather than in melody. They are orators, lecturers and those who sing antiphons and psalms.
2. Those who not only express their thoughts, but who also declaim them in long and short syllables according to a metric plan, as in the case of poets.
3. Those devoted to the histrionic and mimic art, and who move with bodily gestures in imitation of musical sound.
4. Those who create sweet melody with mutually sonorous intervals. These are truly called musicians and singers.

Finally, in his discussion of instrumental music we find some curious and interesting trivia.[5] The organ in ancient times, he says, was powered by 'a bag made of two elephant skins attached,' and could be heard from Jerusalem to the Mount of Olives.[6] It is interesting that

---

[3] Ibid., 17.

[4] Ibid., 21.

[5] Ibid., 28ff.

[6] Ibid., 28. From old Jerusalem to the Mount of Olives is not a great distance and before our noisy century probably any instrument could be heard over that distance.

he includes under *tuba* not only the traditional trumpet but also the trombone, reminding the reader that during most of the Renaissance the slide trumpet and early trombone differed in design but not in principle. It is under *tympanum* that he mentions female musicians for the first time in his book, as performers on this instrument he calls them *tympanistria*.

Andreas Ornithoparchus, *Musice active micrologus* (1517)

Andreas Ornithoparchus was associated with several universities, in particular Leipzig and Tübingen. This treatise was widely used as an educational text in sixteenth-century Germany, republished in several editions and even translated and published in English in 1609.[7]

The treatise by Ornithoparchus is unique among early sixteenth-century German treatises in two regards. First, it is almost a source book of quotations from ancient and medieval treatises, indeed he admits 'whatever flowers the volumes of other men had in them, like a bee I sucked them out.'[8]

Ornithoparchus typically cites earlier authors before making his own observations and, if nothing else, it marks him as being well read and very industrious. He recalls that this effort,

> made me travel to many countries, not without financial loss, to search out the Art; these made me often become wearied, when I might have [remained home] at rest; filled with grief, when I might have solaced myself; disgraced, when I might have lived in good reputation; impoverished, when I might have lived in plenty.[9]

Second, this music treatise, more than any other of its time, concentrates on the ethical values of music. The very purpose of his book, he announces, is to provide the youth of all of Germany with a book which would introduce them to good fashions, the honest delights of music and 'little by little stir them to virtuous actions.'[10] He continues with his list of the most important values of Music.

> Among those things by which the mind of man is wont to be delighted, I can find nothing that is more great, that appeals to any age or sex … There is no breast so savage and cruel, which is not moved with the touch of this delight. For it drives away cares, persuades men to gentleness, represses anger, nourishes arts, promotes concord, inflames heroic minds to gallant deeds, cures vice, breeds virtues and nourishes them when they are born and introduces men to good fashion … Therefore this Art is of a holy, sweet, heavenly, divine, fair and blessed nature.

---

[7] By John Dowland, whose work we quote here, in modernized English.

[8] Ornithoparchus, *Musicae active mirologus* and Dowland, *Introduction: Containing the Art of Singing* (New York: Dover, 1973), 157.

[9] Ibid., 117.

[10] Ibid.

Ornithoparchus returns to this subject again at the end of Book I when he discusses the character of the various modes.[11] Dorian, he says, bestows wisdom to and causes chastity in the listener, while Phrygian causes wars and inflames fury. Aeolian calms the tempest of the mind and, after having done so, lulls it to sleep. Lydian sharpens the wit of the dull and moves the mind from earthly to heavenly desires. No wonder Ornithoparchus warns that the musician must diligently observe which mode he plays for specific listeners! The men of our time, he says, know how to do this according to the nature of the occasion.

> But our men of a more refined time do use sometimes the Dorian, sometimes the Phrygian, sometimes the Lydian and sometimes other modes, because they judge that according to differing occasions they are to choose differing modes. And that is not without cause, for every habit of the mind is governed by songs. For songs make men sleepy and wakeful, careful and merry, angry and merciful. Songs heal diseases and produce diverse wonderful effects, moving some to vain mirth, some to a devout and holy joy, yes often to godly tears.

Ornithoparchus, like many theorists before him, begins by dividing music into Mundane, Human and Instrumental Music. Mundane music he finds in the 'harmony caused by the motion of the stars and the violence of the spheres,' which he also relates to elements and climate. Here he quotes a nice phrase, from a lost work by the philosopher, Dorilaus, 'The world is God's organ.'

Again following earlier writers, especially the ancient Greeks, Human Music is associated primarily with the soul of man. In his conclusion he explains the importance of this idea.

> What other power so orders and glues the spiritual strength, which is invested with an intellect, to the mortal and earthly body, than Music, which every man that looks inside himself finds in himself? For everyone prefers what he likes and is disturbed by his dislikes. Hence it is, that we loath and abhor discords, and are delighted when we hear concords of harmony, because we know there is in ourselves the same concord.[12]

Ornithoparchus establishes three categories of musician: performers, poets and critics (those who judge music only by 'speculation and reason'). It is the first category which he discusses at length, following the old Church prejudices against musicians who are 'merely' performers. The basic logic here is that the performer is merely a kind of craftsman who engages in performance while understanding nothing he does. It will be amazing for the modern reader to read his view that just knowing about music is more important than performing music. This is, of course, as absurd as saying that reading a book about tennis or dancing is more important than actually playing tennis or dancing. One would like to think that this is the last time we shall confront this relic of the worst of medieval Scholastic values, but alas this attitude is still found in some universities today. Here is Ornithoparchus on the performing musician.

---

11   Ibid., 156.
12   Ibid., 121.

> The first category deals with instruments, such as harpists, organists and all others who prove their skill by instruments. They are removed from the intellectual part of music, being as servants, and using no Reason, void of all speculation and following their sense only. Now though they may seem to do things with learning and skill, yet it is plain that they have no knowledge, because they do not comprehend what they profess. Therefore we deny that they have Music, which is the Science of making melody. One can have knowledge without practicing and this is a greater end than being an excellent practitioner. We do not associate nimbleness of fingers with Science, which resides in the soul, but rather to practice. If it were otherwise the more one knew about the Art, the more he would automatically become swift in his fingerings.[13]

Ornithoparchus returns to the subject of the importance of musicianship based on theoretical learning in his discussion of mensural music. Now it is the composer who is the object of his attention and he lashes out at those who compose without 'following the rules.' In mid-stream he suddenly recalls having heard some effective music by composers not trained in theoretical knowledge, which is something he cannot quite explain. We know today that theory and notation is left hemisphere of the brain and the experience of music is in the right. It was the lack of this knowledge, together with the fact that the left hemisphere tends to deny the very existence of the right, which explains much of the early attacks on 'practical' musicians by 'speculative' musicians.

> I cannot but scorn certain composers (for so they will be called, though indeed they are Monsters of Music), who, though they know not so much as the first elements of the art, yet proclaim themselves 'the musicians' musician,' being ignorant in all things, yet bragging of all things and do … disgrace, corrupt and debase this art, which was in many ages before honored and used by many most learned, most wise men. They use any signs at their pleasure, neither reckoning of value, nor measure, seeking rather to please the ears of the foolish with the sweetness of the melody … I know such a man, who has been hired to be the organist at the castle in Prague, who though he know not (and I conceal his greater faults) how to distinguish a perfect time from an imperfect, yet maintains publicly that he is writing from the very depth of music …
>
> There are some who make true songs not by art, but by custom, as having happily lived among singers all their life, yet do not understand what they have made, knowing that such a thing is, but not what it is.[14]

Among his comments focusing on education, Ornithoparchus mentions some 'forbidden intervals,' such as the tritone, 'very rare and forbidden to young beginners.' His implication is that only the most experienced composers can use these. He also praises the use of the monochord, 'a rude master which makes learned scholars.' The value of this instrument, apart from ear training is to 'show hair-brained false musicians their errors.'

Ornithoparchus makes some additional interesting observations on performance practice which touch on aesthetics. He wonders why it is that sounds are more pleasing when they are closer to each other, rather than separated by large intervals. And he has noticed that 'high sounds are heard sooner than bass sounds.'

---

[13] Ibid., 123.

[14] Ibid., 169.

> As a sharp sword pierces quickly, whereas a blunt one enters slowly, so when we hear an high forced voice, it strikes into us, but a bass voice is dull, as if it were thrust at one.[15]

Soon he returns to the subject of singing and first contrasts the vocal qualities of various nationalities.

> Various nations have diverse fashions and differ in clothes, diet, studies, speech and song. Hence it is that the English carol, the French sing, the Spaniards weep, the Italians caper with their voices and others bark. But the Germans, I am ashamed to say, howl like wolves … Germany nourishes many cantors, but few musicians. For very few, excepting those which are or have been in the chapel of princes, truly know the art of singing. For those magistrates to whom this charge is given, appoint … young cantors, whom they choose by the shrillness of their voices, not for the cunning of their art, thinking that God is pleased with bellowing and braying.[16]

This, he says, we know is not pleasing to God, for in the Song of Solomon (2:14) one finds 'let me hear your voice, for your voice is sweet.'

Now Ornithoparchus offers some precepts necessary for every singer, for he has noticed many abuses 'some by moving their body indecently, some by gaping unseemly and some by changing the vowels.' Later he returns to this, saying 'the uncomely gaping of the mouth and the ungraceful motion of the body is a sign of a mad singer.'

Most of his precepts stress the importance of the singer knowing the theoretical rules of music. One of these is the necessity of keeping the beat, 'for to sing without law and measure is an offense to God himself.'

> Whole Vigils are performed with such confusion, haste and mockery … that neither one voice can be distinguished from another, nor one syllable from another, nor one verse sometimes throughout a whole Psalm from another. An impious fashion to be punished with the severest correction. Think you that God is pleased with such howling, such noise, such mumbling, in which there is no devotion, no expressing of words, no articulating of syllables?

Ornithoparchus stresses the importance of making the voice coincide in emotion with the words of the text, 'sad when the words are sad and merry when they are merry.' Here he pauses to recognize a curious exception.

> I cannot but wonder at the Saxons (the most gallant people of all Germany …) in that they use in their funerals a high, merry and *joconde* emotion, for no other reason, I think, than that either they hold death to be the greatest good that can befall a man or that they believe the souls return to the original sweetness of music that is in heaven.

In this regard, Ornithoparchus even cautions the singer to be careful to make his singing correspond to the specific nature of holidays, 'least on a slight holiday he make the service too solemn, or too slight on a great one.'

---

[15] Ibid., 198.

[16] Ibid., 208ff.

Finally, we must report Ornithoparchus' assertion that the inventor of music, Tubal (according to the Old Testament), engraved the rules of music on two tablets, one of slate and one of marble. He records having heard that the marble one survived the flood and can be found in Syria.[17]

Nicolaus Listenius, *Musica* (1537)

Nicolaus Listenius (ca. 1500–1550) matriculated at Wittenberg in 1529, when both Luther and Melancthon were teaching there. As a theorist, his most important work was his *Musica*, which was largely a revision of a *Rudimenta musicae* of 1533. This work was one of the two most popular instruction books in Germany during the sixteenth century, and was reissued in numerous editions.

The work is dedicated to Johann Georg, son of Joachim II, the elector of Brandenburg, and it seems rather daring to us when Listenius tells the prince that by cultivating music he will be worthy of his ancestors. In this same Foreword, Listenius provides a moving review of the purpose and virtue of music. Of particular importance is his observation that music is a 'serious art.'

> Many great and serious reasons are established by learned and intelligent men, for all men of genius particularly free princes, must be versed in music and habituated to it. It influences souls to humanity, suavity, even-temper; it restrains all immoderate affections, grief, wrath; it represses violence and obscene desires, for it calms them; as in sounds and songs, so in all the actions of life we may conserve harmony. Hence we see the highest kings in old monuments singing and playing on strings, not only as a pastime for the enjoyment of the arts, but even more, however, making it a serious art, tying music to the harmony of the soul …
> This art invites the soul to virtue.[18]

Listenius begins his book with one of the old medieval definitions, 'Music is the science of singing correctly and well.' However, in his next sentence he clearly dates himself in the Renaissance by stating that the knowledge of music consists of three kinds: theoretical, practical and *poetic*. The theoretical is concerned only with understanding the subject. Hence, he says, the 'theoretical musician' is content in this knowledge and 'presents no example of his work in performance.'

His definition of practical music, which he divides into Choral and Figured, or Mensural, goes considerably beyond the usual definitions given in the university circles in France, England, and Italy, where the term is given to mean little more than simply performance itself. Listenius speaks of something beyond skill and says the performer teaches the listener something more than mere appreciation.

---

[17] Ibid., 125.

[18] Nicolaus Listenius, *Musica*, trans. Albert Seay (Colorado Springs: Colorado College Music Press, 1975), 1.

> Practical, whose goal is doing, is that which delights not only in the intricacies of skill, but extends into performance itself, leaving out no part of the act of performance. Hence the practical musician, who teaches others something more than the recognition of art, trains himself in it for the goal of any performance.[19]

His third kind of knowledge is an aesthetic definition quite new to the Renaissance. Here he is thinking of the meaning left with the listener when the performance is concluded. This he calls '*total* performance.' It is most important and enlightening that he observed that the practical and the poetic always include the theoretical, 'but the reverse is not true.'

> Poetic is that which is not content with just the understanding of the thing nor with only its practice, but which leaves something more after the labor of performance, as when music or a song of musicians is composed by someone whose goal is total performance and accomplishment. It consists of making or putting together more in this work which afterwards leaves the work perfect and absolute, which otherwise is artificially like the dead.[20]

Heinrich Glarean, *Dodecachordon* (1547)

Glarean (1488–1563) of Switzerland did his higher education at the University of Köln where one of his teachers was Cochlaeus. Glarean was a man of many talents as is testified to in numerous letters by Erasmus, who gives the impression that he was unusually proficient in all the Liberal Arts. In letters of recommendation, Erasmus calls Glarean a mathematician, meaning four branches of the Liberal Arts. It was from this perspective that Glarean was interested in music[21] and our guess is that he probably did not think of himself as a performing musician, although on one occasion he so impressed Maximilian I in his singing of a poem that he was made poet laureate. Such a widely talented man is never universally popular and in the fictitious, satirical *Letters of Obscure Men*, of 1515, by Crotus Rubeanus and Ulrich von Hutten, Glarean is described as,

> a 'very headstrong man ... A terrible man, a choleric, for ever threatening fights—and he must be possessed of a devil'[22]

In any case, Glarean was the author of one of the most extensive music treatises of the sixteenth century, a work he had apparently finished writing by 1539. While our interest is in Glarean's open and honest observations on a wide variety of topics related to performance and aesthetics, the treatise was originally widely known for Glarean's extension of the eight

---

[19] Ibid., 3.

[20] Ibid.

[21] Glarean does say, in his prefatory letter to Cardinal von Waldburg, that he had spent twenty years thinking about the musical problems presented in his book. See Glarean, *Dodecachordon*, trans. Clement Miller (American Institute of Musicology, 1965), I, 39.

[22] Letter of 'Demetrius Phalerius to Ortwin Gratius,' in Francis Stokes, trans., *On the Eve of the Reformation* (New York: Harper & Row, 1909), 183.

church modes to twelve, by adding Aeolian and Ionian, together with their plagals.[23] Beyond this, it is a treatise which treats all elements of music theory in very great detail. Glarean, fully aware of this, and perhaps reflecting on his experience in the university, observes at one point,

> Perhaps we have treated this in more detail than is necessary But it had to be done for the state of mind of the masses, to whom nothing is explained sufficiently.[24]

In another place, however, he seems to suggest the difficulty lay with the professors as much as the minds of the masses.

> If by chance this has seemed insufficiently clear to anyone, I beg him to remember how uneducated and unpolished our present age is, that among the highly learned, even among those teaching mathematics, not one in twenty has a clear conception of this matter.[25]

In any case, it is clear that Glarean's purpose was one of education and early in the treatise he cautions the student regarding the broad knowledge necessary to master music.

> I appeal to every earnest youth, I exhort and admonish you, if you desire to be initiated into the secrets of this science and want to become a priest truly worthy of this discipline, you will make use of three principal points without which this study cannot be fully mastered, however much you may speculate, and even may surpass Prometheus himself in observation. The first is that you have the precepts of arithmetic clearly in mind and also those of theory and practice. Then it follows that you cannot be entirely ignorant of the Greek language. For a great many of the terms of this study are Greek. The third is that you have some instrument at hand on which you can measure all sounds by ear.[26]

This last sentence is very important and represents one of the distinguishing hallmarks of this treatise. Many earlier treatises were written from the perspective that music was something to be understood intellectually. For Glarean, no matter how extensively he explains the cerebral definitions, in the end it was a matter of the ear. For this reason he also treats the practicing musician with more respect than did earlier treatises. In a typical passage, Glarean writes,

> Modes are also changed from one into another but not with equal success. For in some cases the change is scarcely clear even to a perceptive ear, indeed, often with great pleasure to the listener, a fact which we have frequently declared is very common today in changing from the Lydian to the Ionian. Those who play instruments and who know how to sing readily the verses of poets according to a musical play, understand this. Indeed, in this way they are frequently worthy of praise if they do it skillfully, especially if they change the Ionian into Dorian. But in other cases the changing seems rough, and scarcely ever without a grave offense to the ears, as changing from the Dorian to the

---

[23] Clement Miller, in 'The Dodecachordon: Its Origins and Influence on Renaissance Musical Thought,' in *Musica Disciplina* (1961), 155ff., traces the influence of this treatise.

[24] Glarean, *Dodecachordon*, I, 79.

[25] Ibid., I, 133. Glarean here was reviewing the history of the development of the cithara.

[26] Ibid., I, 82ff.

Phrygian. And so whenever present day organists encounter this difficulty in changing church songs in such a way, if they are not well trained and quick, they often incur the derision of experienced listeners.[27]

It is also from this perspective that Glarean begins his treatise by reminding the reader that music, as something heard by the ear, came before theory. After stating that music consists of theory and practice, the separation of the speculative and the practical so long favored by early theorists, he observes,

> Since truly all learning consists in demonstration and neither facts themselves can be computed nor tones be written musicians have invented symbols of the tones partly through figures which they now call notes partly through the naming of syllables.[28]

Glarean does not discuss the subject so important to the ancient philosophers, the ability of music to affect the character of the listener. He does, however, comment on the subjective character of the various modes. He seemed to believe that the modes contained specific and unique characters, although he admits there is not universal agreement. As an example of this inconsistency, he points to the *Die Harmonia musicorum instrumentorum*, by Franchinus, where he finds that in one place the author suggests the Phrygian is suitable for 'more agreeable and the lighter subjects,' while later he contends the same mode 'is suitable for incitement to war and therefore is to be portrayed by a fiery color.' Glarean himself finds Phrygian 'more suitable to severe, religious music, as elegies, laments, and funeral music.'[29]

The Ionian mode Glarean associates with dancing and because 'some men attribute a frivolous wantonness to this mode,' he finds it rarely used in older Church music. He obviously liked it, for he speculates,

> On the other hand, I believe that for the last four hundred years it has also been so deeply admired by church singers, that, enticed by its sweetness and alluring charm, they have changed many songs of the Lydian mode into this mode.[30]

Some other descriptions of the character of various modes which we find interesting are of the Lydian, which Glarean calls 'harsh,' and the Hypoionian mode, which he finds 'has great charm in morning songs and love songs, especially in the Celtic tongue which the Swiss

---

[27] Ibid., I, 129.

[28] Ibid., I, 41

[29] Ibid., I, 130.

[30] Ibid., I, 153.

use.'³¹ Later he says that the Dorian has a 'certain sublime and indescribable majesty'³² and Mixolydian he identifies with 'a certain tranquil dignity which both moves and dominates the people.'³³

In summarizing, Glarean adds a few comments on the qualities of the various modes.

> If I am allowed to make a rough judgment concerning this and the preceding modes, I shall say it in a few words: Each mode seems to me to reflect beautifully the customs of the people from which the names are taken. The Athenians were truly Ionians, the Spartans were Dorians; the former, although lovers of pleasant things and students of eloquence, were still always considered capricious. Yet the Spartans, renowned in war and bound by military discipline and the severe laws of Lycurgus, have preserved longer the harsh customs handed down from their ancestors. These modes have the same characteristics. The Ionian, devoted entirely to dancing, contains much sweetness and pleasantness, almost no severity. On the contrary, the Dorian presents a certain majesty and dignity which it is easier to admire than to explain. It is very suitable for [epic] poetry, as I have myself experienced at one time as a youth in Köln in the presence of the celebrated Kaiser Maximilian and many princes, not without the reward of the merited laurel branch (which is said without boasting).³⁴

In another place, however, Glarean seems to weaken any argument that the modes have specific identifiable characters, by suggesting they can be changed in character by the composer.

> Yet, it cannot be denied that antiquity has changed these modes, but undoubtedly the nature of modes can be turned in another direction, so that a mode which seems light in character can be used with not much difficulty for serious subjects (provided that a propitious talent is at hand), and on the contrary, a serious mode can be used for light subjects.³⁵

Poor Glarean was at heart an old fashioned Churchman, born too late. He probably did not realize that his great book on modes had come near the end of the period of their functional use for general composition. But he must have been aware that Church music was rapidly changing. He preferred simple, sincere plain chant in the Church, in part for reasons which he gives following an interesting discussion of his theory that the music of the original Christians was in the Aeolian mode.

> But now it is worthwhile to observe ... with how much simplicity, also with how much seriousness the songs of the first church musicians were undertaken, with all ostentation completely removed, with all shallowness excluded, in a word, with such grace that everyone must approve them unless he does not possess any hearing How justly we ought to be ashamed to have degenerated in such a degree from this!³⁶

---

31 Ibid., I, 163, 173.

32 Ibid., II, 257.

33 Ibid., II, 262.

34 Ibid., I, 155ff.

35 Ibid., I, 164ff.

36 Ibid., I, 143.

Contrary to modern music history texts, polyphonic music did not dominate the sixteenth-century scene. Outside the Church it was now regarded as archaic and the humanists were attacking it for reasons of their own. Glarean was probably not too concerned about this as he sometimes reveals his own skepticism toward polyphonic music. Speaking of the Hyperaeolian mode, he gets off track and suggests that the ancients could have written polyphonic music but elected not to. He knew that was not true, but he is carried away by his passion against modern music.

> And yet our present time, affected as it were by tedium of all kinds and seeking novelties in every possible way, has arranged songs of this mode polyphonically, and at times shows us something ingenious it thinks it has invented that had been unknown to the ancients; but in fact, antiquity had not neglected this as unknown, but as unworthy for the ears of learned men.[37]

As he continues, he seems to say, if we are going to have polyphonic music, why can't it at least be in the style of those fifteenth-century masters.

> Nonetheless, one still finds songs of this sort among composers who sink to such absurdities in their immoderate thirst for fame. I believe the reason for this error is that they, while despising the ancients, are pleased only with new things; thus we seek glory at present in a way in which we absolutely should not. In poetry, it is a fine thing to follow distinguished masters, as Virgil did not hesitate to follow Theocritus, Hesiod, and Homer. Yet in music, good god, how shameful this seems to some, if anyone should attempt to follow either Josquin des Prez, nearly comparable to Virgil in this matter, or Johannes Ockeghem, a very erudite man, or Pierre de la Rue, a most pleasing musician, although these men have expressed the nature of song with ingenuity and artistry, and have justly merited surpassing praise. In fact, in our time there are those who, just as they disdain the ancients, will not examine a song unless it has just recently come from a writer, still glowing hot from the anvil, as it were. Further, since they think it unseemly to imitate anyone, however much he is learned, and since all the old modes had been used, they turn of necessity to inventing novelties which, however, are foolish and bungling.

Glarean returns to his doubts about polyphony in a lengthy discussion of the differences between what he calls *phonasci* and *symphonetae*. His meaning for these terms he gives in a letter of 1538.

> I call a *phonacus* the inventor of a simple melody in some mode, a *symphoneta* the one who adds the remaining voices.[38]

Glarean concludes a long defense of chant by pointing to two specific objections he finds in those cases where chant has been turned into polyphony. First, he suggests that this is done sometimes just because the singers are ashamed to sing something so routine as a tenor and

---

[37] Ibid., I, 150ff.
[38] Letter to Johannes Aal, quoted in Miller, 'The Dodecachordon,' 160.

want to be heard in the higher voices. This he condemns as arrogance and vanity, 'as the perversity of singers is usually called.' Second, he complains of the unsuccessful attempts he has apparently heard in the improvisation of polyphony over a chant.

> For how often do you find, I should like to know, three or even two who will sing polyphony with you? I speak from experience, for something is always intervening at these times, some weariness or trouble is always at hand. Those who are skilled in this matter want to be asked, but one who does not understand it stands by, somewhat downcast, while the others are singing, either because he wished he were also able to sing or because he was ashamed that he had not learned this skill, or because he disdains what he neither understands nor attains; those who have progressed in this skill to some extent but are not sure of themselves, and their number is great, repeatedly make errors in singing, which produces great disgust among the skilled. Thus it is rare that even three can harmonize together in this manner.[39]

We should mention that in another place Glarean objects to another instance of improvisation, where singers improvise at the end of a chant, cadencing on the wrong tone. Which, he says, 'certain singers plainly do for pleasure ... and to turn up their noses at the listener.' Then he adds, somewhat sarcastically,

> But someone will say that nobody is so stupid not to understand that a song is corrupted in this way. Well, why then does the corruption generally occur in the Nicene Creed, also in the Lord's Prayer, and has no one at all observed this? Is the ear really more discerning in our time than formerly?[40]

If Glarean is thus discouraged at the lack of popularity of the old chants, in the following chapter he also is discouraged with contemporary efforts to compose. First, he issues a challenge, which is basically a recommendation for the values of Humanism. Based on the information he has given, Glarean asks one,

> to see if he can invent a harmony, or as it is usually said, a tenor, according to some form of a song in these odes, which tenor will sound sweetly in the ears, with words added suitably, and which will take hold of the heart and leave keen stimuli in the soul of the listener, in which the strength of its nature seems to have been expressed, and lastly, into which the mind of man may sometimes break, as if aroused from sleep.[41]

Having devoted his first two books to chant, Glarean now turns to polyphonic music. However, as we have indicated above, his heart was not really in this style and thus his explanations are relatively brief and taken mostly from the theorist Franchinus. He excuses his brevity by noting that there is no precedence for this style in antiquity and neither does he recognize anyone distinguished after Josquin.

---

[39] Ibid., I, 209.

[40] Ibid., I, 196.

[41] Ibid., I, 209ff.

As a mathematician, he was undoubtedly disturbed by the lack of universal practice in polyphonic music. He finds some symbols, such as the maxima, no longer in use and seems uncomfortable that the entire system of mensuration has no example in antiquity and is a matter 'almost dependent on the decision of ordinary singers.'[42] He also finds the whole question of the beat and tempo a practice which varies from country to country.[43] In this regard the reason he gives for the alla breve symbol is interesting.

> Whenever musicians wish to accelerate the *tactus*, which they consider should be done when they believe the hearing is fatigued, namely, in order to remove weariness, they draw a line downwards through the circle or semicircle.[44]

It is also interesting that he finds the idea of proportions largely ignored in practice. He admits there have been learned and complex treatises explaining this metrical system, but he says,

> Art ought to be transmitted as the art exists. But even the subject now proclaims that the observance of so many proportions is superfluous; no one, however much he is trained in song, can bear these in mind, and none of the most learned musicians of our time has deigned to adopt them, excepting a very few, in a composition, since there is greater trouble in learning them than there is sweetness or grace in singing them.[45]

Glarean now presents what must have been the most valued portion of his treatise at the time, a lengthy collection of actual music demonstrating the modes he had discussed at length earlier. But before he presents this music, once again he expresses his own doubts about polyphony, especially music in more than four-parts, which he believes was composed,

> not so much for aural pleasure as for the ostentation of the talented. For it could scarcely be possible that the human intellect, distracted by so many and varied sounds, could follow carefully all voices simultaneously ... Indeed, in my opinion, a distinguished [composer] can show the vigor of his talent no less in writing two or three voices than in the accumulation and chattering of many voices. I know it appears otherwise to others, nor do I reprove anyone's judgment; moreover, one may follow what one wishes, and I have stated my opinion.[46]

It is interesting that he was under the impression that polyphony began only about seventy years earlier (he seems unaware of Palestrina).[47]

---

42   Ibid., II, 230.

43   Ibid., II, 232.

44   Ibid., II, 234.

45   Ibid., II, 242.

46   Ibid., II, 248. Interestingly, he says he omits from his collection a five-part 'Stabat mater' by Josquin, because everyone owns a copy of it.

47   Ibid., II, 248.

The one composer of polyphony whom Glarean praises above all others was Josquin, especially because he 'has never brought forth anything which was not pleasant to the ears.' But even Josquin was not above criticism.

> But in many instances he lacked a proper measure and a judgment based on knowledge and thus in some places in his songs he did not fully restrain as he ought to have, the impetuosity of a lively talent, although this ordinary fault may be condoned because of the otherwise incomparable gifts of the man.[48]

For all of the questions which Glarean has raised about polyphonic music, in several of the descriptions he provides for the music he presents in his collection he reveals that he could in fact be deeply moved by such music. It is more significant that, having said several times that one must judge music by the intellect and not by feelings, we cannot help but observe that the works which move him most do so only by the emotions! For example, an 'Elegy of Magdalene' by Michael de Verona, Glarean hears as,

> possessing great emotion and innate sweetness and tremendous power, so that one really believes he hears the weeping of a woman and her following … At the end, through a certain confident hope, it rises so magnificently and is lifted to the heights with such tremendous exultation, and then again, as if wearied and self-reproachful for immoderate joy, it falls back into deep and customary weeping....[49]

And similarly, he mentions a 'Planxit autem David' by Josquin, intended for the mourner, whom Glarean finds,

> at first is wont to cry out frequently, and then, turning gradually to melancholy complaints, to murmur subduedly and presently to subside, and sometimes, when emotion breaks forth anew to raise his voice again and to emit a cry.[50]

Adrian Coclico, *Compendium Musices* (1552)

The Flemish theorist Coclico was engaged as a music teacher at the university in Wittenberg in 1545. Although he remained only a brief time, due to lack of funds, he was popular not only with students but with Melanchthon. Coclico has left a very important treatise from this period, for it not only documents the shift away from the old Scholastic complexities of speculative music to the more modern emphasis on expressive, practical musicianship, but it is the first music treatise in one thousand years which clearly departs from the old Church con-

---

[48] Ibid., II, 264.

[49] Ibid., II, 258ff.

[50] Ibid., II, 269.

cept that music is a branch of mathematics.⁵¹ Indeed, in his 'Preface to Nordic Youth' he suggests that traditional books on music do not even treat what he calls the 'art' of music, 'which is seen more in practice than in rules.'⁵²

Coclico begins by stating his purpose as teaching 'correct, smooth and elegant singing.'

> I see today German youth not only ignorant of the traditions of music, of which many praises will be expounded elsewhere, but also ruined and kept back from the true force and reason of singing. As long as they pass over the memorizing of precepts, for them to learn to sing rapidly and correctly cannot be done.⁵³

He quickly adds a significant qualification to the last sentence, noting,

> I would say that whoever keeps his students too long on precepts and theory lacks judgment and evidently is ignorant of the goal of music.

Coclico, no doubt from experience, is quite specific regarding the qualities which the student must bring to his study. He again stresses that it is performance not speculative music which produces a musician.

> First, adolescents or better, boys, … should bring to their teacher a great zeal and desire for learning music, together with their natural enthusiasm, so that they may listen as eagerly and attentively as possible to whoever teaches and guides. For, if anyone by his nature is perhaps more estranged from the love of music or he may not have wanted to learn what he should, I cannot sensibly promise great things for him. He, however, who is possessed by a certain single-minded zeal for learning and does not have forces of nature repelling him from music, if they have molded him skillfully and carefully, this person I hold myself committed that he will be an excellent musician. In a Greek proverb it is beautifully stated: Love teaches music. Then, if the boy has this proposed goal for himself, so that he will become a better performer than theorist, I would not want to load him down with many precepts and almost overwhelm him. He who wishes first to explore all the reasonings of speculative music and turns himself to this rather than to singing; he will, in my opinion, only arrive at the hoped for and preset goal much later on.⁵⁴

Later he adds an observation which might be found in any era,

> But I do not know how it happens that our youth not only despises work and does not submit well to good recommendations, but even grows angry.⁵⁵

---

51   In Adrian Coclico, *Musical Compendium*, trans. Albert Seay (Colorado Springs: Colorado College Music Press, 1973), 30.

52   Ibid., 1.

53   Ibid., 5.

54   Ibid., 5ff.

55   Ibid., 7.

Coclico promises his book will give the necessary rules and knowledge which the student needs, but he seems eager to get beyond this to the purpose of the study. It is particularly important that he defines this purpose here as being to give pleasure and to exhilarate the listener, as well as stressing that it is the *ear* which must judge.

> When he has learned these things clearly and rapidly, he will then begin to sing, not only as [the music] is written but also with embellishments, and to pronounce skillfully, smoothly and meaningfully, to intone correctly and to place any syllable in its proper place under the right notes.
>
> As a singer, he will study especially how to please the ears of men and how to inspire pleasure in them, as well as admiration and favor for himself. He will also be continually guided by the judgment of his ears. The ears easily understand what is done correctly or badly and are truly the masters of the art of singing. What difference is there, I ask, between a dog's barking and he who does not hear or does not notice what and how he sings?
>
> To be avoided are the vices of certain nations, which, if they stay in us, must be corrected by zeal and industry. Insane clamor and huge roaring and that noise like the voice of certain ignorant men, lacks grace. While they weep, scream or bark, they please no one, they take away all pleasure from their hearers and deprive themselves of praise. A smooth song truly seeks this end, which the musician looks and hunts for, namely, to delight and to exhilarate.[56]

Almost as an afterthought, Coclico provides his credentials. His own study was with that 'most noble musician, Josquin,' from whom he learned 'incidentally, from no book.'

Now Coclico sets the framework for the 'rules' portion of his book by explaining that he divides musicians into four categories. We read his discussion as a virtual history of music, with a clear emphasis on the values of the sixteenth century. The first were the original musicians who discovered music, including Greek mythical figures, figures from the Old Testament and medieval theorists. These, he says, 'were only theorists.'[57]

The second type he calls mathematicians, and seems to have in mind the polyphonic Church composers of the fifteenth century. Everyone knows their compositions, he admits.

> But these men did not pursue the goal of music. Even if they understand the force of this art and also compose, they do not honor the smoothness and sweetness of song. What is worse, when they hope to spread their invented art widely and make it more outstanding, they rather defile and obscene it. In teaching precepts and speculation they have specialized excessively and, in accumulating a multitude of symbols and other things, they have introduced many difficulties. Disputing much a long time, they never arrived at the true rationality of singing.

The third type are the most outstanding musicians, who 'join theory and practice in the best and learned way.' These men, among whom he lists numerous sixteenth-century composers, understand 'how to embellish melodies, to express in them all the emotions of all kinds.'

---

[56] Ibid., 6.

[57] Ibid., 8.

The fourth type he calls poets, but he means those artistic singers who compose, improvise and sing 'smoothly, ornately and artfully for the delight of men.' He adds that he finds such singers particularly in France and Belgium and, once more, stresses that such ability rests more upon the practical than the theoretical.

Coclico now begins the theoretical portion of his book, but he repeatedly renews his criticism of rules-based learning. No sooner has he begun writing of scales, than he stops and observes that this can only be understood in performance.

> I have wished to train this boyish industry in music through but few words and precepts on that account, so that no youth running to the books of musician-mathematicians will waste his life in reading them and never arrive at the goal of singing well.[58]

Similarly, he barely introduces his discussion of mensural rules, when he promises to leave out 'a mass of definitions, lest boys staying for a longer time on precepts arrive too late at the purpose of singing well.'

> For this reason I do not cease to dissuade [students] from remaining tied to the prolix writings of musician-mathematicians who have drawn up so many types of signs of augmentation and diminution, from which no fruit, but rather controversy and discord arises.[59]

Having made this digression, he continues with some fascinating first-hand observations. Of great importance here is his emphasis on learning through performance itself, rather than through the conceptualization of music.

> In Belgian cities, where prizes are given to singers and, because of the prizes to be gained, no procedure or labor is undertaken unless it pertains to the goal of singing well, no music is written down or prescribed by precept.
> My teacher, Josquin des Pres, never rehearsed or wrote out any musical procedures, yet in a short time made perfect musicians, since he did not hold his students back in long and frivolous precepts, but taught precepts in a few words at the same time as singing through exercise and practice ...
> Josquin did not judge everyone capable of the demands of composition. He felt that it should be taught only to those who were driven by an unusual force of their nature to this most beautiful art.[60]

Once again, after giving his subject as the rules of prolations, he is able to produce only two sentences before returning to his chief concern.

> I have wanted something here planned for adolescents so that they will not stick to the books of musician-mathematicians, who have contrived an infinite number of other signs and have turned away the souls of adolescents from the true use of music, making something clear in itself obscure, as when they write so many things about proportions of minor inequality, or sesquitertia.[61]

---

[58] Ibid., 10.

[59] Ibid., 16.

[60] Ibid., 16.

[61] Ibid., 18.

Coclico again interrupts his presentation of the rules of composition, this time to comment on the qualities of the fine singer. He first recommends that the student choose a teacher who sings beautifully and smoothly, who sings by,

> special natural instinct and makes Music joyful by the ornaments of [improvisation], at the same time omitting throat clearings, shouting and other absurdities, leading most noble Music into the hatred of men.[62]

He again points to Belgium and France as the most likely source for fine singing and observes that in Germany the knowledge of such singing is rarely found. He cautions that the singing must come from the throat and that the student will not be able to do this unless he 'sweats and works a great deal.'

When discussing counterpoint, Coclico implies that in Germany polyphonic music had become unpopular among many musicians.

> If anyone makes mention of counterpoint and demands it in a perfect musician, they destroy it with a more than snarling distaste, impudently asserting it as truth that many improper and corrupt types [of intervals] occur in counterpoint, ones that offend the ears and have no place in compositions.

Coclico admits the basic contention, but finds the reason for their views in their improper appreciation of the style.

> I agree that counterpoint offends their ears, for theirs are like those of asses, to whom nothing is agreeable except that which they produce as braying or makes a sound like braying. If it has offended the ears of men, why not more those of Josquin, Pierre de la Rue and their successors, whose ears were most delicate? ...
>
> But knowledge has no enemy except the ignorant and, since the despisers of this art are ignorant of the practice of music, their foolishness easily adds many allies.
>
> A boy should curse the perverse judgment of these men as utter nonsense, and, as with the prince-singers, should hold as true that he will never become a perfect musician without the knowledge and use of counterpoint.[63]

Later he mentions that Josquin compared those inferior in counterpoint to trying to fly without wings.

After a brief discussion of intervals, Coclico briefly mentions improvisation, which he recommends should first be studied in note to note practice of the intervals, followed by more 'florid counterpoint.'[64] This art, he advises, requires constant practice. Later, he gives ability in improvisation even more weight.

---

[62] Ibid., 20.

[63] Ibid., 21.

[64] Ibid., 23.

> The first requirement of a good singer is that he should know how to sing counterpoint by improvisation. Without this he will be nothing.[65]

Perhaps because of the rules he has been presenting, Coclico now pauses to make the point that the urge to compose must be an inspired compulsion, not simply the next step after learning the necessary rules.

> [The Student] should be led to composing by a great desire, and by a certain natural impulse he will be driven to composition, so that he will not taste food nor drink until his piece is finished, for, since this natural impulse so drives him, he accomplishes more in one hour than others in a whole month. Composers to whom these unusual motivations are absent are useless.[66]

Returning to the art of singing, Coclico mentions the difficulties in singing multi-part polyphony. One must learn how to do this by study with a practical musician, otherwise 'he will leave in shame and be laughed at.' And, he adds, 'even if [the student] reads books for ten years, he will not advance at all without use and practice.'

---

[65] Ibid., 24.

[66] Ibid.

PART 3
COMMENTARY ON PERFORMANCE

Contemporary Reflections on the Aesthetic Values of Music

> *What are you doing, O envious Death? The golden voice has been silenced, the golden voice of Ockeghem, the voice that could move even stones, the voice that so often resounded in the vaulted nave with fluid and subtly modulated melodies, soothing the ears of the saints in heaven and likewise piercing the hearts of earthborn men.*
>
> *What are you doing, O envious Death? You are unjust precisely because you deal justly with everyone. It would be enough for you to take away indiscriminately the things that belong to mankind. Music is something divine. Why do you violate the divine?*[1]

IN THE ABOVE ODE COMPOSED BY ERASMUS (1466–1531) upon hearing of the death of Ockeghem (1410–1497), we see some of the common themes which distinguish the discussion of music during the Renaissance as compared to that found in the literature of the Middle Ages. In particular, it is the phrase, 'piercing the hearts of men,' which is so characteristic of the Renaissance. And this is because the Renaissance in music is synonymous with Humanism in music, a return to the communication of feeling as the principal purpose of music. This was in direct opposition with the medieval Church's attempt to make music a branch of mathematics. The men at the beginning of the fourteenth century who coined the terms 'ars nova' and 'ars antiqua' had this distinction very much in mind.

Of course there were some representatives of the 'ars antiqua,' especially those who continued to write scholastic-mathematical treatises on music, who still didn't get it. Even by the sixteenth century we find Andreas Ornithoparchus, who was associated with several German universities, in his *Musice active micrologus* of 1517 lashing out at those composers who are not following the old medieval rules. He is very confused how such a man as the organist in Prague, who fails to follow the old rules, still can describe himself as 'writing from the very depth of music.'

> I cannot but scorn certain composers (for so they will be called, though indeed they are Monsters of Music), who, though they know not so much as the first elements of the art, yet proclaim themselves 'the musicians' musician,' being ignorant in all things, yet bragging of all things and do...disgrace, corrupt and debase this art, which was in many ages before honored and used by many most learned,

---

[1] 'An Epitaph for the Superlative Musician Jan Ockeghem,' in *The Collected Works of Erasmus* (Toronto: University of Toronto Press, 1992), LXXXV, 77.

> most wise men. They use any signs at their pleasure, neither reckoning of value, nor measure, seeking rather to please the ears of the foolish with the sweetness of the melody ... I know such a man, who has been hired to be the organist at the castle in Prague, who though he know not (and I conceal his greater faults) how to distinguish a perfect time from an imperfect, yet maintains publicly that he is writing from the very depth of music.[2]

How very different was the perspective of music by the man who, in 1555, wrote this review of a performance of the lute player, Francesco da Milano.

> He made the very strings to swoon beneath his fingers and transported all who listened into such gentle melancholy that one present buried his head in his hands, another let his entire body slump into an ungainly posture with members all awry, while another, his mouth sagged open and his eyes more than half shut, seemed, one would judge, as if transfixed upon the strings, and yet another, with chin sunk upon his chest, hiding the most sadly taciturn visage ever seen, remained abstracted in all his senses save his hearing, as if his soul had fled from all the seats of sensibility to take refuge in his ears where more easefully it could rejoice in such enchanting symphony.[3]

Not only does this review symbolize the great change in values which had taken place during the Renaissance, but its focus is on the most significant characteristic which separates music of the Renaissance from that of the Middle Ages—the contemplative listener. The references to the contemplative listener follow where the purpose of music is to express feeling. It is for this reason that we first encounter the contemplative listener during the 'Pre-Renaissance,' the period in the thirteenth century when a confluence of new ideas brought down the curtain on the Dark Ages.

As we have indicated above, the phrase used by Erasmus, 'piercing the hearts of men,' seems so characteristic of the Renaissance. The basic message here, that music based on feeling is something that reaches inside a man, also reflects a new recognition of the importance of music itself. In almost identical language as Erasmus' 'piercing the hearts of men,' Pietro Aretino uses the expression 'penetrated my heart' to make the same point about the power of music.

> There is no doubt ... that our pleasures are the panders of our senses, and that being the case, the things which Franceschina sang yesterday to the tune of her lute, penetrated my heart with so sweet a sort of musical persuasion, that I must needs come to the point of amorous conjunction.
>
> Certainly in this lady are found all three kinds of beauty; that of the body, that of the mind, and that of the voice, wherefore those who are wise, note the first with their eyes, the second with their mind, and the third with their ears. Yea, through the means of the above-named senses, she so pleases the spirits of anyone who hears her, understands her, and sees her that he dwells in heaven, not on earth.

---

[2] Ornithoparchus, *Musicae active mirologus* and Dowland, *Introduction: Containing the Art of Singing* (New York: Dover, 1973), 169.

[3] Pontus de Tyard, *Solitaire second* [1555].

And in another place, 'music goes to the core of my soul.'

> While I was being so greatly complimented, the great virtue of music arrived, music which went to the core of my soul. There were four singers, who were looking in a book, and another fellow with a silver lute, which was tuned to their voices. They sang: 'Divine eyes, so calm, so pure.'[4]

Of course the thought of music going to one's heart or soul is powerfully expressed in songs of love. In a poem much in the spirit of the troubadour songs of the Pre-Renaissance, Thomas Campion describes the reactions of the listener:

> And as her lute doth live or die,
> Led by her passion, so must I.
> For when of pleasure she doth sing,
> My thoughts enjoy a sudden spring;
> But if she doth of sorrow speak,
> Even from my heart the strings do break.[5]

George Chapman also provides a remarkable portrait of a listener of a love song.

> Never was any sense so set on fire
> With an immortal ardor, as mine ears;
> Her singing to the strings doth speech inspire
> And numbered laughter, that the descant bears
> To her sweet voice; whose species through my sense
> My spirits; to their highest function rears;
> To which, impressed with ceaseless confluence,
> It useth them as proper to her power,
> Marries my soul, and makes itself her dower.[6]

One might say that Medieval music was aimed at the ears, but Renaissance art music was intended for the heart. It is a point Spenser made in his *The Faerie Queene*, where the mythical musician, Arion, performs music which draws not only the ears, but the hearts of the listeners as well.

> Then there was heard a most celestial sound
> Of dainty music, which did next ensue
> Before the spouse: that was Arion crowned;
> Who, playing on his harp, unto him drew
> The ears and hearts of all that goodly crew.[7]

---

[4] Pietro Aretino, *Dialogues*, trans. Raymond Rosenthal (New York: Marsilio, 1971), 54ff.

[5] Thomas Campion, 'When to her Lute,' in Robert Bender, ed., *Five Courtier Poets of the English Renaissance* (New York: Washington Square Press, 1967), 316.

[6] George Chapman (1559–1634), 'Ovid's Banquet of Sense,' in Emrys Jones, ed., *The New Oxford Book of Sixteenth Century Verse* (Oxford: Oxford University Press, 1991), 682.

[7] Edmund Spenser, *The Faerie Queene*, Book IV, Canto XI, xxiii.

Sometimes we get the impression, in the Renaissance, that men had longed for this kind of music. So it seems in Spenser's 'Colin Clouts Come Home Again,' where he speaks of 'greedy ears' and 'hungry ears.'

> Who all the while, with greedy listfull ears,
> Did stand astonished at his curious skill,
> Like heartless deer, dismayed with thunder's sound.[8]
>
> ......
>
> 'Hark then, ye jolly shepherds, to my song,'
> With that they all began to throng about him near,
> With hungry ears to hear his harmony.[9]

All of these kinds of poems speak of the contemplative listener for it is the single most important characteristic of the highest musical experience. A beautiful and vivid description of the performance of art music in sixteenth-century English fiction is found in Sir Philip Sidney's *The Countesse of Pembrokes Arcadia*. He is clearly aware of the principle of the contemplative listener, whom he calls quite as accurately, those with 'unpossessed minds of attention.'

> The music was of cornetts, whereof one answering the other, with a sweet emulation, striving for the glory of music, and striking upon the smooth face of the quiet lake, was then delivered up to the castle walls, which with a proud reverberation, spreading it into the air; it seemed before the harmony came to the ear, that it had enriched itself in its travel, the nature of those places adding melody to that melodious instrument. And when a while that instrument had made a brave proclamation to all unpossessed minds of attention, an excellent consort followed immediately of five viols, and as many voices; which all being but orators of their master's passions, bestowed this song upon her, that thought upon another matter.[10]

The new Renaissance climate for contemplative listeners made possible music with a wider rage of emotions. In particular we associate with the sixteenth century a new emphasis on sad emotions and one finds reference to this in all types of literature. In Lyly's play, *Endimion*, Geron enters singing, and although we are not given the song, we know its character by the opening lines of his son, Eumenides.

> EUMENIDES. Father, your sad music, being tuned to the same key that my hard fortunes is, has so melted my mind, that I wish to hang at your mouth's end till my life's end.
> GERON. These tunes, Gentleman, have I been accustomed with these fifty Winters.[11]

And in George Peele's play, *The Arraignment of Paris*, Mercury requests the company be quiet, while Oenone sings a song of woe.

---

[8] Edmund Spenser, 'Colin Clouts Come Home Again,' lines 7ff.

[9] Ibid., lines 51ff.

[10] Sir Philip Sidney, *The Countesse of Pembrokes Arcadia*, in *The Prose Works of Sir Philip Sidney*, ed. Albert Feuillerat (Cambridge: Cambridge University Press, 1962), Book III, xv.

[11] John Lyly, *Endimion*, III, iv.

MERCURY. She singeth; sirs, be hushed a while.[12]

Given such strong and somber emotions it is easy to understand the necessity of a singer being in the proper mood to sing such music, for the performance of music is so closely tied to one's own feelings. A character in *The Trials of Persiles and Sigismunda*, who says that 'it's the shared opinion of everyone who's heard me sing that I have the best voice in the world,' observes,

> 'If this weren't more a time to be moaning than singing, I'd easily prove the truth of this to you. But if things improve and my tears have a chance to dry, I'll sing, and while they may not be happy songs, at least they can be sad dirges that will cast their spell as they're sung and make you happy as you cry over them.' Feliciana's words made everyone want to hear her sing as soon as possible, but they didn't dare plead with her to do it because, as she herself had said, the time wasn't right.[13]

And speaking of these stronger emotions in Renaissance music, we remind the reader that a fundamental goal of Humanism in music was getting rid of polyphony, which made it impossible for the listener to be moved by the text. This was due not only to the general density of musical lines, but because one heard four or more different words at any given moment. In this regard there is a charming observation by Baldassare Castiglione (1478–1529) in his famous book on the courtier. In speaking of friendship, Castiglione says it is dangerous to have more than two real friends. 'The reason for this is that, as you know, harmony is more difficult to achieve with several instruments than with two.'[14]

Humanism wanted to replace polyphony with a simple melody accompanied by harmony which supported the emotion of the melody. One of the steps toward effective composition of this nature was the functional bass line which supports chords in the modern sense. This is reflected in a poem by John Lyly, composed ca. 1575–1580, which speaks of music not sounding well unless the bass line can be heard.

> The lofty trees whose branches make sweet shades
> Whose arms in Spring are richly dighte with flowers
> Without the root their glory quickly fades
> And all in vain comes pleasant April showers.
> No love can be at all without the heart
> Nor Music made except the Bass takes part.
>
> The princely towers whose pride exceeds in show
> If their foundations be not strong and sound
> Are subject to the smallest winds that blow
> And highest tops are brought to lowest ground.
> No field is sweet where all is scorched with drought
> Nor Music good when so the bass is out.[15]

---

[12] George Peele, *The Arraignment of Paris*, III, i.

[13] Miguel de Cervantes, *The Trials of Persiles and Sigismunda*, trans. Celia Weller and Clark Colahan (Berkeley: University of California Press, 1989), III, iv.

[14] *The Courtier*, trans. George Bull (New York: Penguin Books, 1967), II, 138.

[15] John Lyly, in *The Complete Works of John Lyly*, ed. Warwick Bond (Oxford: Clarendon Press, 1967), III, 452ff.

Inseparable from the new awareness of the contemplative listener in the Renaissance was a new awareness of the audience in general. This takes several forms, one, for example, being a circumstance familiar even today is mentioned by a Galilei:

> I thank you in the highest degree for your praise; and in order not to fall into that common vice of musicians, I will begin without being begged, and will stop when I see that I am beginning to bore you.[16]

Another aspect of audience attention is influenced by the duration of the concert. There was some discussion of this during the Renaissance, one example being found in Antonio Sebastiano's, *The Art of Poetry* of 1563. Minturno makes some interesting comments on the length of a dramatic performance, relative to the attention of the audience. In general, he states that the performance should be not less than three hours nor more than four,

> lest neither too great brevity rob the work of its beauty and leave the desire of the hearers unsatisfied, nor excessive length deprive the poem of its proportion, spoil its charm, and render it boresome to the beholders. And indeed the wise poet should so measure the time with the matter to be presented that those who hear the work should rather deplore its brevity than regret having remained too long to listen.[17]

With respect to Renaissance art music, especially vocal art music, one thinks of the upper class, which, by the sixteenth century, generally adopted the idea that some knowledge of music was an important facet of the well-rounded man. The best extant discussion of this new aspect of society is found in the *Il Cortigiano* (*The Courtier*) by Castiglione. In the course of the following discussion he mentions several of the topics we discuss in this essay, including the disapproval of polyphony, the importance of good intonation, various aspects of the audience and, of course, the importance of self-education in music. The character, Gaspare, begins this discussion:

> 'There exist many different kinds of music, both vocal and instrumental. So I would be gratified to hear which is the best of all and on what occasion the courtier should perform.'
>
> 'Truly beautiful music,' answered Federico, 'consists, in my opinion, in fine singing, in reading accurately from the score and in an attractive personal style, and still more in singing to the accompaniment of the viol. I say this because the solo voice contains all the purity of music, and style and melody are studied and appreciated more carefully when our ears are not distracted by more than one voice, and every little fault, too, is more clearly apparent, something which does not happen when a group is singing, because then one singer covers up for the other. But above all, singing poetry accompanied by the viol seems especially pleasurable, for the instrument gives the words a really marvelous charm and effectiveness. All keyboard instruments, indeed, are harmonious, because their consonances are perfect and they make possible many effects which fill the soul with sweetness and melody. And no less delightful is the playing of a quartet, with the viols producing music of great

---

[16] Vincenzo Galilei, *Fronimo* [1584], trans. Carol MacClintock (Neuhasen-Stuttgart: Hanssler-Verlag, 1985), 32.

[17] Quoted in, Barrett Clark, *European Theories of the Drama* (New York: Crown, 1959), 57. Sebastiano, known as Minturno, was bishop of Ugento and represented that town in the Council of Trent.

skill and suavity. The human voice adds ornament and grace to all these instruments, with which I think it is good enough if our courtier has some acquaintance (though the more proficient he is the better) without concerning himself greatly with [the aulos] which both Minerva and Alcibiades rejected, because it seems [to] have something repulsive about [it]. Then as to the occasions when these various kinds of music should be performed, I would instance when a man finds himself in the company of dear and familiar friends, and there is no pressing business on hand. But above all, the time is appropriate when there are ladies present; for the sight of them softens the hearts of those who are listening, makes them more susceptible to the sweetness of the music, and also quickens the spirit of the musicians themselves. As I have already said, one should avoid playing in the presence of a large number, especially of the common people. But in any case, everything should be tempered by discretion; for it is just not possible to imagine all the circumstances possible, and if the courtier is a good judge of himself he will adapt himself to the occasion and will know when his audience is in the mood to listen and when not; and he will act his own age, for it is certainly most unbecoming and unsightly when an old grey-haired gentleman, who is toothless and wrinkled, takes up the viol and plays and sings in front of a gathering of ladies, even if his performance is quite good. This is because the words of songs are nearly always amorous, and in old men love is altogether ridiculous; although it sometimes seems that Cupid along with the other miracles he works delights in melting even the icy hearts of the old.'

Then the Magnifico replied: 'Do not rob such poor old men of this pleasure, Federico; for I have known men of advanced years who possess the most perfect voices and are accomplished musicians, and far more so than some young men.'

'It is not my wish,' answered Federico, 'to rob them of this pleasure, but it certainly is my wish to rob you and these ladies of the chance to laugh at their absurdity; and if old men have the desire to sing to the viol, then let them do so in private with the object of shedding from their minds the disturbing thoughts and bitter vexations of which life is full, and of tasting the divinity which, I believe, Pythagoras and Socrates attributed to music. And even if they do not practice it themselves, if they have cultivated a taste for music they will enjoy it far more than those who know nothing about it. After all, very often, because he exercises them a great deal, a blacksmith whose body is otherwise puny will have stronger arms than someone who is more robust; likewise, someone whose ears have been trained to listen to harmony will understand it better and more readily and appreciate it more intelligently than others whose hearing may be very sharp and sound but whose ears are untrained in the varieties of musical consonances; for the modulations of music have no significance for ears that are unaccustomed to them, though admittedly music can tame even a wild animal. This, then, is the pleasure that old men may suitably take in music.'[18]

Another familiar discussion of the members of the upper class participating in musical performance is found in the famous *The Decameron* by Boccaccio. In *The Decameron*, the group of young aristocrats which people this book are often described as participating in the performance of music after the evening meal. A typical example, one of many, occurs on the evening before the stories of the first day,

the tables being cleared away, the queen (the person in charge for the day) bade that instruments of music be brought, for all the ladies knew how to dance, as also the young men, and some of them could both play and sing excellently well. Accordingly, at her bidding, Dyoneo took a lute and Fiammetta a viol and began softly to sound a dance; whereupon the queen and the other ladies, together

---

[18] *The Courtier*, II, 120ff

> with the two young men ... struck up a round and began to dance with slow pace a roundelay; which ended, they fell to singing amorous and merry tunes. They continued thus till it seemed to the queen time to go to sleep.[19]

Benvenuto Cellini, in his autobiography, describes precisely such a concert.

> The supper was followed by a short concert of delightful music, voices joining in harmony with instruments; and forasmuch as they were singing and playing from the book ...[20]

Two listeners in particular, Cellini reports, 'dropped their earlier tone of banter, exchanging it for well-weighed terms of sober heartfelt admiration.'

Chaucer left a brief picture of such aristocratic music inside the palace:

> And, Lord! the hevenyssh melodye
> Of songes, ful of armonye,
> I herde aboute her trone ysonge
> That al the paleys-walles ronge![21]

One scholar believes the the majority of middle-class men and women also sang and performed on instruments.[22] If this were the case it might help make sense of the very wide range of topics sung by a solo singer mentioned by Pietro Aretino in his *Dialogues*:

> NANNA. Then a skillful rebec player appeared and, having tuned his instrument, sang some strange tales.
> PIPPA. May God save you, what did he sing about?
> NANNA. He sang of the hostility that heat has for cold, and cold for heat. He sang of why the days of summer are long and those of winter short. He sang of the link between lightning and thunder, thunder and the flash, the flash and the cloud, the cloud and the clear sky. He sang about where the rain stays when the weather is good, and where good weather goes when it rains. He sang of hail, hoar frost, snow and mist. He sang, I believe, of the woman who rents out rooms, who refrains from laughter when her lodgers weep, and of another woman who refrains from weeping when they laugh; and at the end he sang about the fire which flickers in the butt-end of a glowworm, and as to whether a grasshopper chirps with its body or its mouth.[23]

Among the working class, the songs of Sacchetti enjoyed great popularity. He himself was a good musician and set many of his poems to music himself. Symonds suggests that these pastoral part-songs were a harbinger of the madrigal as we know it in the sixteenth century.[24]

---

[19] *Decameron*, trans. John Payne (Berkeley: University of California Press, 1982), I, 25ff.

[20] Addington Symonds, trans., *The Life of Benvenuto Cellini* (New York: Scribner's, 1914), I, xxx.

[21] 'The House of Fame,' III, 1395.

[22] Quoted in John Larner, *Culture and Society in Italy, 1290–1420* (New York: Scribner's, 1971), 172.

[23] Aretino, *Dialogues*, 242.

[24] John Addington Symonds, *Renaissance in Italy* (New York: Capricorn Books, 1964), I, 135.

Cervantes (1547–1616) goes farther and makes a point of the universality of music when he mentions, in his masterpiece, *Don Quijote*,

> know that even in the mountains and woods there are people who understand music.[25]

Another manifestation of the importance of listening in the Renaissance was a new recognition of the characteristics of good performance. Already in the fourteenth century we find Petrarch recognizing the importance long and laborious practice.

> Saw too a race of melodious singers, all of them masters,
> Content to stand under its shade and fashion the rarest of garlands.
> And on that greensward I too have learned—for much avails practice
> Long and laborious—how to vary my notes, singing many
> Albeit modest songs, and have dared to crown my own temples
> Finally with that same leafage.[26]

We also find some interesting references to the elements of good performance in the anonymous poem, 'The Pearl,' where there is a passage which describes the new music (*a note full new*) which will be sung by the 44,000 souls permitted to enter heaven, as mentioned in the book of Revelations. In this ideal music we find the goals of a full and clear performance, noble (*gentle*) character, in tune and something beyond what one might expect from earthly performers.

> I heard them sound forth a note quite new.
> To hear that was most pleasingly dear!
> As harpers harp upon their harps,
> That new song they sang full clear,
> In resounding tones—a gentle utterance!
> Full fair in unison they caught the modes ...
> Nevertheless, none was ever so skilled,
> Despite all the crafts that ever they knew,
> Who of that song might sing a note
> Except that company.[27]

In a work by the fifteenth-century English poet, Lydgate, we encounter an ensemble of gods playing music in honor of Cupid. Here, after man is told to be still, Lydgate lists all the instruments of the minstrels, indeed, he says, more than any man could name. Then he defines what makes an exceptional performance, that which has no discords, is in tune, with good ensemble and no errors in rhythm. No one, Lydgate observes, could be so sorrowful or oppressed with heaviness that he would not have been comforted by this music.

---

[25] Miguel de Cervantes, *Don Quijote*, trans. Burton Raffel (New York: Norton, 1995), I, xi.
[26] 'Remedies for Fortune Fair and Foul,' trans. Conrad Rawski (Bloomington: Indiana University Press, 1991), X, 366ff.
[27] Anonymous, 'The Pearl,' trans. Mary Hillmann (College of Saint Elizabeth Press, 1959), 877ff.

And yt syt nat me to be stille
But tel, how they wer provyded
Of Instrumentys of Musyke,
For they koude the practyke
Of al manner Mynstralcye
That any man kan specifye;
For ther wer rotys of Almanye
And eke of Arragon and spayne,
Songes, stampes, and eke dauncys,
Dyuers plente of pleauncys,
And many vnkouth notys newe
Of swiche folkys as lovde trewe,
And Instrumentys that dyde excelle,
Many moo than I kan telle:
Harpys, fythels, and eke rotys,
Wel accordyng with her notys,
Lutys, Rubibis, and geterns,
More for estatys than taverns,
Orgnys, cytolys, monacordys.
And ther wer founde noo discordys,
Nor variance in ther sovns,
Nor lak of noo proporsiouns,
Ther was so noble accordaunce;
And for folkys that lyst daunce
Ther wer trumpes and trumpetes,
Lowde shally and docetes,
Passyng of gret melodye,
And floutys ful of armonye,
Eke Instrumentys high and lowe
Wel mo than I koude knowe,
That I suppose, ther is no man
That aryght reherse kan
The melodye that they made:
They wer so lusty and so glade …
Ther melodye was in all
So heuenly and celestiall
That ther nys hert, I dar expresse,
Oppressed so with hevynesse,
Nor in sorrow so y-bounde,
That he sholde ther ha founde
Comfort hys sorrowe to apese
To a-settle his hert at ese.[28]

---

[28] *Lydgate's Reson and Sensuallyte*, ed. Ernst Sieper (London: Oxford University Press, 1901), lines 5564ff.

Finally we should mention a treatise by Tomas de Sancta Maria, published in 1565, which offers a few aesthetic rules for 'beautiful playing.' These include playing cleanly, in good time and with taste. He also suggests that choice of fingerings should reflect tempo.[29]

It is no wonder that we begin to find many specific references to fine musicians during the Renaissance, something also found in the literature of the ancient civilizations but not in the Middle Ages. In 1570, for example, the poet Benedetto Varchi recalls being moved by hearing the solo singer, Silvio Antoniano.

> I never heard anything that moved me more inside and seemed more wonderful (and I am old and I have heard a few things) than the singing extemporaneously to the lira of M. Silvio Antoniano, when he came to Florence.[30]

The singer Fomia is described, when she appeared as Cleopatra in an intermedio given in Piccolomini's *Alessandro* in 1558, by one listener as follows:

> [Fomia] when she sings, cannot be compared to any earthly thing, but to the heavenly harmony.[31]

Giustiniani mentions a cornett virtuoso, Luigi del Cornetto of Ancona, 'who played marvelously.' We find an insight into the volume of this instrument, when Giustiniani recalls,

> he played the Cornett with such moderation and exactitude that it astonished many gentleman present who liked music, because the Cornett did not overshadow the sound of the Cembalo.[32]

He also observed that the art of playing the flute in the German style, 'with grace and nicety,' was not known in Italy, although he singles out the noble, Giulio Cesare of Oriveto, 'who plays upon this instrument, to the amazement of those who hear him.'[33] Giustiniani was thinking of such soloists when he observed that many had achieved considerable profit.

> At present there are many people who, with the profession of music, have earned more than a thousand *scudi* of income; one cannot begin to name them all.[34]

With such rising expectations for performance, it follows that during the Renaissance one finds a new respect for the player as an artist. In the Letters Patent of Baïf's Academy issued by Charles IX of France in 1570, there is some language which is particularly interesting in this

---

[29] *Libro llamado Arte de ta–er fantasia ass' para tecla como para vihuela*, quoted in Gustave Reese, *Music in the Renaissance* (New York: Norton, 1959), 630.

[30] Quoted in Claude V. Palisca, *Humanism in Italian Renaissance Musical Thought* (New Haven: Yale University Press, 1985), 375.

[31] Quoted in Nino Pirrotta and Elena Povoledo, *Music and Theatre from Poliziano to Monteverdi* (Cambridge: Cambridge University Press, 1982), 198.

[32] Vicenzo Giustiniani, *Discorso sopra la Musica* [ca. 1628], trans. Carol MacClintock (American Institute of Musicology, 1962), 79.

[33] Ibid., 80.

[34] Ibid.

regard. When performances are underway, in particular singing, the listeners must not speak, whisper, nor make any noise. No one can enter during a song, but must await its conclusion. It is interesting that the listeners were not to approach the musicians in the private place where they prepared before the performances.

But, as always, there were performances which were not so noteworthy. There is a note in the records of the Scuola de San Rocco for 16 July 1531, which promises,

> to change the players of harp and lute that served us badly to those players who were at the School on Corpus Christi Day.[35]

And then, there is this curious observation by Bruno.

> In these times the lyre has become the principal instrument for charlatans, by means of which they win over and hold their audience and more easily sell their pills and vials, just as the rebec has now become the instrument of blind mendicants.[36]

But, of course, we have been thinking mostly of art music in the above discussion. When it comes to entertainment music entirely different aesthetic expectations come into play, as Erasmus points out:

> Where pleasure's the object, the worst speaker deserves praise no less than the best, because he's no less entertaining; just as the only singer who gives pleasure is one who sings exceptionally well or exceptionally badly.[37]

---

35 Denis Arnold, 'Music at the Scuola di San Rocco,' *Music and Letters* 40, no. 3 (July, 1959): 232, http://www.jstor.org/stable/729389

36 Giordano Bruno, *The Expulsion of the Triumphant Beast*, trans. Arthur Imerti (New Brunswick: Rutgers University Press, 1964), 181 [II, iii].

37 'Convivium fabulosum' [1524], in *The Colloquies of Erasmus*, trans. Craig Thompson (Chicago: University of Chicago Press, 1965), 256.

Contemporary Comments on Performance Practice

THE DEVELOPMENT OF MUSIC during the Renaissance was quite remarkable. From the early Renaissance we have only a relative handful of extant multi-part scores and by the end of the Renaissance we have uncounted published scores. The Renaissance began with music still chained to the Church's artificial nonsense about music being a branch of mathematics and by the end of the Renaissance Humanism had defeated the Church and nearly everyone once again understood that the communication of emotions was the entire point of music. It would be left to the Baroque Period to try to figure how music did this.

We can even see this transformation in so rational and theoretical a subject as form. The forms of medieval music had all been driven by function. By the late sixteenth century the discussion of form was taking place in a new language, a more subjective language that dwelt with style and feeling.

Consider, for example, the often quoted definition of Concerto by Bottrigari.[1] The word concerto, which had first been used solely to mean an ensemble, as in *Concerti di Milano*, has now taken on a new meaning, a humanistic meaning. He points out that the word now means 'contention or conflict' and does not derive from the verb 'consero,' which means 'to graft, to sow and plant together.' Thus for this period we understand an instrumental composition using dialogue technique to be 'concerto' and one in a motet style to be 'concenti.'

Michael Praetorius agreed with the definition of the term itself, which he says derives from *concertare*, 'to compete with one another.' Again, his definition speaks of real live people, not some academic definition.

> Let us imagine several of the best and most competent musicians singing or playing on various instruments—such as cornetts, trombones, recorders or transverse flutes, cromornes, bassoons or dulcians, racketts, viols, large and small violins, lutes, harpsichords, regals, positives, or organs—alternating in the manner of choirs and striving, as it were, to outdo one another.[2]

For Praetorius, who had studied in Italy with Giovanni Gabrieli, 'concerto' was a style in a multi-voice composition in which separate choirs alternate, 'a dialog in which different voices or instruments are combined.'[3] In an apparent reference to Church polyphony, he adds that the pleasure comes not from the craft (mathematics) involved, but from the variety and color of the sound itself. When he adds, 'more properly a composition is called a concerto if a high and a low choir are heard in alternation and together,' we can see the roots of the *concertato* style.

---

[1] Hercole Bottrigari, *Il Desiderio*, trans. Carol MacClintock (American Institute of Musicology, 1962), 20.

[2] *Syntagma Musicum* (facsimile publication by Barenreiter Kassel, 1958), 5.

[3] Ibid., 4. For 'Concerto' he gives *concertatio* in Latin and *ein Concert* in German. He also adds that *Cantio*, *concentus* and *symphonia* all mean at this time, 'a composition for several voices.'

Curiously, when Praetorius speaks of the English practice, he reverts to an older use of this term, meaning simply a group of players. It almost appears here as if he thought the English were too polite and formal.

> The English call this a Consort, from *consortium*, as when several people with various instruments such as harpsichord, large lyra, double harp, lute, theorbo, pandora, *penorcon*, cither, viol, small violin, transverse flute or recorder, sometimes also a soft trombone or rackett, play together quietly and softly, forming a pleasant and harmonious relationship with one another.[4]

In the case of the Motet, Praetorius seems at a loss to fulfill his earlier promise of explaining 'Italian terms which are so puzzling to many musicians.' It strikes us odd that he, not to mentions several Italian treatises he cites, did not recognize this as a French word. 'Opinions vary regarding the origin of the word *motet*,'[5] he says as he proceeds to give some possibilities which are incorrect. Philip de Monte, he maintains, thought it derived from *mutare*, 'to alter,' as in changing verses. Others believed it came from *modo tecta*, 'obscure as to mode' or even from *moda* in Italian for 'fashion.' We never read the correct answer,[6] but in the process Praetorius does provide a more humanistic description of the style of the motet, in particular 'elegance' and a work which 'moves one most profoundly by its seriousness and artfulness.' Praetorius also points out that this form is sometimes confused with Concerto, but he recognizes a distinction in style.

> The concerti should be set for several choirs and composed quite plainly, without particular elaboration and imitative passages; the motet, however, should be written with greater artfulness and care and for not more than eight voices.[7]

Bottrigari concludes his discussion of forms with the complaint that the current performers were not supplying enough contrast in emotional content in their performances.

> The chief [abuse] is the indifference with which they compose the *cantilene*, finding no difference between delightful and lascivious compositions, or between funeral, lugubrious ones and those which ought to serve the divine cult, invoking, thanking and praising the omnipotent majesty of God and His Saints.[8]

Once form began to become associated with feeling it would be only a matter of time before we begin to see the roots of the so-called architectural forms of the later Classical Period. For a particular pleasure found in the right hemisphere (where the emotional and experiential understanding of music is also found) is the pleasure of 'here I am back home

---

[4] Ibid.

[5] Ibid., 6ff.

[6] 'Motet,' of course, comes from *Mot*, French for 'word.'

[7] Ibid., 8ff. He adds the interesting observation that Gabrieli has composed works for up to sixteen voices which are 'motets' in style, but organized into choirs as concerti in form.

[8] Bottrigari, *Il Desiderio*, 44.

again.' Nothing whatsoever of this nature is found in the left hemisphere of the brain. And this is the basis of the pleasure in hearing architectural forms, such as ABA, and including da capos and recapitulations. One first finds this in the early examples of the *concertato* technique, but also in more simple alternation of color. One sees this, for example, in Robert Greene's pastoral romance, *Menaphon*, where the text of Menaphon's song is given, we are told that he played something on his pipe between every stanza of the poem, since he could not, of course, play and sing at the same time.[9]

Perhaps another root of the later architectural forms was in echo songs, such as the very well-known one by Orlando di Lasso. In Sidney's *The Countesse of Pembrokes Arcadia* a singer sings an echo song, producing both parts by the following technique.

> Which he in part to satisfy, began an Eclogue between himself and the *Echo*: framing his voice in those deserted places, as what words he would have the *Echo* reply, unto those he would sing higher than the rest, and so kindly framed a disputation between himself and it.[10]

In addition to the development of more humanistic forms during the Renaissance, there were also some fascinating developments in notation. And it is important to note that these developments came not from the contemplation of some scholastic theorist, but reflected actual practice by living musicians. A perfect example is one of the origins of the fermata sign.

It is our understanding today that a modern ritard. was unknown to Renaissance music. But, how then is the listener to know the composition is coming to an end? Often the Renaissance composer accomplished this by creating the effect of a fermata through a gradual lengthening of note values at the final cadence. But Praetorius suggests making, in performance, a fermata on the next-to-last harmony, which he suggests was common practice by fine musicians! He adds that he hesitates to mention this, since everyone knows it.

> It is not very commendable and pleasant when singers, organists, and other instrumentalists from habit hasten directly from the penultimate note of a composition into the last note without any hesitation. Therefore I believe I should here admonish those who have hitherto not observed this as it is done at princely courts and by other well-constituted musical organizations, to linger somewhat on the penultimate note, whatever its time value—whether they have [already] held it for four, five, or six *tactus*—and only then proceed to the last note.

This practice is confirmed in the famous sixteenth-century dance treatise by Thoinot Arbeau[11] (1519–1595), although, if the translation is accurate, it appears he recommends the fermata *after* the penultimate chord. In his discussion of the capriole Arbeau mentions,

---

[9] Robert Greene, *Menaphon* [1589], in *The Life and Complete Works of Robert Greene*, ed. Alexander Grosart (New York: Russell & Russell, 1964), VI, 40.

[10] Sir Philip Sidney, *The Countesse of Pembrokes Arcadia*, in *The Prose Works of Sir Philip Sidney*, ed. Albert Feuillerat (Cambridge: Cambridge University Press, 1962), I, Book II, xxix.

[11] Reese, *Music in the Renaissance*, 564, gives his real name as Jehan Tabourot.

> You have observed in a musical composition how musicians pause for a moment after the penultimate chord before playing the final chord in order to make an agreeable and harmonious ending.[12]

One of the most interesting recommendations regarding improved notation by Praetorius is one of the earliest articulation symbols, the slur mark. He suggests that complex ligatures should be replaced with the slur indication. Ligatures are usually presented in modern literature as having been a kind of shorthand for scribes and we know of no place where there is a suggestion that there was a phrase association, such as would be indicated by a slur. In retrospect, therefore, Praetorius' observation invites a review of the use of the ligature in fifteenth-century music and before.

Another notational recommendation by Praetorius is made in reference to the necessity of *musica ficta*, the necessary alterations when changing modes, or to avoid the tritone, Praetorius advises the composer that this should *not* be left to the performers.

> Composers would do well, as an excellent precaution, to indicate clearly the two chromatic signs, the *cancellatum* [sharp sign] and *rotundum* [flat sign] whenever they are to be employed, in order to prevent hesitation or doubt. This is useful, convenient, and also most necessary to keep singers from becoming confused, as well as for the benefit of ignorant town musicians and organists who cannot read music, let alone sing correctly.[13]

Some of Praetorius' recommendations are of a very practical nature, having their origin in his own experience as a conductor, such as advising that everyone should start expressing in numbers the number of rests in the various parts. He observes that he has learned from experience, 'not without some embarrassment,' that this is necessary as musicians are inclined not to pay strict attention or are sometimes caught up in listening to the music.[14]

Since it would be a long time after the sixteenth century before the practice of notating measure numbers, there was no fast means of determining the length of a composition. Praetorius had apparently had occasion to find himself in the awkward position of finding himself with a composition too long due to the sermon lasting too long, or some other unanticipated factor. Therefore, he made it a habit to count the number of breves in a composition and notate it at the end of his score. Then, when planning the music for a service, by glancing at a chart he had worked out, he could immediately determine how long it would take to perform the composition.[15] This, he observes, is important so as not to delay the remaining church ceremonies. Similarly, he describes a system of marking cuts,[16] in case the latter does not work, which enables the musicians to stop in a hurry,

---

[12] Thoinot Arbeau, *Orchesography*, trans. Mary Evans (New York: Kamin Dance Publishers, 1948), 92.

[13] Praetorius, *Syntagma Musicum*, 31.

[14] Ibid., 33ff.

[15] Ibid., 88. He had found, for example, that a composition of 640 breves required one hour to perform.

[16] Ibid., 35.

in case the conductor finds the composition before or after the sermon threatens to last too long—since a musician is likely to overdo things.

Yet another notational question raised by Praetorius was the meter signatures at the beginning of compositions, a subject for which Praetorius finds a general lack of agreement. The comments he makes in passing are quite valuable, as for example his observation that the slower common time signature is used in madrigals and the faster alla breve sign is used in motets.[17] However, he has noticed that in *all* the compositions of Gabrieli, he uses only the alla breve sign. In the works of Viadana, he finds the alla breve sign in compositions with text and the common time sign in instrumental works. His own opinion, agreeing with what he has found in the works of Lassus and Marenzio, was that,

> the common time sign should be used for those motets and other sacred compositions which have many black notes, in order to show that the beat is to be taken more slowly ... Anyone, however, may reflect upon such matters himself and decide, on the basis of text and music, where the beat has to be slow and where fast.

In concerti, where madrigal and motets *styles* are found, it is necessary to change tempo. Here, instead of using the common time and alla breve signs, Praetorius suggests it might be better to employ the new practice of using Italian words, such as *adagio*, *presto*, etc.[18]

Praetorius also had concerns for the metric symbols known as proportional signs. Praetorius was unaware that this practice, in which each new time signature was based on the previous one, resulting in the individual notes becoming faster and faster, was nearly dead. Again no doubt reflecting his own public conducting experience he warns that under this system the conductor might end up beating so fast that,

> we make the spectators laugh and offend the listeners with incessant hand and arm movements and give the crowd an opportunity for raillery and mockery.[19]

And, of course, he is right. It reminds us of some modern conductors who, insecure in their feel for the pulse, subdivide every $\frac{5}{8}$ or $\frac{7}{8}$ bar in sight. The result is that instead of allowing the melody flow, they look like a Japanese Benihana chef chopping up his food.

Praetorius was also one of the earliest writers to comment on performance aspects which are influenced by the acoustics of the hall. One such topic he discusses has to do with his recommended seating plan for singers.

> I have always put the sopranos together with the tenors and the altos with the bass ... The reason is that I have not only seen most other composers do the same, but that it is because of the harmony and the intervals. If the singers stand close to each other and have to read and sing from one part, sopranos and tenors will produce pleasant sixths and the alto and basses fifths and octaves. Otherwise a singer

---

[17] Ibid., 48ff.
[18] Ibid., 51.
[19] Ibid., 74.

> would fill the other's ears with unpleasant fourths, the usual progressions between soprano and alto, or tenor and alto, spoiling the music and making singing distasteful, particularly if the performers carrying the other two parts are not placed near enough to complete and round out the harmony.
>
> Nevertheless I do not want to dictate to anyone in this or other matters, but merely to give my own modest ideas and to tell what I have found to be good from my own experience; for everyone will have his own ideas and will act accordingly.[20]

Another acoustical recommendation is quite interesting as it deals with a specific aspect of what experienced conductors today call the pyramid problem, the necessity to create an artificial balance in order to overcome the listener's brain's tendency to emphasize higher partials. Curiously, this is one of two places in his book where Praetorius switches from German into Latin,[21] suggesting that he considered this information a 'secret' only for those conductors who are educated. He had noticed that, under the influence of how we *think* we hear music, as mentioned above, that final releases of chords tend to sound unbalanced, with lots of upper partials and no bass, resulting almost in hearing the chord in a different inversion. The solution for this, as experienced conductors today know, is to stagger the releases, with the upper voices simply ending before the lower ones. Our only surprise in the recommendation by Praetorius is the extent to which he did this, although if one imagines the performance in a large reverberant cathedral the effect would no doubt be wonderful.

> As a piece is brought to a close, all the remaining voices should stop simultaneously at the sign of the conductor or choir master. The tenors should not prolong their tone, a fifth above the bass or lowest voice ... after the bass has stopped. But if the bass continues to sound a little longer, for another two or four *tactus*, it lends charm and beauty to the music [*Cantilenae*], which no one can deny.

That tempo in the sixteenth century was a decision made by the performer, and not the composer, may surprise some readers. Praetorius clearly recommends[22] a level of rubato rarely mentioned in other treatises, although the practice becomes common in the Baroque Period. First he makes two general rules, that a performance must not be hurried and that all note values must be observed. Then he adds,

> But to use, by turns, now a slower, now a faster beat, in accordance with the text, lends dignity and grace to a performance and makes it admirable ... Some do not want such mixture of [tempi] in any one composition. But I cannot accept their opinion, especially since it makes motets and concerti particularly delightful, when after some slow and expressive measures at the beginning several quick phrases follow, succeeded in turn by slow and stately ones, which again change off with faster ones.

The purpose of this he says is to avoid monotony and he adds the same advice relative to dynamics.

---

[20] Ibid., 90.

[21] The other place is his recommendation regarding the addition of a fermata before final cadences.

[22] Ibid., 79ff.

Besides, it adds much charm to harmony and melody, if the dynamic level in the vocal and instrumental parts is varied now and then.[23]

Later Praetorius returns to dynamics, mentioning that the Italians are beginning to use *forte*, *piano*, etc., to mark changes within a concerto. It is interesting that, in this case at least, he seems to suggest the two, dynamics and tempo, go together.

> I rather like this practice. There are some who believe that this is not very appropriate, especially in churches. I feel, however, that such variety [in dynamics] and change [in tempo] are not only agreeable and proper, if applied with moderation and designed to express the feelings of the music, and affect the ear and the spirit of the listener much more and give the concerto a unique quality and grace. Often the composition itself, as well as the text and the meaning of the words, requires that one [change] at times—but not too frequently or excessively—beating now fast, now slowly, also that one lets the choir by turns sing quietly and softly, and loudly and briskly. To be sure, in churches there will be more need of restraint in such changes than at banquets.[24]

It is also interesting here, that Praetorius gives one Latin term, *lento gradu*, which he says was understood to mean that the voice was both softer and slower.

Praetorius above speaks of adding 'grace to a performance,' which is a new word reflecting the growing sophistication of Renaissance music. This word is also used by Giustiniani, who makes 'grace' the most distinguishing quality of a gentleman. Although supposing it to be a gift of God, he finds grace the chief virtue in the beauty of women, in the behavior of the gentleman, in speech and among artists. In the performance of music, he defines grace as follows.

> For in the voice as well as for instruments, one will be able to offer the same reasons for grace and melody saying, by way of definition, that singing with grace is nothing other than a close observance of the style and rules of singing and of those rules for using the voice or playing a good instrument so that it shall not be unpleasant or awkward. It is this grace that customarily brings pleasure and delight to the ears of persons of judgment. And so one can say that a person does not have a good voice but sings with grace as, for example, I will mention Cardinal Montalto, who played and sang with much grace and feeling even though his appearance was more martial than Apollonian, and who had a scratchy voice …
>
> And that it is true that grace in singing is a quality provided by nature and not by art…may be seen from the fact that sometimes a singer appears pleasing to one person and tiresome to another; and on the contrary a stupid singer pleases when he ought not to. And the same effect is seen also in other things, especially in the bordellos of Spain and Africa in which there is not a woman that does not find a market, however ugly she may be.[25]

---

[23] Later he mentions, with regard to concerti, that a softer dynamic level can also be achieved by simply not having as many instruments doubling in a particular choir. [Ibid., 128 (108)].

[24] Ibid., 132 (112).

[25] Vicenzo Giustiniani, *Discorso sopra la Musica* [ca. 1628], trans. Carol MacClintock (American Institute of Musicology, 1962), 73ff.

We find the word 'grace' again in Galilei, where it is called 'one of the proper aims of music of our time.' In his *Fronimo*, Galilei has a lutanist say,

> Further, I have never committed [such] errors ... nor have I spoiled or impeded the order of fugues so that they could not be heard entirely. Rather have I proceeded to help them (if I can use that word in such a connotation) by making the voices clear and by augmenting the parts and the whole with sonority, beauty and grace in the best possible way that I knew how and was able to do, in order to completely delight the sense of hearing—which is indeed the proper aim of Music in our time— without any regard to inducing in the souls of the hearers one virtuous habit rather than another, as formerly the ancient Greek writers had it.[26]

In this treatise on intabulation for the lute, Galilei uses the word 'grace' also with respect to otherwise technical solutions. He says, for example, that to repeat a note without reason 'would cause the refined ear no little annoyance.'[27] In another place, a lutanist tells him that he chose to repeat a note in a tenor part of a canzone 'for very good reason, because striking it again brought to delicate ears a *je ne sais quoi* of sadness.'[28] Galilei that the lutanist might omit repeated notes 'for more grace,' and 'to furnish some novelty of the ear—which, like all the other senses, is fed by it.'[29] Similarly, that the use of rests, depending on their use, can result in 'grace' or 'dullness.'[30]

By the way, in this same book Galilei makes reference to having known of transcriptions for lute of music in which the original had as many as '40, 50 and 60 parts.'[31] No one today knows of sixty-part Renaissance music. Such implied aesthetic freedom in transcription during the Renaissance also extended to freedom in doubling of parts in performance, as we can see in an account by Bastiano de Rossi of an 1589 intermezzo for Bargagli's *La Pellegrina*, which included 'symphony a 6' which was actually played by,

> six lutes, three large and three small, a psaltery, a bass-viol with three tenor viols, four trombones, a *cornetta*, a transverse flute, a zither, a mandola and a *sopranino di viola* played most excellently by Alessandro Striggo.[32]

But of all the subjects discussed during the Renaissance relative to performance practice the most important centered on the performer's duty to add emotion to the extant music. Chaucer, in the thirteenth century, used a word never found in medieval music, 'loud singing.' We believe he meant by this 'enthusiasm' and that was his way of referring to emotion, or heart-

---

[26] Vincenzo Galilei, *Fronimo* [1584], trans. Carol MacClintock (Neuhasen-Stuttgart: Hanssler-Verlag, 1985), 61ff.

[27] Ibid., 54.

[28] Ibid., 55.

[29] Ibid., 171.

[30] Ibid., 54.

[31] Ibid., 159.

[32] Nino Pirrotta and Elena Povoledo, *Music and Theatre from Poliziano to Monteverdi* (Cambridge: Cambridge University Press, 1982), 220.

felt singing. In the 'Canterbury Tales,' the carpenter's wife sang 'loud and lively'[33] and we are told that even a trumpet was not half so loud as the two-part songs sung by the Pardoner and the Sumner.[34] The parish clerk, Absalom, sometimes sang in a 'loud treble,'[35] but when he was thinking of love he sang in a small and gentle voice with good harmony from his gittern.

> He syngeth in his voys gentil and smal,
> 'Now, deere laady, if thy wille be,
> I praye yow that ye wole rewe on me,'
> Ful wel acordaunt to his gyternynge.[36]

Singing with enthusiasm was also one of the concerns of Martin Luther, who wrote in his preface to the Babst *Hymnal* of 1545,

> Thus there is now in the New Testament a better service of God, of which the Psalm [96] here says: 'Sing to the Lord a new song …' For God has cheered our hearts and minds through his dear Son, whom he gave for us to redeem us from sin, death, and the devil. He who believes this earnestly cannot be quiet about it. But he must gladly and willingly sing and speak about it so that others also may come and hear it. And whoever does not want to sing and speak of it shows that he does not believe and that he does not belong under the new and joyful testament, but under the old, lazy, and tedious testament.[37]

Being responsible for adding the emotional character to performance may have been one of the things Galilei had in mind when he warned the player,

> And let it not come into your mind to try to defend yourself with the silly excuse of some who say they did not feel called upon to do more than that which they found written or printed.[38]

This seems evident when he continued by saying that the player's goal toward the composer should be to communicate 'not only what he says but often what he wished to say.' There is no more remarkable, indeed startling, testimonial to the importance of the performer's emotional role than a following passage in which Galilei wonders if the fact that the lute cannot sustain a pitch hinders emotions. The lutanist answers that the instruments most capable of this is the organ, but he has found on the contrary that such virtuosi of the organ, such as Claudio di Correggio and Gioseffo Guami,

---

33 'The Miller's Tale,' 3257.

34 'Prologue, The Canterbury Tales,' 669.

35 'The Miller's Tale,' 3332.

36 Ibid., 3360.

37 *Luther's Works* (St. Louis: Concordia, 1961), LIII, 332ff.

38 Ibid., 83.

not by failure of their art and knowledge but by the nature of the instrument, have not been able, cannot, and never will be able to express the harmonies for *affetti* like *durezza, mollezza, asprezza, dolcezza*—consequently the cries, laments, shrieks, tears, and finally quietude and rage—with so much grace and skill as excellent players do on the lute.[39]

Testimonials to the emotional quality of performance are also reflected in works of fiction. In a Romance by Lodge, his *Forbonius and Prisceria*, there is a description of a singer singing a 'mournful melody' and we are told he made his lute 'tunable to the strains of his voice.' His listener responded to 'his manifold sighs, aspects, and motions, whereunto he applied his actions.'[40]

Sometimes we find the criticism of a musician who does not appropriately convey feeling in his performance. Such an example is found in Greene's *Metamorphosis*, where Morpheus is deeply depressed by love. He takes his lute to play 'certain melancholy dumps' and some ladies stand quietly behind him 'to hear what humor the man was in' and heard him sing this 'mournful madrigal.'

> Rest thee desire, gaze not at such a Star,
> Sweet fancy sleep, love take a nap awhile …

But Marpesia, of whom he was singing, 'drew him abruptly from his passions,' criticizing him as follows,

> … for Phidias … playing on his pipe, and yet tears dropping from his eyes, as mixing his greatest melody with passions: but I see the comparison will not hold in you, for though your instrument is answerable to his, yet you lack his lukewarm drops, which show, though your music be as good, yet your thoughts are not so passionate.[41]

We should add here two more minor references to performance practice during the Renaissance. No topic is debated with more heat today than whether vibrato was used in early performance. We add to this debate a statement found in Lyly's *Gallathea*, where an Alchemist, in discussing the precision necessary to his art, says of his workers that when they blow on the fire, 'must beat time with their breath, as musicians do with their breasts.'[42]

Shakespeare makes only one reference to contemporary performance practice. This, a criticism of poor rhythm, is found in *Richard II*, following a stage direction reading, 'The music plays,' when the king observes,

> Music do I hear?
> Ha, ha! Keep time. How sour sweet music is
> When time is broke and no proportion kept![43]

---

39 Ibid., 87.

40 Thomas Lodge, *The Delectable History of Forbonius and Prisceria* (London: Shakespeare Society, 1853), 85ff.

41 Robert Greene, *Metamorphosis* [1588–1591], in *The Life and Complete Works of Robert Greene*, IX, 98ff.

42 John Lyly, *Gallathea* [1592], III, ii.

43 *Richard II*, V, v, 41ff.

It must have been inevitable that with the increasing evidence of contemplative listeners there was a growing concern over the problem of tuning during the Renaissance. By the sixteenth century the problem had become a central problem in performance practice. It was, for example, one of the principal reasons why the host of new wind instruments were made by the 'case,' that is, a consort made by the same maker at the same time to facilitate playing in tune as an ensemble.[44] Thus we begin to find attacks on the ancient contentions about tuning and the division of the octave. Giovanni Spataro, in his 'Errori di Franchino Gafurio da Lodi,' of 1521, says that the old Pythagorean concepts, in so far as modern performance practice is concerned, 'is altogether useless, deceptive, and futile.'

Lodovico Fogliano, in his 'Musica theorica,' of 1529, approached his study of music not on the basis of earlier theorists, but on the basis of his own observations. Hence he defines consonance simply as 'that which is pleasing to the ears.' Thus he expanded intervals considered consonant to include the sixths as well as intervals larger than an octave, which he says are delightful and are used by all composers of part music, organists and singers, 'as anyone moderately learned in this discipline knows.' Tuning, for him, should be done by the sense of hearing, not according to mathematics.

But for some sixteenth-century musicians the ensemble problems in tuning when using the string instruments, which used the old tetrachord system, was more trouble than it was worth. Better, Bardi says, to just leave these instruments out.

> More than once I have felt like laughing when I saw musicians struggling to put a lute or viol into proper tune with a keyboard instrument, for aside from the octave these instruments have few strings in common that are in unison, since until now this highly important matter has gone unnoticed or, if noticed, unremedied. In your consorts, then, you will as far as possible avoid combining lutes or viols with keyboard instruments or harps.[45]

Galilei, in his book on lute intabulation, admits that lutanists had come under criticism because of their old tetrachord system of tuning and that singers, in particular, hesitated to sing with them. But, in his view the old system of tuning gave the lute greater flexibility, with its greater possibilities within the octave, and from this greater sophistication in expressing emotions.

> I should reply to them thus. Since the most noble and least imperfect instrument in use today must remain excluded, (because of the insolence of some of those for whom it has become such) and therefore become an ignoble and most imperfect instrument, what will it be in the hands of those persons? Since they cannot use it with voices, by what means can they convey the meaning of the affections of the soul with greater efficacy than can be done with the well tempered sound alone? O thought unworthy of a reasonable man![46]

---

44 One who recommended adoption of the consort principle as a solution to tuning was Bottrigari, see *Il Desiderio*, 21.

45 Bardi, 'Discourse on Ancient Music and Good Singing,' in Oliver Strunk, *Source Readings in Music History* (New York: Norton, 1950), 297

46 Vincenzo Galilei, *Fronimo*, 165ff.

In any case, he says, 'if this defect had been capable of being remedied it would have been foreseen long before this.'

The most engaging and vivid discussion of the solutions of the problems faced by musicians in an environment where three different tuning systems were in use is found the *Il Desiderio* (1594) by the nobleman-musician, Hercole Bottrigari. In this dialogue, we meet Gratioso Desiderio, a cultured nobleman, but one with little knowledge of the theory of music, as he admits.

> I have never done any theoretical study in matters of music, but have only paid attention to the pleasure and delight afforded my sense of hearing by the composition and sound, as is the usual practice in our time.[47]

He has just left an afternoon concert by a large ensemble of some forty instrumentalists and encounters another nobleman, Alemanno Benelli, whose authority on music he respects. The latter has missed the concert because he took a nap, assuming the concert would begin later.

Desiderio explains to Benelli that he has left the concert with 'increased confusion in my mind,' and indeed that he often experiences such disappointment when hearing large ensembles.

> Having gone a number of times to hear various and diverse musical concerts by voices accompanied by different instruments, I have never experienced the great pleasure which I had imagined and supposed, and which, in fact I had hoped to experience. And today particularly, when I attended this one, such was the case; because, having seen a great apparatus of different kinds of instruments—among them a large Clavicembalo and a large Spinet, three Lutes of various forms, a great number of Viols and a similar large group of Trombones, two little Rebecs and as many large Flutes, straight and traverse, a large Double Harp and a Lyre—all for accompanying many good voices—there where I had thought I would hear a celestial harmony I heard confusion rather than the contrary, accompanied by a discordance, which has offended me rather than given me pleasure.[48]

Benelli responds that since he knows Desiderio has a good ear, it is possible that in fact he heard discord rather than concord, confusion rather than union and that probably the ensemble was out of tune. Desiderio doubts this,

> since all the musicians who were performing are excellent artists. I know them well, and all are capable of acting as conductors, as sometimes I have seen them do in similar concerts. Therefore there must be some other reason.[49]

Benelli then proceeds to explain the problem which arises from the three different tuning systems in use. First, there are the 'stable' instruments, organs, keyboards and harps, which are tuned to Just Intonation and 'can produce only the pure diatonic scale which pleases most

---

[47] Hercole Bottrigari, *Il Desiderio*, 26.

[48] Ibid., 12ff.

[49] Ibid., 14.

CONTEMPORARY COMMENTS OF PERFORMANCE PRACTICE 161

people, or seems to please them.'[50] When what he calls 'stable but alterable instruments' play with the 'stable' instruments, it is therefore necessary for these players to alter their pitches in order to correspond to the keyboard instruments.

> The stable but alterable instruments are all those which, after they have been tuned by the diligent player, can be changed, augmented or diminished in some degree, according to the good judgment of the player as he touches their frets a little higher or a little lower. This occurs with the Lute and Viol, even though they may have the stability of their frets. The same thing happens with the wind instruments, such as the straight and traverse Flutes and straight and curved Cornetts. Even though they may have a certain stability because of their holes, the accomplished player can nonetheless use a little less or a little more breath and can open the vents a little more or a little less, bringing them closer to a good accord. Expert players do this. The instruments which are completely alterable are those which have neither fingerboards nor holes—Trombones, Ribechini, Lire, and the like. These, having ordinarily neither frets nor openings, can wander here and there, according to the will of the player.

Benelli also mentions that he has spoken with the makers of flutes and cornetts and found that they construct these instruments with the holes placed according solely to their ear 'aided by nature,'[51] in other words using the overtone series like singers. Benelli then gets to the real problem, which was that some strings still tuned on the basis of the old tetrachords, which resulted in completely different divisions of the octave, with varying values of steps and half-steps. After illustrating this by a demonstration, Benelli adds an extraordinary observation regarding instances where in some circumstances keyboard players are forced to transpose their music in order to play with one of the strings tuned in the ancient system. He apparently suggests that when a keyboard must transpose a major key to a key impossible in Just Intonation, they played in the parallel minor!

> The players of the entirely stable instruments, as the Clavicembalo, Organ, and others, however excellent they may be, when they wish to transpose a tone lower or higher, or a semitone lower or higher, cannot do so in all places on their instrument. And here is the reason. When it is necessary to play the semitone commonly called major, since they lack it on their instruments they must needs play the one commonly called minor, whence the listeners and they themselves feel that their sense of hearing is offended.[52]

For Praetorius, the tuning problems he faced in his conducting experience were all problems which he felt could have been avoided by more diligent performers. Being an organist, he could not understand why all those players could not tune their instruments and 'warm-up' at home, before they come to perform!

> But it creates great confusion and din if the instrumentalists tune their bassoons, trombones, and cornetts during the organist's prelude and carry on loudly and noisily so that it hurts one's ears and gives one the jitters. For it sounds so dreadful and makes such a commotion that one wonders what kind

---

[50] Ibid., 15ff.

[51] Ibid., 16.

[52] Ibid., 19.

of mayhem is being committed. Therefore everyone should carefully tune the cornett or trombone in his lodging before presenting himself at the church or elsewhere for performance and he should work up a good embouchure with his mouthpiece [at home] in order that he may delight the ears and hearts of the listeners rather than offend them with such cacophony.

And even if you tune carefully, Praetorius found that pitch was subject to the personalities of the performers.

> This point above all must be carefully kept in mind in all concerti, by instrumentalists as well as singers. No one must cover up and outshout the other with his instrument or voice, though this happens very frequently, causing much splendid music to be spoiled and ruined. When one thus tries to outdo the other, the instrumentalists, particularly cornett players with their blaring, but also singers through their screaming, they cause the pitch to rise so much that the organist playing along is forced to stop entirely. At the end it happens then that the whole ensemble through excessive blowing and shouting has gone sharp by a half, often indeed a whole tone and more.[53]

---

[53] *Syntagma Musicum*, 148ff.

Comments on Renaissance Improvisation

Today most 'classical' musicians think of improvisation as something added to a composition or a special skill to be applied in certain measures. We tend to forget that for many centuries before the advent of modern notation *all* music was improvised. Likewise, we tend to forget that early Renaissance music was not that far removed in time from the period when there was still no agreed upon notational system. This is very clear, to cite one example, when one considers how few fourteenth-century Italian organ manuscripts exist. If there were no manuscripts, what were all those organists in fourteenth-century Italy doing? Gustave Reese adds that the absence of even later works by many famous sixteenth-century organists may be explained by a practice of improvisation.[1] He also finds this the intent of a Venetian decree of 1546 that no canons or priests should interrupt performing organists, but should remain quiet and patiently await the end of a piece.

Since traditional musicology has always been based on extant music, the impression one might gain from traditional texts is that there was that music somehow disappeared in Italy ca. 1350. One of the very best Renaissance scholars felt the need to address this impression.

> It is not surprising to me that no attempt to solve the case of the missing Quattrocento music has led to a satisfactory answer. It has been my contention that the secret, if there is one, is in the island, not in the gap that divides it from the continent. For the island is largely a mirage of our historical perspective, a tiny object magnified by our faith in the written tradition, at best a floating island, not only surrounded but also supported by the waves of a sea now opaque to our eye, once full of light, of life, and of sound—the sound of unwritten music.[2]

What he means is that the extant written music, namely Church music, was really just one kind of music performance. Pirrotta hastens to add that we must not assume that the 'unwritten' music of the fourteenth century was only monophonic.[3]

Palisca, another distinguished authority on fourteenth-century Italian music, adds that much of the music which is extant is music from the Low Countries and not Italian at all.

---

[1] Gustave Reese, *Music in the Renaissance* (New York: Norton, 1959), 544.

[2] Nino Pirrotta, 'Ars Nova and Stil Novo,' in *Music and Culture in Italy from the Middle Ages to the Baroque* (Cambridge: Harvard University Press, 1984), 28, where he devotes a more lengthy argument to this contention.

[3] Nino Pirrotta and Elena Povoledo, *Music and Theatre from Poliziano to Monteverdi* (Cambridge: Cambridge University Press, 1982), 26.

> Style as a criterion is particularly misleading in the Italian Renaissance, because some of the most characteristic music of the period is not preserved in writing, and much of the written music exhibits style elements of undeniably transalpine origin. But this should not lead us to the conclusion that the Renaissance was a northern phenomenon.[4]

In fact, it may well have been the case that in the fourteenth century that the very thought that music was something you read from a page was still not entirely accepted. One finds, for example, contemporary statements which imply that the written notes had not yet obtained the kind of legitimacy we bestow on them today. A case in point is Jean de Muris's (ca. 1290–1350) treatise, 'Ars nove musice,' an important early university text in the old Scholastic mathematical model, in which we find the following comment on the subject of 'ancient' notation:

> For reasons which we shall pass over, their symbols did not adequately represent what they sang.

A similar reference to music which cannot be represented by notation is found in the *Practica musicae* by Franchino Gaffurio (1451–1518):

> Further, sounds which cannot be written down are committed to memory by usage and practice so that they will not be lost, for their delivery flows imperceptibly into the past.[5]

Vincenzo Galilei, in his *Fronimo* of 1584, goes further, advising that it is the duty of the musician *not* to play what is written down.

> And let it not come into your mind to try to defend yourself with the silly excuse of some who say they did not feel called upon to do more than that which they found written or printed.[6]

The two reasons he gives for his premise are quite valid, aesthetically. First, written and printed music often has errors, which of course one should not aspire to play, but more important the player's goal toward the composer should be to communicate 'not only what he says but often what he wished to say.'

Thomas Lodge's (1558–1625) *Euphues' Shadowe* includes a song within a Romance which is interesting because it suggests that poets were also participating in improvisation. In this case, musicians first performed an instrumental version of a madrigal. At its conclusion one of the guests extemporized a madrigal poem to the melody which had just been performed.[7]

---

4   Claude V. Palisca, 'An Italian Renaissance in Music?,' in *Humanism in Italian Renaissance Musical Thought* (New Haven: Yale University Press, 1985, 4ff.

5   *The Practica musicae of Franchinus Gafurius*, trans. Irwin Young (Madison: University of Wisconsin Press, 1969), 18.

6   Vincenzo Galilei, *Fronimo* [1584], trans. Carol MacClintock (Neuhasen-Stuttgart: Hanssler-Verlag, 1985), 83.

7   Thomas Lodge, *Euphues' Shadowe, The Battle of the Senses* [1592].

Even by the Baroque Period we find some writers suggesting that even for the listeners something was lacking in music when it became a matter of reading from the page. John Donne (1573–1631), in a letter of ca. 1600 suggests the listeners prefer improvised music to that read from a page ('sett' music).

> For both listeners and players are more delighted with voluntary than with sett musicke.[8]

For most modern readers the biggest surprise is that improvisation was also prevalent in the performance of early Church music, for few music history books dare to discuss this topic.[9] The one early writer who did discuss this at some length was Johannes Tinctoris (1435–1511), one of the greatest of the early theorists. His term for improvisation is *super librum* and in one of his more explicit references to this, Tinctoris suggests the improvisation was primarily done against the tenor and suggests some pre-agreement among the singers results in a more profitable result.

> But, with two or three, four or many, harmonizing *super librum*, one is not subject to the other, for, indeed, it suffices that each of them make consonances with the tenor with those thing that pertain to the law and arrangement of concords. I do not, however, think it disgraceful, but rather most laudable, if, agreeing among themselves on a similarity of assumption and arrangement of concords, they sing prudently, or thus they make of their harmonizing a fuller and more suave [effect].[10]

Later in this same treatise, Tinctoris, seems to suggest *variety in performance* as a primary virtue of improvisation. More extraordinary, given our understanding from traditional school texts dealing with the Renaissance, is his final thought below. He suggests that in a chanson, a song in which melody would be the chief characteristic, there is less improvisation than in motets. And not so much improvisation in motets as in the performance of the Mass!

> Variety must be most accurately sought for in all counterpoint, for, as Horace says in his *Poetics*: 'One who sings to the kithara is laughed at if he always wanders over the same string.' Wherefore, according to the opinion of Cicero, as a variety in the art of speaking most delights the hearer, so also in music a diversity of harmonies vehemently provokes the souls of listeners into delight; hence Aristotle, in his *Ethics*, does not hesitate to state that variety is a most pleasant thing and human nature in need of it.
>
> Also, any composer or improviser of the greatest genius may achieve this diversity if he either composes or improvises now by one quantity, then by another, now by one perfection, then by another, now by one proportion, then by another, now by one conjunction, then by another, now with syncopations, then without syncopations, now with *fugae*, then without *fugae*, now with pauses, now without pauses, now diminished, now as written. Nevertheless, the highest reason must be adhered to in all these, although I have kept silent about improvisation [*super librum*], which can be

---

[8] John Donne, Letter [ca. 1600], quoted in *Selected Prose*, ed. Helen Gardner (Oxford: Clarendon Press, 1967), 109.

[9] Reese, in *Music in the Renaissance*, 143 does admit 'the prominent role [improvisation] played in the musical life of the time.' Reese also suggests that much of the idioms of later style were first worked out in improvisation.

[10] *The Art of Counterpoint*, trans. Albert Seay (American Institute of Musicology, 1961), 105.

diversified by the will of those improvising; nor do so many and such varieties enter into one chanson as so many and such in a motet, nor so many and such in one motet as so many and such in one mass.[11]

In his treatise, *De Inventione et Usu Musicae*, Tinctoris actually points to a more specific tradition, called *cantus regalis*, in which some improvisation was done above plain chant.[12]

Finally, he suggests that the most successful musician is the one who 'composes with constant effort or sings *super librum*.' He concludes this discussion with the interesting observation that he has never known one successful composer or improviser who began his practice after the age of twenty.[13]

Tinctoris' suggestion that the 'most successful' Church singer was identified by his ability to sing in improvisation is also confirmed by Adrian Coclico in his *Compendium Musices* of 1552.

> The first requirement of a good singer is that he should know how to sing counterpoint by improvisation. Without this he will be nothing.[14]

Bottrigari also provides an extraordinary account of the improvisation of singers, including during the Church service. It is important to notice he confirms the reference by Tinctoris to the tradition of improvisation over chant.

> BENELLI. Because of the presumptuous audacity of performers who try to invent improvisation [*passaggi*], I will not say sometimes, but almost continuously, all trying to move at the same time as if in an [improvisation] contest, and sometimes showing their own virtuosity so far from the counterpoint of the musical composition they have before them that they become entangled in their dissonances—it is inevitable that an insupportable confusion should occur. This increases so greatly as they continue, that even those (and you see clearly how far this caprice and mania has gone) who play the low part, and the Bass, do not remember—not to say are ignorant of the fact—that it is the base and the foundation upon which the *cantilena* was built. And not standing firm beneath it, as the fabric requires, they go on up, they add nonsensical passages and allow themselves, because they enjoy it, to go so far as not only to pass into the Tenor part but even into that of the Contralto. Even this not sufficing, they go almost to that of the Sopranos, climbing in such a way to the top of the tree that they can't come down without breaking their necks …
>
> Meanwhile the other parts go vacillating, all being in great peril of falling to earth, without hope of having any succor …
>
> DESIDERIO. That explains why I have often heard similar discords and confusions made by the singers in Church when they improvise counterpoint above the *cantus fermus* of the Introit, which because of it often becomes almost odious and ridiculous at the same time.
>
> BENELLI. You may take it for certain that if it is very difficult to do a thing well, even if it is done thoughtfully and carefully, how much easier it is to do it badly if one does it without thought and in haste and, I will add, without any taste, as seems to me to be clearly seen today in all our singers and players. Here is proof of it—they are no sooner in the place where they have to make music than

---

[11] Ibid., 139.

[12] Reese, *Music in the Renaissance*, 147.

[13] *The Art of Counterpoint*, 140ff.

[14] Adrian Coclico, *Musical Compendium*, trans. Albert Seay (Colorado Springs: Colorado College Music Press, 1973), 24.

> immediately, even if they are late in appearing, they want to rush off to some other place; and while they are singing or playing, they are still able to jabber, laugh, and make jokes with their neighbors. Furthermore, whether the music is sung or played, they have only one kind of expression, so to speak, whether it's a good Madrigal or a Motet; and they are not interested in anything else.[15]

Bottrigari's objection to improvisation in church seems to have been over its quality, but of course there were some who objected in general to improvisation in the church. The fourteenth-century writer, Paolo Cortese, complained that there was so much improvisation he could no longer tell what mode the music was in.[16] The well-known sixteenth-century Italian theorist, Zarlino, in Part Three of his *Le Istitutioni Harmoniche* objects in general to improvisation.

> Matters for the singer to observe are these: First of all he must aim diligently to perform what the composer has written. He must not be like those who, wishing to be thought worthier and wiser than their colleagues, indulge in certain improvisation [*diminutioni*] that is so savage and so inappropriate that they not only annoy the listener but are ridden with thousands of errors, such as many dissonances, consecutive unisons, octaves, fifths, and other similar progressions absolutely intolerable in composition. Then there are singers who substitute higher or lower tones for those intended by the composer, singing for instance a whole tone instead of a semitone, or vice versa, leading to countless errors as well as offense to the ear. Singers should aim to render faithfully what is written to express the composer's intent, intoning the correct steps in the right places.[17]

Later in this book, Zarlino once again condemns improvisation.

> I have heard at times some presumptuous persons—I will not call them fools—who were arrogant enough to add an extra part not only to a composition of two voices but even of up to twelve, solely to impress the audience with a skill they did not even possess.... They manage to convince those as foolish as themselves that they are performing miracles. The true worth of such performances, however, will be obvious to anyone of good taste. If these improvisations were to be written down, they would be found to contain a thousand errors against common rules and to be full of innumerable dissonances.[18]

Giovanni de' Bardi, in his 'Discourse on Ancient Music and Good Singing,' confirms the widespread practice of improvisation in secular music, mentioning that he had even heard improvisation in the bass part.

> When singing alone, whether to the lute or [cembalo] or to some other instrument, the singer may contract or expand the time at will, seeing that it is his privilege to regulate the time as he thinks fit. To [improvise] upon the bass is not natural, for this part is by nature slow, low, and somnolent. Yet it

---

[15] Hercole Bottrigari, *Il Desiderio*, trans. Carol MacClintock (American Institute of Musicology, 1962), 61ff.

[16] 'De cardinalatu libri tres,' quoted in Pirrotta, 'Ars Nova and Stil Novo,' 103.

[17] Gioseffo Zarlino, *The Art of Counterpoint*, trans. Guy Marco and Claude Palisca (New Haven: Yale University Press, 1968), 110ff.

[18] Ibid., 221.

> is the custom to do this. I know not what to say of it and am not eager to praise or to blame it, but I would counsel you to do it as little as possible and, when you do, at least to make it clear that you do it to please someone …
>
> Then you will bear in mind that the noblest function a singer can perform is that of giving proper and exact expression to the canzone as set down by the composer, not imitating those who aim only at being thought clever (a ridiculous pretension) and who so spoil a madrigal with their ill-ordered [improvisation] that even the composer himself would not recognize it as his creation.[19]

Vicenzo Giustiniani, in discussing singers in Florence, also mentions improvisation in the bass line.

> And they all sang, whether bass or tenor, with a range consisting of many notes, and with exquisite style and [improvisation] and with extraordinary feeling and a particular talent to make the words clearly heard.[20]

He also mentions the fine women singers of Mantua and Ferrara and their 'exquisite improvisation delivered at opportune points, but not in excess.'[21]

And speaking of secular music, Arbeau, in his famous dance treatise, indicates the instrumentalists accompanying the dance were free to improvise. The goal of the improvisation, according to Arbeau, was to produce a result which was 'most pleasing and euphonious' and 'to please themselves.'[22]

If any of the above is surprising to the modern reader, he will no doubt be positively shocked to read the suggestion by Michael Praetorius that a singer did not even have to sing the first note as written by the composer! Although little known today, Praetorius seems to suggest that this practice, which he calls 'Intonatio,' was fairly common. *Intonatio*, he writes,

> refers to the manner in which a vocal piece is started. Opinions vary about this, some wanting to start the tone on the proper written pitch, some a second below, but in a way that the pitch is gradually raised. Some prefer to begin on the third, some on the fourth, some with a delicate and soft voice. All these methods, for the most part, are designated by the term *accentus*.[23]

Unfortunately, for all the evidence of the practice of improvisation during the Renaissance, there are few extant materials which address what these musicians did specifically. Caccini's treatise[24] gives excellent examples for singers of the first generation of opera and must represent customs familiar to the late Renaissance.

---

19 Giovanni de' Bardi, 'Discourse on Ancient Music and Good Singing,' in Oliver Strunk, *Source Readings in Music History* (New York: Norton, 1950), 299ff.

20 Vicenzo Giustiniani, *Discorso sopra la Musica* [ca. 1628], trans. Carol MacClintock (American Institute of Musicology, 1962), 70ff.

21 Ibid., 67ff.

22 Arbeau, *Orchesography*, trans. Mary Evans (New York: Kamin Dance Publishers, 1948, 39.

23 *Syntagma Musicum*, III.

24 Giulio Caccini, *Le Nuove Musiche*, ed. H. Wiley Hitchcock (Madison: A-R Editions, 1970).

We are fortunate to have what is in effect a record of actual instrumental improvisation in the sixteenth century, the *Il Vero Modo di Diminvir* (1584) published by Girolamo Dalla Casa, conductor of the Venetian Civic Wind Band.[25] He was the most famous cornett player of the sixteenth century and at the end of his life he decided to leave a testament of his improvisation. This volume gives the reader a key which refers to a known chanson, motet or madrigal by another composer, but not the actual music. The only actual music here is the improvisation which Dalla Casa played, as an additional voice, above the indicated multi-part composition by someone else. So, for study or performance purposes, one has to first find the original composition and then place Della Casa's part above it. Our observations after studying our own copy of this book is that the improvisation is done primarily at cadential points and the style appears to be that which vocal treatises call *passaggi*, of a rapid, flowing diatonic nature.

Most contemporary discussion relative to the nature of Renaissance vocal improvisation only has its focus on the importance of adhering to the emotions of the text. We will quote a typical example, a poem 'Musiciens qui chantez a plaisir,' known through its setting as a chanson by Hubert Waelrant of Antwerp. We have selected this example because it also offers some advice which might be of value to the modern musician who is asked to improvise and who has had little or no instruction in the art of doing this.

> Musicians, you who sing at will, who improvise, divide the note;
> Take a tone most sweet and slow signifying what the song means.
> Keep in tune like the linnet who takes pleasure in her graceful song.
> Be alert of ears and eyes or otherwise keep silent;
> And take good care not to sing unless you have had plenty to drink![26]

---

[25] 'Capo de Concerti delli stromenti di fiato della Illustriss. Signoria di Venetia.'

[26] Quoted in Jane Bernstein, *French Chansons of the Sixteenth Century* (University Park: Pennsylvania State University Press, 1985), 165.

Bibliography

Part 1: The Dawn of a New Era

Chapter 1 On Music and Society in the 14th Century

Boccaccio. *L'Ameto*. Translated by Judith Serafini-Sauli. New York: Garland, 1985.
Francesco de Sanctis. 'Boccaccio and the Human Comedy.' Quoted in *The Decameron*. Translated by Mark Musa and Peter Bondanella. New York: Norton, 1977.
Larner, John. *Culture and Society in Italy, 1290–1420*. New York: Scribner's, 1971.
Machaut, Guillaume de. *Remedies for Fortune Fair and Foul*. Translated by Conrad Rawski. Bloomington: Indiana University Press, 1991.
Machaut, Guillaume de. *Remede de Fortune*. Translated by James Wimsatt and William Kibler. Athens: The University of Georgia Press, 1988.
Marchetto of Padua. *Lucidarium*. Translated by Jan W. Herlinger. Chicago: University of Chicago Press, 1985.
Reese, Gustave. *Music in the Middle Ages*. New York: Norton, 1940.
Robinson, James. *Petrarch, The First modern Scholar and Man of Letters*. New York: Putnam, 1914.
Smithers, Don L. *The Music and History of the Baroque Trumpet*. London: Dent.
Strunk, Oliver. *Source Readings in Music History*. New York: Norton, 1950.
Wooldridge, H. E. *The Oxford History of Music*. London, 1929.

Chapter 2 On the 'Well-rounded Man'

Aretino, Pietro. *Dialogues*. Translated by Raymond Rosenthal. New York: Marsilio, 1971.
Boccaccio. *Concerning Famous Women*. Translated by Guido Guarino. New Brunswick: Rutgers University Press, 1963.
Boccaccio. *The Decameron*. Translated by Mark Musa and Peter Bondanella. New York: Norton, 1977.
Chubb, Thomas. *The Letters of Pietro Aretino*. New Haven: Shoe String Press [Archon Books], 1967.
Galilei, Vincenzo. *Fronimo* [1584]. Translated by Carol MacClintock. Neuhasen-Stuttgart: Hanssler-Verlag, 1985.
Giraldi Cinthio, *Discorso intorno al comporre dei romanzi*. Translated in Henry Snuggs, *Giraldi Cinthio On Romances*. Lexington: University of Kentucky Press, 1968.
Giustiniani, Vicenzo. *Discorso sopra la Musica* [ca. 1628]. Translated by Carol MacClintock. American Institute of Musicology, 1962.
Greene, Robert. *A Quip for an Upstart Courtier* [1592]. In *The Life and Complete Works of Robert Greene*. Edited by Alexander Grosart. New York: Russell & Russell, 1964.

Greene, Robert. *Mourning Garment* [ca. 1590].

Greene, Robert. *The Royal Exchange* [1590].

Guicciardini, Francesco. *Maxims and Reflections*. Translated by Mario Domandi. New York: Harper Torchbooks, 1965.

Lope de Vega. *El mayordomo de la duquesa de Amalfi*. Translated by Cynthia Rodriguez-Badendyck. Ottawa: Dovehouse, 1985.

Lope de Vega. *La Dorotea*. Translated by Alan Trueblood and Edwin Honig. Cambridge: Harvard University Press, 1985.

Lope de Vega. *Peribanez*. Translated by Jill Booty. In *Lope de Vega, Five Plays*. New York: Hill and Wang, 1961.

Lyly, John. *Euphues and his England*. Edited by Morris Croll. New York: Russell & Russell, 1964.

Lyly, John. *The Complete Works of John Lyly*. Edited by Warwick Bond. Oxford: Clarendon Press, 1967.

Montaigne, Michel. *Essays*. Translated by M. A. Screech. London: Penguin, 1993.

More, Thomas. *The Complete Works of St. Thomas More*. New Haven: Yale University Press, 1984.

Nashe, Thomas. *Pierce Penilesse His Supplication to the Devil* [1592]. In *The Works of Thomas Nashe*. Edited by Ronald McKerrow. Oxford: Blackwell, 1966.

Navarre, Marguerite. *The Prisons*. Translated by Hilda Dale. Reading: Whiteknight's Press, 1989.

Palisca, Claude V. *Humanism in Italian Renaissance Musical Thought*. New Haven: Yale University Press, 1985.

Putnam, Samuel. *The Works of Aretino*. New York: Covici, 1926.

Rabelais, François. *Pantagruel*. Translated by Donald Frame. Berkeley: University of California Press, 1991.

Shakespeare. *As You Like It*.

Shakespeare. *Hamlet*.

Shakespeare. *Richard*.

Shakespeare. *The Tragedy of Troilus and Cressida*.

Shakespeare. *The Winter's Tale*.

Shakespeare. *Twelfth Night or What You Will*.

Spenser, Edmund. *The Faerie Queene*.

Stubbs, Phillip. *The Anatomy of the Abuses in England* [1583]. Edited by Frederick Furnivall. London: The New Shakespeare Society, n.d..

Tasso, Torquato. 'Malpiglio, or On the Court.' In Carnes Lord, trans., *Tasso's Dialogues*. Berkeley: University of California Press, 1982.

Chapter 3 In Praise of Women

Aretino, Pietro. *Il Marescalco*. Translated by Leonard Sbrocchi. Ottawa: Dovehouse, 1986.

Bottrigari, Hercole. *Il Desiderio*. Translated by Carol MacClintock. American Institute of Musicology, 1962.

Brant, Sebastian. *The Ship of Fools*. Translated by Edwin Zeydel. New York: Columbia University Press, 1944.

Cartwright, Julia. *Beatrice d'Este*. Freeprot, NY, 1899 and London, 1928.

Cartwright, Julia. *Isabella d'Este*. London, 1915.

Cochlaeus, Johannes. *Tetrachordum Musices*. Translated by Clement Miller. American Institute of Musicology.

Fenlon, Iain. *Music and patronage in sixteenth-century Mantua*. Cambridge University Press.

Giustiniani, Vicenzo. *Discorso sopra la Musica* [ca. 1628]. Translated by Carol MacClintock. American Institute of Musicology, 1962.

Glixon, Jonathan. 'Music at the Venetian Scuole Grandi, 1440–1450.' In *Music in Medieval and Early Modern Europe*. Edited by Iain Fenlon. Cambridge: Cambridge University Press, 1981.

Noyes, Ella. *Story of Milan*. London, 1908.

Pirrotta, Nino and Elena Povoledo. *Music and Theatre from Poliziano to Monteverdi*. Cambridge: Cambridge University Press, 1982.

Shakespeare. *Much Ado About Nothing*.

Shakespeare. *Othello*.

Shakespeare. *The Taming of the Shrew*.

Vessella, Alessandro. *La Banda*. Milan, 1935.

Part 2: Commentary on the New Renaissance Values

Chapter 4 On Music and Society in the 15th Century

Blunt, Anthony. *Artistic Theory in Italy, 1450–1600*. Oxford: Clarendon Press, 1959.

Carpenter, Nan Cooke. *Music in the Medieval and Renaissance Universities*. Norman: University of Oklahoma Press, 1958.

Christine de Pizan. *Christine's Vision*. Translated by Glenda McLeod. New York: Garland Publishing, 1993.

Christine de Pizan. *The Book of the Body Politic*. Translated by Kate Forhan. Cambridge: Cambridge University Press.

Christine de Pizan. *The Epistle of the Prison of Human Life*. Translated by Josette Wisman. New York: Garland Publishing, 1984.

D'Amico, John. *Renaissance Humanism in Papal Rome*. Baltimore: Johns Hopkins University Press, 1983.

Gundersheimer, Werner. *Ferrara*. Princeton, 1973.

Kristeller, Paul. 'Music and Learning in the Early Italian Renaissance.' *The Journal of Renaissance and Baroque Music* (1947).

Lockwood, Lewis. 'Strategies of Music Patronage in the Fifteenth Century: the Cappella of Ercole I d'Este.' In Iain Fenlon, ed., *Music in Medieval and Early Modern Europe*. Cambridge: Cambridge University Press, 1981.

Lydgate, John. *Lydgate's Reson and Sensuallyte*. Edited by Ernst Sieper. London: Oxford University Press, 1901.

Medwall, Henry. *Nature*.

Nicholas of Cusa. *On Learned Ignorance*. Translated by Jasper Hopkins. Minneapolis: Banning Press, 1981.

Pierre de Ronsard. *Livre des mélanges* [1560].

Pirrotta, Nino and Elena Povoledo. *Music and Theatre from Poliziano to Monteverdi*. Cambridge: Cambridge University Press, 1982.

Polk, Keith. 'Instrumental music in the Urban Centres of Renaissance Germany.' In *Early Music History*, VII.

Reese, Gusstave. *Music in the Renaissance*. New York: Norton, 1959.

Stinger, Charles. *The Renaissance in Rome*. Bloomington: Indiana University Press, 1985.

Thompson, James. *Economic and Social History of Europe in the Later Middle Ages*. New York, 1931.

Tinctoris, Johannes. In *Dictionary of Musical Terms*. Translated by Carl Parrish (New York: Free Press of Glencoe, 1963.

Tinctoris, Johannes. *Concerning the Nature and Propriety of Tones*. Translated by Albert Seay. Colorado Springs, 1976.

Tinctoris, Johannes. *Proportionale Musices*. Translated by Albert Seay in *Journal of Music Theory* 1, no. 1 (1957): 22–75, http://www.jstor.org/stable/843090

Valla. 'De Musica.' Quoted in Claude V. Palisca, 'An Italian Renaissance in Music.' In *Humanism in Italian Renaissance Musical Thought*. New Haven: Yale University Press, 1985.

Gafurius, Franchinus. *The Practica musicae of Franchinus Gafurius*. Translated by Irwin Young. Madison: University of Wisconsin Press, 1969.

Chapter 5 Johannes Tinctoris on Music

Baines, Anthony. 'Fifteenth-century Instruments in Tinctoris's *De Inventine et Usu Musicae*.' *The Galpin Society Journal* 3 (1950): 19–26, http://www.jstor.org/stable/841898

Reese, Gustave. *Music in the Renaissance*. New York: Norton, 1959.

Tinctoris, Johannes. *Concerning the Nature and Propriety of Tones*. Translated by Albert Seay. Colorado Springs, 1976.

Tinctoris, Johannes. *Proportionale Musices*. Translated by Albert Seay in *Journal of Music Theory* (1957).

Tinctoris, Johannes. *The Art of Counterpoint*. Translated by Albert Seay. American Institute of Musicology, 1961.

Tinctoris, Johannes. *Dictionary of Musical Terms*. Translated by Carl Parrish. New York: Free Press of Glencoe, 1963.

Chapter 6 On Music and Society in the 16th Century

Agrippa, Henry Cornelius. *Of the Vanitie and Uncertaintie of Arts and Sciences*. Edited by Catherine Dunn. Northridge: California State University, Northridge Press, 1974.

Ascham, Roger. *The Schoolmaster* [1570]. Edited by Lawrence Ryan. Ithaca: Cornell University Press, 1967.

Ascham, Roger. *The Whole Works of Roger Ascham*. Edited by Rev. Giles. London: John Russell Smith, 1864.

Blunt, Anthony. *Artistic Theory in Italy, 1450–1600*. Oxford: Clarendon Press, 1959.

Bottrigari, Hercole. *Il Desiderio*. Translated by Carol MacClintock. American Institute of Musicology, 1962.

Furnivall, F., ed. *Miscellaneous, Series VI, Shakespere's England, Nr. 2*. Vaduz: Kraus Reprint, 1965.

Gosson, Stephen. *The Schoole of Abuse* [1579]. Edited by Edward Arber. London, 1868.

Greene, Robert. *The Life and Complete Works of Robert Greene*. Edited by Alexander Grosart. New York: Russell & Russell, 1964.

Jackson, Samuel. *Huldreich Zwingli*. New York: Putham, 1901.

Lodge, Thomas. *A Defence of Poetry, Music and Stage-plays*. London: Shakespeare Society, 1853.

Lyly, John. *The Complete Works of John Lyly*. Edited by Warwick Bond. Oxford: Clarendone Press, 1967.

Monson, Craig. 'Elizabethan London.' In Iain Fenlon, ed., *The Renaissance*. Englewood Cliffs: Prentice Hall, 1989.

Morley, Thomas. *A Plain and Easy Introduction to Practical Music*. Edited by R. Alec Harman. New York: Norton, n.d..

Nashe, Thomas. *The Anatomie of Absurditie* [1589]. In *The Works of Thomas Nashe*. Edited by Ronald McKerrow. Oxford: Blackwell, 1966.

Northbrooke, John. *A Treatise Against Dicing, Dancing, Plays, and Interludes* [1577]. London: The Shakespeare Society, 1843.

Peacham, Henry. *The Complete Gentleman*. Edited by Virgil Heltzel. Ithaca: Cornell University Press, 1962.

Reese, Gustave. *Music in the Renaissance*. New York: Norton, 1959.

Sidney, Philip. *The Prose Works of Sir Philip Sidney*. Edited by Albert Feuillerat. Cambridge: Cambridge University Press, 1962.

Stinger, Charles. *The Renaissance in Rome*. Bloomington: Indiana University Press, 1985.

Stubbs, Philip. *The Anatomy of the Abuses in England* [1583]. Edited by Frederick Furnivall. London: The New Shakespeare Society, n.d.

Watkins, Glenn. *Gesualdo, The Man and His Music*. Chapel Hill: The University of North Carolina Press, 1973.

Chapter 7 Polyphony, the Child of Mathematics, is left on the Steps of the Church

Castiglione, Baldassare. *The Courtier*. Translated by George Bull. New York: Penguin Books, 1967.

Cochlaeus, Johannes. *Tetrachordum Musices*. Translated by Clement Miller. American Institute of Musicology, 1970.

Coclico, Adrian. *Musical Compendium*. Translated by Albert Seay. Colorado Springs: Colorado College Music Press, 1973.

Galilei, Vincenzo. *Fronimo* [1584]. Translated by Carol MacClintock. Neuhasen-Stuttgart: Hanssler-Verlag, 1985.

Glarean, *Dodecachordon*. Translated by Clement Miller. American Institute of Musicology, 1965.

Heartz, Daniel. 'The Chanson in the Humanist Era.' In *Current Thought in Musicology*. Austin: University of Texas Press, 1976.

Lockwood, Lewis. 'Strategies of Music Patronage in the Fifteenth Century: the Cappella of Ercole I d'Este.' In Iain Fenlon, ed. *Music in Medieval and Early Modern Europe*. Cambridge: Cambridge University Press, 1981.

Miller, Clement. *Hieronymus Cardanus, Writings on Music*. American Institute of Musicology, 1973.

Palisca, Claude V. *Letters on Ancient and Modern Music*. American Institute of Musicology, 1960.

Palisca, Claude V. *Humanism in Italian Renaissance Musical Thought*. New Haven: Yale University Press, 1985.

Pirrotta, Nino. In *Music and Culture in Italy from the Middle Ages to the Baroque*. Cambridge: Harvard University Press, 1984.

Praetorius, Micheal. *Syntagma Musicum*. Facsimile of the original German publication. Bärenreiter Kassel, 1958.

Reese, Gustave. *Music in the Renaissance*. New York: Norton, 1959.

Strunk, Oliver. *Source Readings in Music History*. New York: Norton, 1950.

Chapter 8 On Music and Society in the 16th Century

Aretino, Pietro. *Dialogues*. Translated by Raymond Rosenthal. New York: Marsilio, 1971.

Chubb, Thomas. *The Letters of Pietro Aretino*. New Haven: Shoe String Press [Archon Books], 1967.

Cunningham, Caroline. *Estienne du Tertre, 'Scavant Musicien,' Jean d'Estree, 'Joueur de Hautbois du Roy,' and the Mid-Sixteenth Century Franco-Flemish Chanson and Ensemble Dance*. Dissertation, Bryn Mawr, 1969.

Freedman, Richard. 'Paris and the French Court under Francois I.' In *The Renaissance*. Englewood Cliffs: Prentice Hall, 1989.

Galilei, Vincenzo. *Fronimo* [1584]. Translated by Carol MacClintock. Neuhasen-Stuttgart: Hanssler-Verlag, 1985.
Guicciardini, Francesco. *Maxims and Reflections*. Translated by Mario Domandi. New York: Harper Torchbooks, 1965.
Heartz, Daniel. 'The Chanson in the Humanist Era.' In *Current Thought in Musicology*. Austin: University of Texas Press, 1976.
Heartz, Daniel. *Pierre Attaingnant Royal Printer of Music*. Berkeley, 1969.
Hooker, Richard. *The Works of Mr. Richard Hooker*. Oxford: Clarendon Press, 1888.
Jackson, Samuel. *Huldreich Zwingli*. New York: Putham, 1901.
Lesure, François. *Musicians and Poets of the French Renaissance*. Translated by Elio Gianturco. New York: Merlin Press, 1955.
Machiavelli. *Machiavelli, the Chief Works*. Translated by Allan Gilbert. Durham: Duke University Press, 1965.
Palisca, Claude V. *Humanism in Italian Renaissance Musical Thought*. New Haven: Yale University Press, 1985.
Regiomontanus. *Regiomontanus on Triangles*. Translated by Barnabas Hughes. Madison: The University of Wisconsin Press, 1967.
Sidney, Philip. *The Prose Works of Sir Philip Sidney*. Edited by Albert Feuillerat. Cambridge: Cambridge University Press, 1962.
Stokes, Francis, trans. *On the Eve of the Reformation*. New York: Harper & Row, 1909.
Strunk, Oliver. *Source Readings in Music History*. New York: Norton, 1950.
Zarlino, Gioseffo. *The Art of Counterpoint*. Translated by Guy Marco and Claude Palisca. New Haven: Yale University Press, 1968.

Chapter 9 Erasmus on Humanism

Erasmus. *The Collected Works of Erasmus*. Toronto: University of Toronto Press, 1992.
Erasmus. *Epistles*. London, 1901.

Chapter 10 On Music and Society in the 16th Century

Agrippa, Henry Cornelius. *Of the Vanitie and Uncertaintie of Arts and Sciences*. Edited by Catherine Dunn. Northridge: California State University, Northridge Press, 1974.
Bodin, Jean. *Method for the Easy Comprehension of History*. Translated by Beatrice Reynolds. New York: Columbia University Press, 1945.
Bodin, Jean. *Six Books of the Commonwealth*. Translated by M. J. Tooley. New York: Macmillian, 1955.
Carpenter, Nan Cooke. *Music in the Medieval and Renaissance Universities*. Norman: University of Oklahoma Press, 1958.
Erasmus, Desiderius. *The Collected Works of Erasmus*. Toronto: University of Toronto Press, 1992.

Luther, Martin. *Luther's Works*. St. Louis: Concordia, 1961.
Palisca, Claude. *Letters on Ancient and Modern Music*. American Institute of Musicology, 1960.
Reese, Gustave. *Music in the Renaissance*. New York: Norton, 1959.
Stokes, Francis, trans. *On the Eve of the Reformation*. New York: Harper & Row, 1909.
Vives, Juan. *Vives: On Education*. Translated by Foster Watson. Cambridge: University Press, 1913.

Chapter 11 On Sixteenth-Century German Music Treatises

Carpenter, Nan Cooke. *Music in the Medieval and Renaissance Universities*. Norman: University of Oklahoma Press, 1958.
Ornithoparchus. *Musicae active mirologus* and Dowland. *Introduction: Containing the Art of Singing*. New York: Dover, 1973.
Listenius, Nicolaus. *Musica*. Translated by Albert Seay. Colorado Springs: Colorado College Music Press, 1975.
Glarean, Heinrich. *Dodecachordon*. Translated by Clement Miller. American Institute of Musicology, 1965.
Stokes, Francis. *On the Eve of the Reformation*. New York: Harper & Row, 1909.
Miller, Clement. In 'The Dodecachordon: Its Origins and Influence on Renaissance Musical Thought.' In *Musica Disciplina* (1961).

Chapter 12 Contemporary Reflections on the Aesthetic Values of Music

Anonymous. *The Pearl*. Translated by Mary Hillmann. College of Saint Elizabeth Press, 1959.
Aretino, Pietro. *Dialogues*. Translated by Raymond Rosenthal. New York: Marsilio, 1971.
Arnold, Denis. 'Music at the Scuola de San Rocco.' *Music and Letters* 40, no. 3 (July, 1959): 229–241, http://www.jstor.org/stable/729389
Baccaccio. *Decameron*. Translated by Payne. Berkeley: University of California Press, 1982.
Bender, Robert, ed. *Five Courtier Poets of the English Renaissance*. New York: Washington Square Press, 1967.
Bruno, Giordano. *The Expulsion of the Triumphant Beast*. Translated by Arthur Imerti. New Brunswick: Rutgers University Press, 1964.
Castiglione, Baldassare. *The Courtier*. TRanslated by George Bull. New York: Penguin Books, 1967.
Cervantes, Miguel. *Don Quijote*. Translated by Burton Raffel. New York: Norton, 1995.
Cervantes, Miguel. *The Trials of Persiles and Sigismunda*. Translated by Celia Weller and Clark Colahan. Berkeley: University of California Press, 1989.
Clark, Barrett. *European Theories of the Drama*. New York: Crown, 1959.
Erasmus, Desiderius. *The Collected Works of Erasmus*. Toronto: University of Toronto Press, 1992.

Erasmus, Desiderius. *The Colloquies of Erasmus*. Translated by Craig Thompson. Chicago: University of Chicago Press, 1965.

Galilei, Vincenzo. *Fronimo* [1584]. Translated by Carol MacClintock. Neuhasen-Stuttgart: Hanssler-Verlag, 1985.

Giustiniani, Vicenzo. *Discorso sopra la Musica* [ca. 1628]. Translated by Carol MacClintock. American Institute of Musicology, 1962.

Jones, Emrys, ed. *The New Oxford Book of Sixteenth Century Verse*. Oxford: Oxford University Press, 1991.

Larner, John. *Culture and Society in Italy, 1290–1420*. New York: Scribner's, 1971

Lydgate, John. *Lydgate's Reson and Sensuallyte*. Edited by Ernst Sieper. London: Oxford University Press, 1901.

Lyly, John. *The Complete Works of John Lyly*. Edited by Warwick Bond. Oxford: Clarendon Press, 1967.

Lyly, John. *Endimion*.

Ornithoparchus. *Musicae active mirologus* and Dowland. *Introduction: Containing the Art of Singing*. New York: Dover, 1973.

Palisca, Claude V. *Humanism in Italian Renaissance Musical Thought*. New Haven: Yale University Press, 1985.

Peele, George. *The Arraignment of Paris*.

Petrarch. *Remedies for Fortune Fair and Foul*. Translated by Conrad Rawski. Bloomington: Indiana University Press, 1991.

Pirrotta, Nino and Elena Povoledo, *Music and Theatre from Poliziano to Monteverdi*. Cambridge: Cambridge University Press, 1982.

Pontus de Tyard. *Solitaire second* [1555].

Reese, Gustave. *Music in the Renaissance*. New York: Norton, 1959.

Sidney, Philip. *The Prose Works of Sir Philip Sidney*. Edited by Albert Feuillerat. Cambridge: Cambridge University Press, 1962.

Spenser, Edmund. *The Faerie Queene*.

Symonds, John Addington, trans. *The Life of Benvenuto Cellini*. New York: Scribner's, 1914.

Symonds, John Addington. *Renaissance in Italy*. New York: Capricorn Books, 1964.

Chapter 13 Contemporary Comments on Performance Practice

Arbeau, Thoinot. *Orchesography*. Translated by Mary Evans. New York: Kamin Dance Publishers, 1948.

Bottrigari, Hercole. *Il Desiderio*. Translated by Carol MacClintock. American Institute of Musicology, 1962.

Chaucer. *The Canterbury Tales*.

Galilei, Vincenzo. *Fronimo* [1584]. Translated by Carol MacClintock. Neuhasen-Stuttgart: Hanssler-Verlag, 1985.

Giustiniani, Vicenzo. *Discorso sopra la Musica* [ca. 1628]. Translated by Carol MacClintock. American Institute of Musicology, 1962.
Greene, Robert. *Menaphon* [1589]. In *The Life and Complete Works of Robert Greene*. Edited by Alexander Grosart. New York: Russell & Russell, 1964.
Greene, Robert. *Metamorphosis* [1588–1591].
Lodge, Thomas. *The Delectable History of Forbonius and Prisceria*. London: Shakespeare Society, 1853.
Luther, Martin. *Luther's Works*. St. Louis: Concordia, 1961.
Lyly, John. *Gallathea* [1592].
Pirrotta, Nino and Elena Povoledo, *Music and Theatre from Poliziano to Monteverdi*. Cambridge: Cambridge University Press, 1982.
Praetorius, Michael. *Syntagma Musicum*. Bärenreiter Kassel, 1958 (facsimile).
Shakespeare. *Richard II*.
Sidney, Philip. *The Countesse of Pembrokes Arcadia*. In *The Prose Works of Sir Philip Sidney*. Edited by Albert Feuillerat. Cambridge: Cambridge University Press, 1962.
Strunk, Oliver. *Source Readings in Music History*. New York: Norton, 1950.

CHAPTER 14 COMMENTS ON RENAISSANCE IMPROVISATION

Arbeau. *Orchesography*. Translated by Mary Evans. New York: Kamin Dance Publishers, 1948.
Bernstein, Jane. *French Chansons of the Sixteenth Century*. University Park: Pennsylvania State University Press, 1985.
Bottrigari, Hercole. *Il Desiderio*. Translated by Carol MacClintock. American Institute of Musicology, 1962.
Caccini, Giulio. *Le Nuove Musiche*. Edited by H. Wiley Hitchcock. Madison: A-R Editions, 1970.
Coclico, Adrian. *Musical Compendium*. Translated by Albert Seay. Colorado Springs: Colorado College Music Press, 1973.
Donne, John. Letter [ca. 1600]. *Selected Prose*. Edited by Helen Gardner. Oxford: Clarendon Press, 1967.
Gafurius, Franchinus. *The Practica musicae of Franchinus Gafurius*. Translated by Irwin Young. Madison: University of Wisconsin Press, 1969.
Galilei, Vincenzo. *Fronimo* [1584]. Translated by Carol MacClintock. Neuhasen-Stuttgart: Hanssler-Verlag, 1985.
Giustiniani, Vicenzo. *Discorso sopra la Musica* [ca. 1628]. Translated by Carol MacClintock. American Institute of Musicology, 1962.
Lodge, Thomas. *Euphues' Shadowe, The Battle of the Senses* [1592].
Palisca, Claude V. *Humanism in Italian Renaissance Musical Thought*. New Haven: Yale University Press, 1985.

Pirrotta, Nino. 'Ars Nova and Stil Novo.' In *Music and Culture in Italy from the Middle Ages to the Baroque*. Cambridge: Harvard University Press, 1984.

Pirrotta, Nino and Elena Povoledo. *Music and Theatre from Poliziano to Monteverdi*. Cambridge: Cambridge University Press, 1982.

Praetorius, Michael. *Syntagma Musicum*.

Reese, Gustave. *Music in the Renaissance*. New York: Norton, 1959.

Strunk, Oliver. *Source Readings in Music History*. New York: Norton, 1950.

Tinctoris, Johannes. *The Art of Counterpoint*. Translated by Albert Seay. American Institute of Musicology, 1961.

Zarlino, Gioseffo. *The Art of Counterpoint*. Translated by Guy Marco and Claude Palisca. New Haven: Yale University Press, 1968.

About the Author

Dr. David Whitwell is a graduate ('with distinction') of the University of Michigan and the Catholic University of America, Washington DC (PhD, Musicology, Distinguished Alumni Award, 2000) and has studied conducting with Eugene Ormandy and at the Akademie für Musik, Vienna. Prior to coming to Northridge, Dr. Whitwell participated in concerts throughout the United States and Asia as Associate First Horn in the USAF Band and Orchestra in Washington DC, and in recitals throughout South America in cooperation with the United States State Department.

At the California State University, Northridge, which is in Los Angeles, Dr. Whitwell developed the CSUN Wind Ensemble into an ensemble of international reputation, with international tours to Europe in 1981 and 1989 and to Japan in 1984. The CSUN Wind Ensemble has made professional studio recordings for BBC (London), the Köln Westdeutscher Rundfunk (Germany), NOS National Radio (The Netherlands), Zürich Radio (Switzerland), the Television Broadcasting System (Japan) as well as for the United States State Department for broadcast on its 'Voice of America' program. The CSUN Wind Ensemble's recording with the Mirecourt Trio in 1982 was named the 'Record of the Year' by The Village Voice. Composers who have guest conducted Whitwell's ensembles include Aaron Copland, Ernest Krenek, Alan Hovhaness, Morton Gould, Karel Husa, Frank Erickson and Vaclav Nelhybel.

Dr. Whitwell has been a guest professor in 100 different universities and conservatories throughout the United States and in 23 foreign countries (most recently in China, in an elite school housed in the Forbidden City). Guest conducting experiences have included the Philadelphia Orchestra, Seattle Symphony Orchestra, the Czech Radio Orchestras of Brno and Bratislava, The National Youth Orchestra of Israel, as well as resident wind ensembles in Russia, Israel, Austria, Switzerland, Germany, England, Wales, The Netherlands, Portugal, Peru, Korea, Japan, Taiwan, Canada and the United States.

He is a past president of the College Band Directors National Association, a member of the Prasidium of the International Society for the Promotion of Band Music, and was a member of the founding board of directors of the World Association for Symphonic Bands and Ensembles (WASBE). In 1964 he was made an honorary life member of Kappa Kappa Psi, a national professional music fraternity. In September, 2001, he was a delegate to the UNESCO Conference on Global Music in Tokyo. He has been knighted by sovereign organizations in France, Portugal and Scotland and has been awarded the gold medal of Kerkrade, The Netherlands, and the silver medal of Wangen, Germany, the highest honor given wind conductors in the United States, the medal of the Academy of Wind and Percussion Arts (National Band Association) and the highest honor given wind conductors in Austria, the gold medal of the Austrian Band Association. He is a member of the Hall of Fame of the California Music Educators Association.

Dr. Whitwell's publications include more than 127 articles on wind literature including publications in Music and Letters (London), the London Musical Times, the Mozart-Jahrbuch (Salzburg), and 52 books, among which is his 13-volume *History and Literature of the Wind Band and Wind Ensemble* and an 8-volume series on *Aesthetics in Music*. In addition to numerous modern editions of early wind band music his original compositions include 5 symphonies.

David Whitwell was named as one of six men who have determined the course of American bands during the second half of the 20th century, in the definitive history, *The Twentieth Century American Wind Band* (Meredith Music).

A doctoral dissertation by German Gonzales (2007, Arizona State University) is dedicated to the life and conducting career of David Whitwell through the year 1977. David Whitwell is one of nine men described by Paula A. Crider in *The Conductor's Legacy* (Chicago: GIA, 2010) as 'the legendary conductors' of the 20th century.

> 'I can't imagine the 2nd half of the 20th century—without David Whitwell and what he has given to all of the rest of us.' Frederick Fennell (1993)

About the Editor

CRAIG DABELSTEIN began studying the piano at age seven and took up the saxophone at age twelve. Mr Dabelstein has Bachelor of Arts (Music) and Bachelor of Music degrees from the Queensland Conservatorium of Music, where he majored in the performance of classical saxophone repertoire. He also has a Graduate Diploma of Learning and Teaching and a Graduate Certificate in Editing and Publishing from the University of Southern Queensland.

He has held the principal alto and tenor saxophone chairs in the Australian Wind Orchestra and has been an augmenting member of the Queensland Philharmonic Orchestra, the Queensland Symphony Orchestra, and the Queensland Pops Orchestra. For many years he was also a member of the Queensland Saxophone Quartet.

He has been a casual conductor of the Young Conservatorium Symphonic Winds, and has previously been a saxophone teacher at the Queensland Conservatorium of Music. He is a regular conductor of the Queensland Wind Orchestra, having served as their artistic director and chief conductor from 2004 to 2009.

Craig Dabelstein is a research associate for the *Teaching Music Through Performance in Band* series of books, contributing analyses to volumes 7, 8, 1 (rev. edn), and the *Solos with Wind Band Accompaniment* volume. He served as the copyeditor and layout designer of the *Australian Clarinet and Saxophone Magazine* from 2007 to 2009 and he has written many CD and book reviews for *Music Forum* magazine. He is the editor of the second editions of the books by Dr. David Whitwell including *A Concise History of the Wind Band*, *Foundations of Music Education*, *Music Education of the Future*, *The Sousa Oral History Project*, *Wagner on Bands*, *Berlioz on Bands*, *The Art of Musical Conducting*, and the *Aesthetics of Music* series (8 volumes) and *The History and Literature of the Wind Band and Wind Ensemble* series (13 volumes). From 1994 to 2012 he was a staff member at Brisbane Girls Grammar School. He now teaches woodwinds and conducts bands at St. Joseph's College, Gregory Terrace, Brisbane, Australia.

www.ingramcontent.com/pod-product-compliance
Lightning Source LLC
Chambersburg PA
CBHW081353230426
43667CB00017B/2821